The Tragic Empress

The authorized biography

of Alexandra Romanov

by

Countess Sophie Buxhoeveden

ISBN-10   1542570476
ISBN-13   978-1542570473

'The Tragic Empress' was published in its original form as 'The Life and Tragedy of Alexandra Feodorovna, Empress of Russia.'

This book, published by Taylor Street Books, is a re-edited / translated and updated version of the original publication. The additional edits are the copyright of Taylor Street Books, 2016.

Taylor Street Books is also the publisher of other books covering the last days of the Romanovs, including:

'The Funeral Bride'
'The Empress of Tears'
'The Shaken Throne'
'The Pride of Eagles'
'No Greater Crown'

(The 'Autobiography of Empress Alexandra' series, authored by Kathleen McKenna Hewtson)

'The Life and Death of Nicholas & Alexandra,' authored by Maria Mouchanow and Yakov Yurovsky

'We, The Romanovs,' authored by Grand Duke Alexander 'Sandro' Mikhailovich

With many thanks to Charles Klein for sourcing the front cover image for this book.

.

Chapter 1

Early Surroundings: 1879

In the middle of the small, old-fashioned town of Darmstadt, surrounded by quiet, dignified streets belonging to a time long gone by, stands the New Palace.

It was the house Princess Alice of Britain, the second daughter of Queen Victoria, wife of Prince Louis of Hesse-Darmstadt, had built for herself when her first home proved too small for her rapidly increasing family. For a town house, the New Palace had a lovely garden – the site having previously served as the Botanical Gardens – and it was constructed according to the Princess's own tastes, being fashioned as closely as possible after an English house. In that palace the future Empress Alexandra was born.

Although Princess Alice had moved to Germany as a very young girl – she married and left England shortly after the death of her father Prince Albert, the Prince Consort, during whose illness she had been Queen Victoria's great support and comfort – she remained intensely English in her outlook and her attachment to the country of her birth never wavered.. She was always thinking of England and she built and furnished her new home to remind her of the home she had left behind.

"I can't fancy I am in Germany, the house and all its arrangements being so English," the Princess wrote to Queen Victoria on March 20, 1866.

Portraits of all the family were there, from those of King George III and his family to numerous pictures of Queen Victoria, Prince Albert, and of all Princess Alice's brothers and sisters. Sketches of Windsor, Balmoral, and of other places she had loved in her youth were treasured by the Princess at Darmstadt and in turn fostered in her children that love and admiration for England that was to be so strong a trait in all of them. She also insisted that life in the Palace was to be organized along English lines, a regime that continued even after her death.

Although Princess Alice's life proved to be short – she died on December 14, 1878, at the age of thirty-five – it was nevertheless a full one. She saw many things, and judged and analyzed them with the wonderfully clear brain so remarked upon by her contemporaries. Young though she was at the time of Prince Albert's death, she had been her father's favorite companion, and her warm heart and practical mind impelled her toward all the social work she conducted in the small country that became hers by marriage. Even now most of its charitable institutions bear her name. She founded hospitals and women's guilds. She patronized women's unions, when, for the first time in Germany, the question of posts in government offices being filled by women was raised (she was also a good judge of men and had the gift of choosing the right people to carry out her schemes). During the wars of 1866 and 1870 she took an active part in the Red Cross work of Hesse. She founded new hospitals and improved the existing ones. With the help of Queen Victoria, she had the newest and best appliances sent from England.

"Life is meant for work and not for pleasure," she wrote to Queen Victoria on August 29, 1866, but in truth it was in work that her active mind found its greatest pleasure.

The war of 1866 created much bitter feeling in Germany, as civil war always does. Hesse sided with Austria against Prussia, and Prince Louis of Hesse went to war with the Hessian army. The Prussians won and soon Prussian troops had invaded Darmstadt. This was a bitter moment for Princess Alice as she waited helplessly in her palace in Darmstadt where her third daughter, Princess Irene, had just been born. In the ensuing treaty Hesse lost a large part of its territory, the main part of Oberhessen having to be handed over to Prussia. This has never been forgotten by the population and a feeling of coldness towards Prussia is evident to this day. The personal relations of the Hessian Grand Ducal family with that of the then Crown Princess of Prussia (the Empress Victoria) did not suffer, however, and the two sisters were always devoted to each other.

Princess Alice was a woman of many interests with a wide circle of friends, including the great philosopher David Strauss who dedicated to her his work on Voltaire. Intellectual pursuits were always more congenial to her than worldly pleasures, although in person she was always very charming and scrupulously played her part in the social life of Darmstadt.

Meanwhile, her private life was devoted to her husband and their seven children. In her letters to Queen Victoria she continually mentions their little ailments, their quaint sayings, and the trivial things that a mother loves to note. She directed their education, studied their characters, and guided each one individually. The terrible death of her baby boy, Prince Frederick – who was killed by a fall from a window under her very eyes on May 29, 1873 – gave her a moral and physical shock from which she never really recovered, but she braced herself for the sake of her other children

"God is very merciful in letting time temper the sharpness of one's grief and letting sorrow find its natural place in our hearts without withdrawing us from life," she wrote to Queen Victoria.

The little Princess Alix, who was born on June 6, 1872, and who was destined to be one of history's most tragic figures, was christened on July 1, 1872, which happened to be her parents' wedding anniversary. Her full name was Victoria Alix Helena Louise Beatrice and her godparents were the Prince and Princess of Wales (later King Edward VII and Queen Alexandra of Britain), the Tsarevich (later Alexander III and Tsarevna Marie of Russia and Princess Alix's future parents-in-law), Princess Beatrice of Britain, the Duchess of Cambridge, and the Landgravine of Hesse.

The Princess was called "Alix," as being the nearest translation of her mother's name into German, because Princess Alice wished to avoid calling her "Alice" in its English form.

"They pronounce "Alice" too dreadfully in German," she explained on June 17, 1872, adding twelve days later that "they murder my name here, Aliicé they pronounce it."

The little Princess inherited the good looks of all her brothers and sisters and we can catch glimpses of her happy, uneventful babyhood in Princess Alice's letters to Queen Victoria.

August 14th, 1872

Baby is like Ella, only smaller features, and still darker eyes with very black lashes, and reddish brown hair. She is a sweet, merry little person, always laughing and a dimple in one cheek, just like Ernie.

Mention of the Princess Alix's beauty as a baby is made in several later letters. On the occasion of the christening of her little sister, Princess Marie ("May"), Princess Alice wrote to Queen Victoria on July 13, 1874, "Sunny in pink was immensely admired," ("Sunny" being Princess Alix's nickname), and on September 1, 1878, that "Sunny is the picture of robust health."

Princess Alix's sisters, the Princesses Victoria and "Ella" (Elizabeth), were already in the schoolroom when their sister was born, and Princess Irene was by herself, between the nursery and the schoolroom. Princess Alix's babyhood was thus spent mostly with her brother Prince Ernest and her youngest sister Princess May. This beloved elder brother, the originator of all their games, was the object of her deep admiration, and the intimacy of their childhood remained with them all their lives.

Their father did not become reigning Grand Duke until the death of his uncle in 1877, and as both Prince Louis and Princess Alice gave much of their income to charity – the building of the New Palace having already swallowed up the greater part of the capital from Princess Alice's dowry – they were far from rich before his accession to his uncle's title and so the nurseries were large, lofty rooms, very plainly furnished.

Life in both the nursery and the schoolroom followed definite rules laid down by Princess Alice along the same basic lines as those on which she herself had been brought up, including old-fashioned English ideas of hygiene, which were at that time far ahead of those in Germany. Their dress was simple and their food of the plainest. Indeed, they retained all their lives hateful memories of rice puddings and baked apples being served in endless succession.

Mrs. Mary Anne Orchard – "Orchie" to the children – ruled the nursery. She was the ideal head nurse: sensible, quiet, enforcing obedience, not disdaining punishment, kind but firm, and gave the children that excellent nursery training that leaves its stamp on one for life. She had fixed hours for everything and the children's day was strictly divided in such a way as to allow them to take advantage of every hour Princess Alice could spare them. Princess Alice's rooms were on the same floor as the nurseries and the little princesses brought their toys there and played while their mother wrote or read.

Toys were uncomplicated in those days compared with the elaborate ones that modern children have. Princess Alix never cared for dolls – they were not "real" enough; she preferred animals that responded to her caresses – but she delighted in games. Sometimes all the old boxes containing their mother's early wardrobe were brought out for dressing up. The children strutted down the long corridors in crinolines and played at being great ladies or characters from fairy tales, dressed in bright fabrics and Indian shawls, which their grandmother Queen Victoria could not have imagined being put to such a use.

Prince Louis was not able to devote much time to his children, but their rare games with him were a delight and Princess Alix's earliest recollections were of romps in which her big burly soldier-father participated.

The children were full of fun and mischief: they did not always drive decorously in their small pony carriage with a liveried footman at the pony's head, and they sometimes escaped from their nurse's vigilance.

Princess Alix once paid dearly for such an escapade. The children were staying at Darmstadt just after their mother's death and were chasing one another in the garden. Princess Irene and Prince Ernest ran over some high forcing frames, carefully treading only on the stone walls. Princess Alix – who was six at the time – followed them, but tried to run over the glass panes instead, ending up crashing through the glass and receiving bad cuts to her legs, the scars of which she bore all her life.

Winters were spent at Darmstadt, while the summers were mostly spent at the castles of Kranichstein or Seeheim, and it is easy to picture this band of high-spirited children romping among the suites of old fashioned rooms at Kranichstein, racing in the park under the oaks, and standing in deep admiration before the ancient winding staircase on which the life-sized picture of a stag commemorated the spot where a real stag had once sought refuge from a former Landgrave.

Christmas was celebrated partly in the English manner and partly in the German one, and was a family feast in which all the household shared. A huge Christmas tree stood in the ballroom, its branches laden with candles, apples, gilt nuts, pink quince sausages, and all kinds of treasures. Tables were arranged around it bearing gifts for all the members of the family. The servants came in and Princess Alice gave them their presents. There then ensued a family Christmas dinner of the traditional German goose, followed by real English plum pudding and mince pies sent from England. The poor were not forgotten and Princess Alice had gifts sent to all the hospitals. Later,

Empress Alexandra was to bring these same Christmas customs with her to Russia.

Every year, much to the children's delight, the whole family went to Britain, staying at Windsor Castle, Osborne or Balmoral, according to wherever Queen Victoria was in residence at that moment.

Queen Victoria was adored by all her grandchildren as a fond grandmother who did not apply to them the strict rules that had governed her own children, and in England the little prince and princesses of Hesse met up with crowds of cousins, including the children of the Prince and Princess of Wales (later King Edward VII and Queen Alexandra) and those of Princess Alice's sister, Princess Helena. With this merry band, they played around Windsor Castle, wandered in the grounds of Balmoral and Osborne, visited favorite little shops and had their own special friends among Queen Victoria's retainers. They went round to see these old friends every time they came over, and the visit to "the merchants," a small shop between Abergeldie and Balmoral, was never missed.

The "merchants" sold sweets, notepaper, and other small things, and the children would come back from their expedition laden with wonderful purchases, to which the kindly "merchants," an old lady and her sister, would generally add a sweet something. The great delight of the young princesses at being initiated by their old friend and her sister into the secrets of scone-baking was remembered all their lives, and the tales of these adventures, recounted in later days, filled the hearts of the imperial Russian children with longing and envy. "Grandmamma in England" was, to the childish imagination of Princess Alix, a combination of a very august person and Santa Claus. When she returned from England, Princess Alix would talk about her stay for weeks and immediately begin to look forward to the next year's visit.

During the winter at Darmstadt, Princess Alice often used to take her children with her to hospitals and charitable institutions, teaching them from an early age to enjoy giving pleasure to others, and

Princess Alix, when quite tiny, would be asked to take flowers to hospitals on her mother's behalf.

Occasionally other children came to play with the small princesses at Darmstadt, and there were children's parties, but these Princess Alix did not much enjoy. Her natural shyness was already beginning to show itself and she always lingered in the background.

The friend of her babyhood, who remained her most intimate companion until her marriage, was Fraulein Toni Becker. She and Toni played together as babies, and later shared dancing and gymnastic lessons. As they grew older, their intimacy grew also, until by the time Princess Alix "came out," Toni was at the Palace almost every day.

In 1877, Princess Alix's father became the reigning Grand Duke of Hesse on the death of his uncle, the former Grand Duke Louis. This event produced no change in the children's lives, but for Princess Alice it meant a great increase in her public duties and consequently a considerable added strain on her health. In the summer of 1878 she was ordered to Eastbourne to convalesce and took all her children with her, continuing on from there to visit Queen Victoria for a short time. Of Eastbourne Princess Alix had golden memories of crab-fishing, bathing, and sand-castle building. There were, too, delightful games with other children on the beach, for many of Princess Alice's friends were there with children of about the same age as hers.

This was to be the last journey that Princess Alix took with her mother and the last time that Princess Alice was to visit her own country. In the November of that year diphtheria broke out severely in the New Palace, and all the family, with the exception of Princess Ella, went down with it. The first to fall ill was Princess Victoria; Prince Ernest, his sisters, and the Grand Duke followed. Princess Alix became dangerously ill. On November 12, Princess Alice telegraphed to the Queen, "This is dreadful. My sweet precious Alicky so ill. The doctor at once saw that it was a severe case."

At that time serum was unknown and the old-fashioned methods of treatment were powerless against this scourge. It was a case of nature against the disease, and Princess Alice had a terribly anxious time. Queen Victoria sent her own doctor to help the German physicians and several nurses were called in, but, according to her wont when any members of her family were ill, Princess Alice undertook their nursing herself, sitting up whole nights with her children, moving from one sick-bed to the next. All except Princess Victoria were desperately ill. Princess Alix always remembered calling night after night for her mother, who invariably appeared, whatever the hour, to soothe and quieten the child. In spite of all her devotion, the "baby" Princess May died on November 16. Princess Alice managed to keep the other children from the jaws of death, but now her own weakened constitution succumbed to the infection. On December 8 she fell ill in her turn and on December 14 she died, greatly lamented both in Hesse and in England, while to her own family her death was a shattering blow.

Chapter 2

Childhood: 1879-1888

Princess Alix used to say in later years that her earliest recollections were of an unclouded, happy babyhood of perpetual sunshine, then of a great cloud ...

Princess Alice's death left an inexpressible void in the palace and it took a long time before those who remained behind could adjust themselves to a life that had lost the hand that guided it. All the children were moved as soon as possible into the cold, unfamiliar surroundings of the old town Schloss, and from its windows poor little Princess Alix, then barely six, saw her mother's funeral procession wending its way from the New Palace to the family mausoleum at the Rosenhohe.

Prince Louis, now Grand Duke Louis IV, had scarcely recovered from his own severe illness at the time of his wife's death, but he did all in his power to take his wife's place with his motherless children. He was a kind-hearted, honest man, with a wonderfully fair outlook on things and events, and was adored by his children. Naturally he spoilt the youngest a little. Princess Alix seemed so lonely and desolate without her small playfellow, Princess May.

Princess Alice had always had the entire management of the children's education and after her death the Grand Duke scrupulously followed the directions she had given, so that, although she was no more, her influence remained. The princesses' governesses consulted the Grand Duke on minor details, but essentially followed his late wife's ideas.

From this time, too, Queen Victoria took a special interest in her orphaned grandchildren. Both Miss Jackson and Prince Ernest's tutor had to write monthly reports to the Queen, whose signed answers to

Miss Jackson show that she went into every small detail and often gave them definite directions. These letters express the Queen's ideas on feminine education. They may strike the reader as old-fashioned, but Miss Jackson, while keeping within the main guidelines of the Queen's sound advice, evidently adapted them to the exigencies of more modern times.

The first months after her mother's death represented untold misery and loneliness for Princess Alix, and probably laid the foundations of the seriousness that lay at the bottom of her character. She was now quite alone in the nursery; Prince Ernest, who was now ten, had a tutor to keep him at lessons all day, and Princess Irene, who was six years older, had joined the elder princesses in the schoolroom. Princess Alix long afterwards remembered those deadly sad months when, small and lonely, she sat with old "Orchie" in the nursery, trying to play with her new and unfamiliar toys as all her old ones had been burned or were being disinfected. When she looked up, she saw her old nurse silently crying. The deaths of her beloved Princess Alice and of Princess May had nearly broken her faithful heart.

Until this time Princess Alix had been on the whole a cheerful child. It has to be admitted that she had a tendency to be hot-tempered and wilful, but she nevertheless showed great self-restraint even at an early age. She was generous and, even in her babyhood, incapable of any childish falsehood. She had a warm and loving heart, yet was also obstinate and very sensitive. A chance word could hurt her, but even as a small girl she did not show how deeply she had been wounded. This was her character as a child and in many respects presaged the future woman.

Queen Victoria, who loved the Grand Duke of Hesse as a son, urged him to come to her with all his children as soon as possible, and in January 1879 the family went to Osborne for a long stay. Here by degrees they recovered, mentally and physically, and returned to Darmstadt two months later, accompanied by Prince Leopold who had always been a favorite uncle.

17

The two elder Princesses tried to take their mother's place as their father's companions and were constantly with him. The sixteen-year-old Princess Victoria looked after her brother and sisters and acted as mistress of the house. The Grand Ducal family went that first year to Schloss Wolfsgarten, and the new surroundings and the elasticity of youth helped the children to recover their vitality. They returned to the New Palace in the winter of 1879-1880, where Princess Alix began her solitary schoolroom life. She had toiled at her spelling under faithful Orchie's eye; now came the somewhat formidable Fraulein Anna Textor, a relative of Goethe himself, who carried on her education under Miss Jackson's general guidance.

Miss Margaret Hardcastle Jackson, "Madgie" as Princess Alix affectionately called her later, was a broadminded, cultivated woman, who soon gained a strong influence over her pupils, particularly the eldest. She had impressed Princess Alice by her advanced ideas on feminine education in that she attempted not only to impart knowledge to her pupils, but to form their moral characters and widen their views on life. A keen politician, she was always deeply interested in all important political and social questions of the day, and discussed all such matters with the children, young as they were, so as to awaken their interest in intellectual questions and train them to discuss abstract subjects. Gossip of any kind was not allowed by her. It was unfortunate that Miss Jackson felt too old and tired, and had to retire before having quite finished the Princess Alix's education, when her youngest charge was only fifteen, as she would certainly have been able to accustom her to break through her reserve and acquire a simpler and easier outlook on life.

With the thoroughness that ever characterized her, Princess Alix gave her whole energy to her lessons. She always had a strong sense of duty and her teachers certify that she would always willingly give up any pleasure that she thought might prevent her finishing some task for next day. Samples of her handwriting at seven years old show it to be wonderfully neat and firm and she had a very retentive memory.

By the time she was fifteen, she was well grounded in history, literature, geography and all general subjects, particularly those relating to England and Germany. According to her letters to her eldest sister, she toiled without a murmur at dry works like Guizot's 'Reformation de la Litérature,' 'The Life of Cromwell,' and Raumer's 'Geschichte der Hohenstaufen' in nine volumes. Compared with these, 'Paradise Lost,' which she read in the intervals, must have seemed quite light reading! She had a French teacher, and though her accent was fair, she never became thoroughly at home in that language and always felt "cramped," as she said, in it, rendering her at a loss for words. This hampered her later in Russia, where French was the official language at Court. English was, of course, her natural language and she spoke and wrote it to her brother and sisters, and later to her husband and children, and to all those she knew well.

Princess Alix had one of those sensitive natures that respond most readily to music. She adored Wagner and the classics, and when she grew up attended every concert within her reach. Her music teacher was a Dutchman, W. de Haan, at that time Director of the Opera at Darmstadt, who was full of praises for her musical ability.

She played the piano brilliantly but her shyness made her extremely self-conscious whenever she played before people. She told me of the torment she endured when Queen Victoria made her play in the presence of her guests and her suite at Windsor. She said her clammy hands felt literally glued to the keys and that it was one of the worst ordeals of her life.

She did not excel in drawing, but was good at needlework and designed attractive trifles, which she gave to her friends or to charity bazaars. Her interest in art in general developed later under her brother's influence.

Grand Duke Louis IV spent a great deal of time with his children, and in the summer months liked to take them about with him to functions in different towns or on maneuvers. Princess Alix had a very great love for her father and her delight knew no bounds when she was included in these expeditions. She loved her picturesque "Hessenland," cherished recollections of her childhood and early youth spent there, and always in her mind separated Hesse completely from the rest of Germany. She considered Prussia to be a different country and she went to Berlin only twice on short visits before her marriage.

Nearly every autumn the Grand Duke of Hesse took his children to Windsor or Osborne, or more often to Balmoral, for he was a keen sportsman and a good shot. These visits were the best part of the year to his youngest daughter. They developed her mentally, too, as they brought her into contact not only with her cousins but with all of Queen Victoria's entourage, many politicians and the great and good of all descriptions. Listening to their conversations at luncheon, her interest in matters beyond her years was automatically awakened and at thirteen she looked and spoke like a much older girl. Her English point of view on many questions in later life was certainly due to her many visits to England at this most impressionable age. The Grand Ducal family looked upon themselves almost as a branch of the English royal house. They felt at one with it and took part in all the family festivities. For instance, in 1885 Princess Alix's holidays were brought forward to enable her to act as bridesmaid to her aunt, Princess Beatrice, who married Prince Henry of Battenberg on July 23 of that year, which proved to be quite an experience for the thirteen years old princess.

At Wolfsgarten the Grand Ducal family had frequent visits from their English relations: the Prince of Wales (later King Edward VII), the Marquess and Marchioness of Lorne (Princess Louise), Prince Leopold and, most often, Prince Christian and Princess Helena, whose children, Princesses Marie Louise and Helena Victoria, were great friends of Princess Alix. The younger children of the Crown Princess of Germany (later Empress Victoria), the Princesses Sophie and Margarethe, now Queen-Dowager of Greece and Landgravine of Hesse, also came often to Wolfsgarten.

The elder Hesse princesses were fast growing into womanhood. Princess Victoria and Princess Ella came out in 1881, but Princess Alix only heard echoes of their lively entertainments. She had been promoted to share the schoolroom with the fifteen-year-old Princess Irene, but the latter had her own friends and Princess Alix was often left to her own devices. In her immediate surroundings, her two ladies-in-waiting most certainly played a part in the development of Princess Alix's character. These were Baroness Wilhelmine Senarclens Grancy, Lady-in-Waiting to the four princesses, and Fraulein Margarethe (Gretchen) von Fabrice. Baroness Grancy was a woman of the old school: upright, honorable and kind, if perhaps a trifle strict. She was a real friend to the family, and dearly loved little Princess Alix, to whom, as with everyone else, she did not refrain from occasionally giving a piece of her mind. The wiry, hardy, little, old lady was incapable of any insincerity and the embodiment of duty. Never allowing herself a moment's relaxation, she always preached that "one must pull oneself together" and not give in, either physically or morally, and she inculcated this principle into Princess Alix, who was always very hard with herself throughout her life. Her outward manner was short and abrupt, and in those early years Princess Alix may have felt her more of a mentor than a friend.

Fraulein von Fabrice was appointed Princess Alix's special lady-in-waiting when the Princess was sixteen and she herself was in her twenties. She had lived in England as governess to Princess Helena's daughters and her aim was to guide the Princess. She had high and lofty ideals and was very religious, but, as she was shy herself, she could not help the Princess to fight against her timidity. However, her idealism certainly influenced Princess Alix, who formed a great friendship with her, although she soon became reticent in speaking of the things that touched her deeply, fearful of her too demonstrative nature. Toni Becker, her childhood friend, was allowed sometimes to share her thoughts, and the young hereditary Prince Ernest, when he was at home, shared many more. He was the only real friend of her youth, and their childhood love and understanding deepened as the difference in their ages was equalized by time, and when he went to the University she missed him sorely, for she was again alone.

In 1884 there was great excitement among the young people at the Darmstadt palace, for their eldest sister, Princess Victoria, who had always ruled the nursery and had mothered her younger sisters so capably since their mother's death, became engaged to her cousin, Prince Louis of Battenberg. The wedding festivities took place at Darmstadt on April 30, 1884, in the presence of Queen Victoria, the Prince and Princess of Wales, and the German Crown Prince and Crown Princess. The young princesses were so excited by the event that this first break in their family circle was in no way sad, particularly as Princess Victoria promised to return to Darmstadt whenever her sailor husband was at sea.

No sooner had the excitement of this wedding abated, than preparations began for the marriage of the second princess, Ella, who had been engaged for some time to Grand Duke Serge, a brother of Emperor Alexander III of Russia. Princess Ella had known the Grand Duke from childhood as he had often stayed for months at a time at Jugenheim with his mother, Empress Marie, wife of Alexander III. Princess Ella was a very pretty girl, tall and fair, with regular features, and she was the personification of unselfishness, always ready to do anything in order to give pleasure to others. She was cheerful, with a strong sense of humor, and as a child always the peacemaker in the nursery and the schoolroom, a favorite with all her sisters and brothers, and a link between them.

After a visit to England in the spring of 1884, the whole Grand Ducal family went to St. Petersburg for Princess Ella's marriage. Princess Alix, who was only twelve at the time, was full of joy and anticipation at the idea of the journey. Travelling up the long ugly stretches of country from the Russian frontier to St. Petersburg, Princess Alix's impressions of what was to be her country also cannot have been very thrilling ones. But, happily, she was interested in everything, and all the young people arrived in a very cheerful mood at Peterhof, then the residence of the Russian Court. Ella made her state entrance into the capital in a gilt coach drawn by white palfreys which were led by gold-liveried servants. At St. Petersburg the gorgeous marriage ceremonies took place, followed by many festivities, in which Princess Alix, to her chagrin, could not take part, but she was rewarded by the few delightful days that the whole family spent afterwards in Peterhof, where, for the first time, she met her future husband, the Tsarevich Nicholas and his brothers and sisters. The band of young people amused themselves in the gardens and went sight-seeing together, Princess Alix the keenest among them. She could always join in fun thoroughly and could laugh at some joke until the tears streamed down her cheeks, even in later times, but it was never in her to set the laughter going.

Leave-taking from Grand Duchess Ella was sadder than from Princess Victoria: the elder sister's parents-in-law lived in Hesse and there was the prospect of seeing her often, while the distance from Russia was great, so the family circle was reduced that winter at Darmstadt, and was made still smaller by the death of Grand Duke Louis' mother, old Princess Elisabeth. She had many sorrows and had lived a very retired life in her own palace at Darmstadt, devoting much of her time to charitable works, but she had been very kind to her motherless grandchildren and was sincerely mourned by them.

In the spring of 1885, Grand Duke Serge and Grand Duchess Ella came to Wolfsgarten to spend part of the summer there. Prince Louis of Battenberg and Princess Victoria soon joined them with their baby daughter, Princess Alice (later Princess Alice of Greece), a delightful entertainment for Princess Alix. This was the first of a series of happy family meetings that were to take place nearly every year.

The Grand Duke Serge was much liked by his wife's family. He was a real *grand seigneur*, steeped in high culture with the artistic temperament and desire for intellectual pursuits to go with it, although a certain shyness made him seem outwardly stiff and unresponsive.

He took a great liking to little Princess Alix, whom he very much admired. He used to tease her unmercifully and often reduced her to a state of blushing confusion, which she really rather enjoyed.

Grand Duke Louis was always ready to join in his children's fun and liked going about with his four pretty daughters, while Princess Irene acted as hostess for her father.

Princess Alix used sometimes to be allowed, as a great treat, to appear at tea dances which were given for Princess Irene, and in the years 1886-7 she began to see something of the young people of Darmstadt. The year of 1887 was also marked by Queen Victoria's jubilee celebrations, to which Grand Duke Louis took his two youngest daughters. However, as Princess Alix was not yet "out in society," much to her regret she was only allowed to watch the procession in the streets.

Chapter 3

A Young Princess: 1888-1893

In the spring of 1888 came a great turning-point in Princess Alix's life – her confirmation. She was prepared for this by Dr. Sell, a Hessian divine chosen by the Princess Alice to give religious instruction to her children. He was a clever man who soon gained a strong influence over Princess Alix, whose sensitive soul had always had serious leanings. His early teaching laid the foundations of that searching for truth that was the keynote of her spiritual life. He dwelt strongly on the force of the Lutheran doctrine and impressed its tenets on her. This later placed Princess Alix in a great moral dilemma when, loving the Tsarevich and knowing that she was loved by him, she also knew that to marry him she would have to embrace the Orthodox faith.

Dr. Sell's words penetrated deep. Princess Alix's nature was always introspective and now she began to analyze her every action and its right and wrong motives, finding fault with herself and seeking to attain a lofty and abstract ideal. This made her take her whole life very seriously. She was always wrestling with issues, always striving to solve deeper questions in connection with smaller ones, while jealously shielding all this inner life from prying eyes.

After her confirmation, according to the custom of German courts, Princess Alix was considered "out in society" and the great impression made upon her by the religious ceremony did not prevent her from leading the usual life of a young princess and enjoying its opportunities.

A friend of her youth, Minnie Cochrane, told me she was always bright and cheerful at home. When Miss Cochrane would stay at Wolfsgarten, Princess Alix would come into her room while she was dressing in the morning and they would talk on and on. Sometimes, even at that early hour, they would start singing duets to their own banjo accompaniments, which would make them desperately late for breakfast!

Princess Alix was then a tall, slim girl, looking older than her real age because of the serious expression in her beautiful luminous eyes and because of a trace of something sad and wistful about her mouth. It was this sad expression, and not her ready smile, that was always on show in her photographs. Superstitious people might say that hers was a face that bore the stamp of predestination to sorrow. Her regular features retained their resemblance from babyhood to those of Grand Duchess Ella. Both sisters were tall and stately, and had very good complexions, although Princess Alix had beautiful golden hair, while the Grand Duchess' was slightly darker.

The year of 1888 saw another wedding in the family, which brought both married sisters back to Germany. Princess Irene was married to her first cousin, Prince Henry of Prussia, at the palace of Charlottenburg, near Berlin. This was Princess Alix's first visit to the capital of the German Empire, where she created quite a sensation with her beauty.

In the autumn of that year, the Princess' coming-out was celebrated by a ball at the New Palace, for which Grand Duke Serge and Grand Duchess Ella returned specially from Russia. Grand Duchess Ella saw to every detail of her young sister's appearance, encouraging her to wear white muslin, with bunches of lilies of the valley on her hair and dress, for which she was very much admired according to contemporary accounts.

Grand Duchess Ella had extracted from her father the promise that he would revisit her that winter in St. Petersburg, and after Christmas the Grand Duke of Hesse, along with Prince Ernest and Princess Alix, travelled to Russia. Grand Duchess Ella had won over all Russian hearts, both in the Imperial Family and in St. Petersburg society, and all her friends were delighted to welcome her sister and brother.

The Hessian party stayed with Grand Duke Serge and Grand Duchess Ella at their palace on the Nevsky Prospect, which was nearly opposite the Anichkov Palace, the residence of Emperor Alexander III and the Empress Marie. The Tsarevich often used to visit his young aunt informally, jokingly calling her "Tetinka" (Little Aunt). Grand Duchess Ella loved dancing and organized all kinds of entertainments, so that her house was very attractive to her young relatives.

The Tsarevich visited their palace even more often when the Princes of Hesse were there. He had taken a strong liking to Prince Ernest, whom he was deputed to entertain as a foreign guest, and he was greatly attracted by his young aunt's shy little sister. On her side, Princess Alix had quickly fallen in love with the Tsarevich. She hid it carefully and indeed at first did not realize it herself. It was only on her return to Darmstadt that she felt that she had left her heart in Russia.

There was much entertaining at Court and in St. Petersburg that winter. There were many balls to which Grand Duchess Ella took her sister, who danced more than ever again in her life, several of the merriest ones being held by the Empress Marie at Anichkov. Among these was the celebrated *bal noir* which dated back to a moment in history when the Austrian Court had held a grand function during a period of Russian Court mourning, so, in retaliation, a subsequent Anichkov ball went ahead despite the recent death of the then Archduke of Austria. The guests were, however, asked to attend this ball dressed in mourning, the ladies never looking better than when attired in every kind of black gown sparkling with jewels.

There were also concert balls at the Winter Palace and Grand Duchess Ella often took her family to the opera and ballet. Afternoons were spent at the fashionable skating grounds in the Jardin de la Tauride, where Prince Ernest and Princess Alix – with the Tsarevich, his brother Grand Duke George and his sister Grand Duchess Xenia joining them – skated or tobogganed down the ice hills along with the younger members of St. Petersburg society.

Princess Alix enjoyed everything. Her smile and her bright eyes showed this clearly, although her shyness still prevented her from being at ease with the people she met.

Grand Duke Louis IV was happy bear-hunting in the country or shooting with the Russian Emperor, and everyone enjoyed the visit so much that it was extended until Lent when the Hessian princes conscientiously "buried" the Season at the traditional *folle journée* – the last flourish before the season's end, given on the last Sunday of Carnival by the Court. This took place at the Alexander Palace at Tsarskoe Selo, where Princess Alix was to live later as Empress, and was a comparatively small and very select afternoon dance for young people personally known to the Emperor. It was followed by a dinner at six o'clock. A feature of the dinner was the traditional carnival dish of blinis eaten with fresh caviar. After dinner, dancing was resumed and there was a *cotillon* with presents for all the guests. On the first stroke of twelve the band suddenly stopped, dancing ceased, and the Imperial Family and their guests sat down to a "fasting supper," although, if truth be told, the fasting was in name only and merely meant that meat was not included on the menu.

The first week of Lent was, however, a serious matter. No good Russian attended places of amusement during Lent. The theatres were closed and everyone was expected to go devoutly to church to hear the penitential psalms. This Lenten spirit gripped Princess Alix. She loved the quiet days after the rush of pleasures and the last weeks spent in St. Petersburg were those she liked the best, perhaps because she had more opportunities to see the Tsarevich quietly.

After her Russian season, Princess Alix began in earnest her life as a grown-up princess. She received people, presided at dinner parties, went about with the Grand Duke, visited schools and hospitals, and played as far as possible the part of *"Landesmutter"* in the Grand

Duchy. *"Prinzesschen,"* as she was known, was loved by high and low, but the people did not know the suffering every public appearance caused her. Princess Alix's timidity hampered her all her life, for shyness can spell disaster to those in high position. However, she loved dancing and after her first moments of fright had passed off, thoroughly enjoyed going out.

Whenever Prince Ernest came back from the University, he was always ready to arrange pleasures for his sister. Costume balls were then the fashion, and even now the Darmstadters remember the brilliance of a Renaissance Ball at which Princess Alix, dressed in the Renaissance style, looked lovely in pale green velvet and silver with emeralds in her fair hair that flowed down her back according to the fashion of the time.

She always enjoyed dressing up. Somehow it made her feel like another person and helped her to forget her fears. Her face was always serious, however, even when she was amused. Her friend Toni Becker (later Frau Bracht) recounted that she was once at the theater – the theater playing a major role in Darmstadt life – while a very amusing German play was being performed, with Princess Alix watching on from the Grand Ducal box. Fraulein Becker looked up at her friend's face only to see that she retained her habitual half-wistful, half-sad expression, although the next day Princess Alix told her that she had been suppressing her giggles all the time.

With her mother's precepts held strongly in her mind, Princess Alix took a warm interest in all Prince Alice's charities, both public and private. The gifts she gave were mostly of her own making and nearly always meant a drain on her own purse as her allowance was a very small one, and for weeks before Christmas she would work hard making presents for every kind of person, including old retainers, governesses and friends.

In the summer of 1890, the Grand Duke of Hesse went to Russia again, accompanied by Princess Alix, Prince Ernest and Princess

Victoria of Battenberg. This time they did not go to St. Petersburg but to Illinskoe, Grand Duke Serge's country seat in the province of Moscow.

The impression of Russia she gained during this visit probably exercised a great influence on Princess Alix's subsequent fate. If she had not felt that this second stay confirmed the liking she already felt for Russia, she might have stifled her feelings and not have risked marrying into such a different and distant country. All her impressions of rural life and of the nature of Russian peasants arose from this visit to Illinskoe, the only time she ever stayed in a Russian country house.

Illinskoe was very much a Russian country house, like those described by Turgenyev in his novels. Grand Duke Serge and Grand Duchess Ella lived a simple country life there alongside the ladies and gentlemen of their court and a few personal friends who had been invited for extended visits, in the Russian fashion. Grand Duchess Ella loved it all dearly. She was interested in the village people and enjoyed playing lady bountiful. The typical Russian surroundings – the wide expanse of flat meadows, the immense horizons, the vast pine forests, and the grey birches of her garden – attracted her more and more, and she taught her sister to appreciate the peculiar charm of rural Russia as well.

Grand Duchess Ella liked to take her guests on surprise visits to see her neighbors and they would also attend every village fair in the area, to everyone's great enjoyment. It was all so different from anything the Hessians had ever seen and Princess Alix even lost her shyness. She felt at ease with her sister's guests at the simple meals from which etiquette was banished, and got to love the good-natured peasants who welcomed their Grand Duchess' young sister with low bows.

September 18 was St. Elizabeth's Day, the name day of Grand Duchess Ella, and was celebrated by the arrival of many guests, though, to the disappointment of his cousins, the Tsarevich, who had been expected, could not make it.

At the close of their visit, Grand Duchess Ella took her guests to Moscow, where they saw all the sights like ordinary tourists, to Princess Alix's particular delight. With many regrets and numerous boxes of sweets – a photograph taken at the time of their arrival shows them surrounded by empty boxes – Princess Alix returned to Darmstadt, promising to return soon, although she did not in fact do so until late in 1894, when she was obliged to hasten to Emperor Alexander III's death-bed as the Tsarevich's fiancée.

In the winter of 1880, Princess Alix had a glimpse of life beyond the precincts of palaces in the enchanting setting of Southern Europe when her father took her on a visit to see her sister, Princess Victoria of Battenberg, in Malta, where Prince Louis held a naval command. It was Princess Alix's first trip to the Mediterranean and it meant a great deal to such an ardent nature lover. At the same time she came in touch with people in the simple way she loved and she was fêted everywhere. Naval hospitality is well known and Prince Louis' brother officers and their wives devised all kinds of excursions and amusements, and the commander-in-chief, Admiral Sir Anthony Hoskins, gave many parties.

Lieutenant Mark Kerr was attached to the Grand Duke and looked after Princess Alix, who called him her "equerry." The number of dances he had at the balls beat all records. She was delighted with everyone and everything, and became an enthusiast about everything connected with the Navy.

From 1890 up until the death of the Grand Duke, Princess Alix stayed mostly at home, except for an annual visit to England. However, in Darmstadt she built a wider circle of friends and many of the great princely families in the neighborhood came to town for the winter season. She could therefore get to know more girls of her own age, although her childhood playmates were still her favorites.

She also went on several occasions to see her sister Princess Irene at Kiel, and there formed a great intimacy with the latter's young Lady-in-Waiting, Countess Julia ("Juju") Rantzau. Countess Rantzau became one of the Princess' closest friends and was often invited to Wolfsgarten. She was a bright, merry girl who knew how to draw the Princess out. She and Princess Alix had a common love of music and literature, and spent a lot of time together.

Wolfsgarten was a fine old place where large family parties gathered in the summer. Five separate buildings enclosed an inner courtyard. The castle was small but very comfortable. In the great forests surrounding the house, Princess Alix rode and drove her four-in-hand. She handled the reins well and her old friend, Baron Moritz Riedesel zu Eisenbach, her father's equerry, who had taught her, was proud of her achievements.

Princess Alix was always happy when her father and her brother Ernest were around. The Grand Duke was a kind and indulgent parent to all of his children, but he was particularly fond of his youngest one, an affection returned with wholehearted devotion. The older she grew, the more Princess Alix came to understand and admire her father's character. Grand Duke Louis IV was essentially a soldier. He had shown considerable military qualities in the wars of 1866 and 1870 and was beloved by his men with whom he always kept in touch. He took his duties as a ruler seriously and was interested in politics outside of his little grand duchy. He even supported the idea of a united Germany, despite the fact that Hesse had lost so much territory to Prussia. The Grand Duke also loved England and English institutions, and was on the best of terms with all his late wife's relatives.

Sadly, in the beginning of 1892 the Grand Duke suffered from some minor heart trouble which was not considered serious. However, he then had a major seizure while lunching with his family and died nine days later, on March 13, 1892, without ever recovering consciousness. His sudden death came as a terrible blow to Princess

Alix who watched over him day and night while he lay dying, longing for a sign of recognition, for a last word to remember … but in vain. The misery of that time and the awareness that death can often strike without notice were always vivid in her memory. She once told me, thinking of her father, "Death is dreadful without preparation and without the body gradually loosening all earthly ties."

Her father's death was perhaps the greatest sorrow of Princess Alix's life. For years she could not speak of him and, long afterward, when she was in Russia, anything that reminded her of him would bring her to the verge of tears.

After his death, her sisters stayed at Darmstadt long enough to help her to adjust to her new life. Her brother was now the reigning Grand Duke Ernest Louis, and it was to him that she gave all the love that she had previously divided between her father and her brother.

Chapter 4

Engagement: 1894

Over the next two years the bond that had always united the young Grand Duke of Hesse and his sister grew into a complete and harmonious understanding. The Grand Duke looked after his sister assiduously and acted as a father, mother and friend to her. The innate motherliness of the Princess' character meant that she was at her happiest when she could most devote herself to others and she now centered all her thoughts on her brother. She shared his pursuits, identified herself with his interests, and subsumed her life and aspirations for his.

She always did everything with her whole heart and, in carrying out the official duties of a Grand Duchess of Hesse, Princess Alix overtaxed her strength. The shock of her father's death and the fatigues that followed it were too much for her. She was nearing a breakdown and had to be taken by her brother for a cure to Schwalbach, after which they crossed to England in the August.

Her cousins lived almost continually in the Queen's household and there was always a merry band of young people at whichever palace she was residing in. Queen Victoria herself always hoped that Princess Alix would marry in England, and in 1892 she took her with her when she visited the mining districts in Wales. The Princess was intrigued by all that she learned about the life of the miners and insisted on being allowed to go down a mine.

In January 1893, Princess Alix paid her second visit to Berlin for the wedding of two of her cousins, Prince Frederick Charles of Hesse and Princess Margarethe of Prussia. However, she fell ill while she was there with an ear infection and was advised to recuperate in a warmer climate, so her brother took her to Italy in the early spring of

1893. They first went to Florence – where Queen Victoria was staying at the Villa Palmieri – and then to Venice. Both siblings were artistic and fully appreciated the beauties of Italy. Princess Alix was too busy sight-seeing with her relatives, whom she met in great numbers on that trip, to write much, but still she managed to send her old friend and governess Miss Jackson – her "darling Madgie" – "a few lines from your beloved Venice."

> *We have been favored with the finest weather so that you can imagine how enjoyable all has been. It is like a dream, so different to anything one has ever seen. And how interesting the different style of painting to the Florentines ... The delightful sensation of being rowed in a gondola and the peace and quiet. We used to take our tea on some island or other ... What a dream of beauty Florence also ... That view from San Miniato is too exquisite. Now we have once been here, I fear that we shall always long to come again.*

Nevertheless, however much Princess Alix enjoyed the journey and shared her brother's artistic enthusiasm, throughout that year the memory of her father was constantly with her. Her life and frame of mind at this period are seen in another letter to Miss Jackson:

DARMSTADT,
June 3, 1893

DARLING MADGIE,

I send you my most loving thanks for your dear letter and the sweet little book. I ought not to have opened the packet till the 6th, but I could not resist the temptation, I enjoy the little books you send me always so much.

We have come into town for Ernie's audiences and I have been writing, trying on, eating cherries and picking flowers in the Herrengarten, which I have been arranging in the Schloss Kirche, as Toni von Hombergk is going to be married to Pfarrer Erhardt there today, and the church looked so bare without any plants or flowers – now it looks quite friendly.

It is still warm, sunny and bright. We have been rowing on the pond at Kranichstein and fishing. Frau von Westerveller and Marie von Biegeleben came out to us yesterday for a few hours, the visit of the Grand Duke of Baden went off very well last Tuesday. When the Saxons and Austrians come there will be more to do, and I dread it.

Tonight we came in again for a large concert in the theatre, on account of the 25 (or 50) years' existence of the Mozartverein here, and the first time we go to the theatre again, I feel quite upset at the idea.

Oh Madgie dear, if you only knew how too terribly I miss my own Darling – it is too hard to believe that we shall never meet again in this world. But I must not make you sad. I am glad that you are going to Folkestone and so will be near Victoria.

A good long kiss.
Ever your very loving,
P.Q. No. III,
ALIX.

Don't you wish "The Old Man" on a cherry tree ?

Many princes came to Wolfsgarten during these years and Princess Alix saw many more in England as well, but no one had succeeded in touching her heart. She was always faithful to the Tsarevich whom she had loved at first sight. She thought of him as the hero of an ideal romance, but only her friend Toni knew what was in her heart. She knew that the wife of the heir to Russia had to be of the Orthodox faith, and to her the religious question seemed an insurmountable obstacle.

After her father's death, her conscientious scruples troubled her even more, for she had never spoken of the question to him, and she now felt that she could never know what his views would have been.

The Tsarevich had admired her greatly in 1889, but both were too young then – they were only seventeen and twenty-one respectively – for any question of marriage to arise. The Tsarevich was still being treated as a boy by his parents. They did not meet between 1889 and 1892, although they corresponded and exchanged small gifts, and the Tsarevich heard a great deal about Princess Alix from her sister, Grand Duchess Ella. Both she and Grand Duke Serge had always wished for the marriage and she naturally rejoiced at the idea of having her sister in Russia, having guessed Princess Alix's romantic inclinations and seen the attraction she held for the Tsarevich.

Grand Duchess Ella loved Russia and its people, and she had made many friends and was very popular. As her husband was not in direct succession to the throne, she could have retained her Lutheran faith, but the Orthodox Church appealed to her, and of her own free will – her husband never attempted to influence her – she became Orthodox in 1891. She did not, therefore, see the religious question as an impediment.

When the topic of his marriage was raised, the Tsarevich told Emperor Alexander III that he would marry no one but Princess Alix and Grand Duchess Ella resolved to help him. She often talked to him and relayed their conversations to her sister, but there followed for

Princess Alix a time of great mental unrest as her love for the Tsarevich struggled with the religious scruples that she had acquired, without her having really probed the differences of belief that she imagined to be so important.

Events hastened her decision. In the autumn of 1893, her brother Grand Duke Ernest became engaged to his first cousin Princess Victoria Melita of Saxe-Coburg (a daughter of the Duke of Edinburgh). Princess Alix had always dreaded the moment when her adored brother would marry and would no longer need her, a time when the close intimacy of their last few years would inevitably cease, and she was still hesitating as to what to do about it when she travelled to Coburg for their wedding. However, at the last minute, the unexpected news came that the Tsarevich had also decided to attend. They met and he convinced her that she could reconcile her religious beliefs with his.

Love conquered all, and on April 20, 1894, Princess Alix of Hesse and the Tsarevich Nicholas were engaged.

It was a real love match, one of those ideal unions that seem to belong to fairyland, tales of which are handed down through the ages. Their love grew with their life together, drawing them ever closer, and never abated. The Emperor's diaries and the Empress' letters to the Emperor show what they were to each other.

Princess Alix sent a radiant telegram from Coburg to her confidante Toni Becker in which she said she was *"unendlich glucklich"* (supremely happy), and the following letter to her old governess:

PALAIS EDINBURG, COBURG,
April 28, 1894

DARLING MADGIE,

Most loving thanks for your dear letter, which touched me deeply. I am more happy than words can express; at last after these 5 sad years!

You must come and see me, as soon as you can. Next week I arrive at Windsor and then I can tell you all about the wedding, too, and our reception at Darmstadt, where we spent a night and a few hours in the day. The others are all in Church, tomorrow is their Easter.

It is pouring at the present moment, so a good occasion for answering all one's letters and I have not got few, as you can imagine.

With a tender kiss.
Ever your very loving,
P.Q. No. III,
ALIX.

The political advantages of the marriage had never carried weight with Princess Alix. She had followed her heart and the fact that the Tsarevich was the heir to one of the greatest Empires in the world was, as her friend Toni Becker has said, more of a drawback than a blessing.

Her relatives took a more practical view. Queen Victoria, who had come to Coburg for her grandson's wedding, was very pleased with the prospective alliance and did a great deal at the crucial moment to help Princess Alix get over her conscientious scruples. Her voice was to the Princess the echo of that of her mother, and brought with it, too, her revered grandmother's authority. The German Emperor was also strongly in favor of the match, and, although he had never been a particularly intimate friend of either of them, helped them both by suggesting a modification of some of the antiquated formulae of renunciation so as to lessen the religious difficulties for the Princess.

There were, therefore, great rejoicings at Coburg when the engagement was announced and warm telegrams were received from the Emperor and Empress of Russia. The people of Darmstadt, too, were proud at the prospect of their Princess' great marriage, although some of the older ones shook their heads. Russia was far away and the political atmosphere there always seemed heavy with menace to those who remembered the murder of Alexander II. The young Princess had no such forebodings, however. She was intensely happy.

The engaged couple spent a few days at Coburg and then made a day trip to Darmstadt to see Grand Duke Ernest and his bride and to visit the mausoleum at the Rosenhohe. Afterward, the Tsarevich had to return to Russia, and Princess Alix left almost immediately for Windsor with Fraulein von Fabrice.

Here Queen Victoria once more brought her influence to bear, encouraging her granddaughter to engage in serious talks with the Bishop of Ripon, Dr. Boyd Carpenter. The bishop demonstrated to her how many points there were in common between the Orthodox Church and the Church of England, and it was decided that, on her return from a cure in Harrogate, the Emperor of Russia's confessor, Father Yanishev, should come to Windsor to instruct the Princess in the tenets of the Orthodox Church.

In Harrogate, where she underwent a treatment for sciatica, Princess Alix did not lose time, for she at once began to study Russian diligently under the guidance of Mlle. Catherine Adolfovna Schneider, reader to her sister Grand Duchess Ella. "It is amusing, but certainly not easy!" Princess Alix wrote to Miss Jackson about these Russian lessons.

The Princess lived very quietly in Harrogate under the name of Baroness Starckenburg, but her disguise was soon rumbled, much to her chagrin, and she had great difficulty in escaping from the notice of the public, whose interest in her was sometimes very embarrassing. She did not go about much on account of her cure, but her small niece, Princess Victoria of Battenberg's daughter, was with her. So full of interest was the Princess in everyone and everything about her that, when the landlady at her lodgings had twins, she insisted on being named a godparent, the children being appropriately called Nicholas and Alexandra.

Meanwhile, the Tsarevich was waiting impatiently to see his fiancée again, and as soon as the Princess' cure was complete, he set off for England where the Princess was staying with her sister and brother-in-law, Prince Louis and Princess Victoria of Battenberg, at Walton-on-Thames, and there the engaged couple spent a few happy days together. Then they went on to Windsor, where they met all the members of the Royal Family, received congratulations, and saw numerous visitors, among them the aged Empress Eugénie who had been a friend of Grand Duchess Alice and had paid a visit to Prince Ernest and Princess Alix in 1883 when they were in quite a state of isolation in Darmstadt. The little Princess had entertained her charmingly and had been presented with a beautiful doll by the Empress as a reward – too beautiful to play with, alas!

The Tsarevich's simple, engaging manner endeared him to those relatives of the Princess who had yet to meet him. Physically he was very much like his cousin the Duke of York (later King George V), and this resemblance resulted in many amusing mistakes. When the Tsarevich was in England for the Duke's wedding in 1893, many of the guests at a garden party, taking him for his cousin the bridegroom, shook him warmly by the hand and congratulated him effusively. The greatest joke, however, was when one of the gentlemen of the Court made the opposite mistake and, coming up to the Duke whom he took for the Tsarevich, begged him not to be late for his own wedding the next day.

While the Tsarevich and Princess Alix were at Windsor, the present Prince of Wales was born and the Tsarevich was named as one of his godparents. Between rides, tea parties, and dinners, Father Yanishev began his tuition, but it was decided that this had better be postponed until they were back in Darmstadt, as Queen Victoria had a tendency to want to have her grandchildren around her at all times, like any other proud grandmother.

It was an idyllic time for Princess Alix and she always cherished these memories of Windsor and of the brief moments when she and her fiancé were together, although the Queen had strict ideas on chaperonage and never left the engaged couple alone, which must sometimes have been rather trying for the Tsarevich.

He had brought Princess Alix beautiful presents, both from himself and from his father and mother. The pink pearl ring that the Empress always wore was her engagement ring. Her chain bracelet, with a huge emerald, was a present given to her by the Tsarevich at Windsor, as was a necklace of pink pearls; and the Emperor of Russia sent a marvelous sapphire and diamond brooch. The Empress used to recount that when Queen Victoria saw all these splendors, so different from the simple jewelry of her own youth, she would say to her granddaughter, as if she were still a child, "Now, do not get too proud, Alix."

From Windsor, the Queen took the Tsarevich and his fiancée to Osborne. Their stay there could only be short as the Tsarevich had to leave for Russia so as to be present at the wedding of his sister, the Grand Duchess Xenia. From the Emperor's diaries of the time, it is evident how their love was always growing and how hard the separation was for both of them.

After her brief sojourn at Osborne, the Princess returned to Darmstadt and diligently set about preparing for her own marriage, which was planned for some time the following spring, working assiduously with Mlle. Schneider and Father Yanishev to learn Russian and the Orthodox faith. She went into the question of religion with the utmost thoroughness. Father Yanishev once told Grand Duke Ernest that the Princess used to ask him questions on points of theology that were so abstruse that he had never heard them raised even by theologians, and that she often had him in a corner, when, to quote his own words in somewhat faltering German, he could only "scratch like a cat" (*"kratzen wie eine Katze"*) without finding an answer.

Meanwhile, disquieting reports began to arrive concerning the health of Emperor Alexander III. Years of work had sapped his strong constitution and the recent army maneuvers, which he had insisted on attending, had further aggravated his illness. The doctors consequently had ordered him to rest and to depart immediately for the Crimea.

The state of his father's health obliged the Tsarevich to put off his proposed visit to Darmstadt and soon his letters to his fiancée grew more and more despondent. Princess Alix was equally distressed at not being with him at such a time as she knew how devoted he was to his father and could picture his state of mind.

At the beginning of October the Tsarevich telegraphed Princess Alix to summon her to the Crimea. Princess Victoria of Battenberg accompanied her to Warsaw, where the sisters parted, Princess Victoria returning to Malta, and Princess Alix, now accompanied by Baroness Grancy, continuing on alone. On the way south, Grand Duchess Ella joined her, and on October 23 she arrived at Simferopol and was met by the Tsarevich. Princess Alix and he drove the eighty versts between Simferopol and the imperial residence, Livadia, together in an open carriage with Grand Duchess Ella following them in another carriage.

The whole Imperial Family was gathered at Livadia, everyone realizing that the sands of the Emperor's life were running out. The Emperor, however, insisted, on getting up and dressing to do honor to his heir's bride, and greeted the Princess with the greatest kindness.

In the lovely Livadia chapel, the Princess participated in her first Russian Church service, which was one of intercession for the Emperor. There are a few lines written by her in the Tsarevich's diary at that time which speak of this. "I have been able to pray with you in church for your darling father. What a comfort! You near me, all seems easier. I know you will always help me."

Princess Alix had wired to the Tsarevich at the Russian frontier her intention of joining the Orthodox Church on her arrival at Livadia, news which, as he notes in his diary, had given him great joy.

The whole palace was under the influence of the angel of death and the family scarcely dared leave the house for fear of a sudden collapse. The end came on November 1. In the presence of the whole Imperial Family, Father John of Kronstadt read the last prayers to his dying sovereign. Then Emperor Alexander III passed away and the Tsarevich became the new emperor, Nicholas II.

Chapter 5

Marriage and First Year in Russia: 1894-5

The next morning, the new Emperor, the Dowager-Empress and Princess Alix attended Holy Communion in the Livadia chapel. It was perhaps the most momentous day in Princess Alix's life so far in that she had been received into the Orthodox Church by Father Yanishev that morning.

The body of Emperor Alexander III lay in state at Livadia for nearly a week while the complicated funeral ceremonies were being planned and prepared in Moscow and St. Petersburg. According to a Ukase of the new Emperor Nicholas II, her fiancé, Princess Alix had become "the truly believing Grand Duchess Alexandra Feodorovna" and her name, as the Emperor's betrothed, was coupled with his in the litanies of the Church.

The new Emperor was overburdened with work and with the weight of overwhelming new responsibilities, and clung to Princess Alix and would not hear of her returning to Darmstadt, as had been planned, to wait for a wedding in the spring. The question of an immediate marriage was raised, and, feeling that it would have been the wish of the late Emperor, the Dowager-Empress asked that it take place before Alexander III's funeral. The Emperor's uncles, however, opposed this, considering the event to be of too much importance in the eyes of the nation for such a private ceremony. The Ministers supported this opinion and it was settled that the marriage should take place at the earliest possible date at the Winter Palace at St. Petersburg and that the Princess should not return to Hesse.

On November 8, the funeral cortège left Livadia, the Black Sea fleet acting as convoy. Princess Alix travelled with the young Emperor and the Dowager-Empress in the imperial train that took

Alexander III's body from Sebastopol to Moscow and St. Petersburg. It was a long, sad journey lasting several days and at every large station, and every town, immense crowds, headed by the local authorities, were waiting. The Imperial Family would disembark and long, solemn funeral ceremonies were held.

The rest of the Imperial Family was assembled at St. Petersburg to meet the funeral train and Princess Alix's first entrance into her future capital was in a weary funeral procession in contrast to the usual state entrance of a Grand Ducal bride. The memory of Grand Duchess Ella's fairytale procession must have struck her as she sat in her mourning coach, rocking on its springs like a ship in distress for the long four hours' drive. This sorrowful atmosphere could not have failed to depress her and seemed a dire portent for the new reign.

The body of the late Emperor now lay in state in the cathedral at the Peter and Paul Fortress. Services were held twice daily. The endless litanies that were incomprehensible to her and the woeful chants and prayers of the complicated funeral ceremonial seemed to Princess Alix like a long, sad dream through which she felt that she must keep up her courage for the sake of her fiancé. Her very genuine grief revealed the warm side of her nature to her new relatives, but that whole time was always blurred in her memory.

The Princess could, of course, see very little of the young Emperor at St. Petersburg, as State duties claimed him when he wasn't in church, so she waited impatiently for the fast-approaching day of her wedding when she would be able to be with him constantly and be of real help to him. The severing of her home ties was made easier to her than would have been the case under ordinary conditions as she did not return to Darmstadt but rather spent the twelve days before her marriage in the company of Grand Duchess Ella.

The wedding took place on November 26, a week after the late Emperor's funeral. It also happened to be the Dowager-Empress' birthday, and so a relaxation of Court mourning for the day was allowed. Many princes who had come for the funeral remained for the wedding; among them the bride's brother the Grand Duke of Hesse, the Prince and Princess of Wales, and Prince Henry and Princess Irene of Prussia.

On the wedding morning, the Dowager-Empress, a pathetic figure dressed, like the bride, in white, took her future daughter-in-law from the Serge Palace to the Winter Palace in the great chapel of which the ceremony was to take place. Princess Alix was dressed for her wedding in the Malachite drawing room of the Winter Palace. Her hair was done in the traditional long side curls in front of the famous gold mirror of the Empress Anna Ioannovna, before which every Russian Grand Duchess dresses on her wedding day. The chief dressers of the ladies of the Imperial Family assisted and handed her the crown jewels, which lay on red velvet cushions.

The Dowager-Empress herself placed the diamond nuptial crown on the bride's head. She wore numerous splendid diamond ornaments and her dress was a heavy Russian Court dress of real silver tissue, with an immensely long train edged with ermine. From her shoulders flowed the imperial mantle of cloth-of-gold, lined with the same royal fur. These robes were carried by chamberlains and were so heavy that, when the marriage ceremony was over and the Imperial Family had retired to the Malachite room with their guests, the Grand Duke Ernest saw his sister standing motionless and alone in the middle of the room (the Emperor having left her for a moment), unable to move a step! The train was so heavy that, when it was not carried by the chamberlains, she was almost pinned to the ground by its weight.

We see her impression of the ceremony in the following letter to her sister:

PALAIS ANICHKOV
December 10th, 1894.

The ceremony in church reminded me so much of '84, only both our fathers were missing – that was fearful –

47

no kiss, no blessing from either. But I cannot speak about that day nor of all the sad ceremonies before. One's feelings you can imagine. One day in deepest mourning, lamenting a beloved one, the next in smartest clothes being married. There cannot be a greater contrast, but it drew us more together, if possible.

Aunt Minny [the Dowager-Empress] is so sweet and patient in her great grief. She touches one with her gentleness.

To-day was again a hard day, the fortieth day at the fortress. We two have just now been for five days at Tsarskoe, alone with a lady and gentleman, the rest and quiet did one good. We walked and drove and enjoyed the beautiful country air. Here we get out but little, as Nicky sees people almost all day and then has to read through his papers and to write. Only tea we have together, all the other meals upstairs with the rest.

I cannot yet realize that I am married, living here with the others, it seems like being on a visit. The rooms are quite comfortable: Nicky's old ones and two others with nice light furniture and chintzes we chose. We are trying to make designs for our rooms at the Winter Palace. My two new ladies seem nice – the young one is C. Lamsdorff's sister.

It was horrid saying good-bye to the dear ones when they left again for home – poor Gretchen! But one must not think of that. For my Nicky's sake I must be good, so as to cheer him up.

If I only could find words to tell you of my happiness daily it grows more and my love greater. Never can I thank God enough for having given me such a treasure. He is too good, dear, loving and kind, and his affection for his mother is touching, and how he looks after her, so quietly and tenderly.

No festivities of any kind followed the marriage ceremony. It took place in the morning and immediately afterward the young imperial couple drove to the Anichkov Palace, enthusiastically cheered on by the huge crowds that lined their route, stopping at the Kazan Cathedral on their way to pray before the greatly venerated icon of Our Lady. The Empress in later years often went to this cathedral between the services with one of her ladies in attendance. She used to kneel in the shadow of a pillar, unrecognized by the few people in the church, who did not guess who the lady was who so unobtrusively bought a taper and put it before the icons.

Their marriage had been arranged so hastily that no preparations had been made for the young couple in any of the palaces. Alexander III had lived almost entirely at Gatchina, an hour's distance from St. Petersburg, and had used the small Anichkov Palace in the capital in winter. The Winter Palace at St. Petersburg was the official residence of the emperors of Russia, consisting of a series of gigantic halls, flanked at both sides by vast suites of apartments. No one had lived in it since the death of Alexander II in 1881 and it was used only for balls and receptions. The new Emperor Nicholas II meant to live in the rooms of his great-grandfather, Nicholas I, but these had to be thoroughly renovated. In the meantime, the young couple accepted the hospitality of the Dowager-Empress and it was settled that two rooms should be added to the Emperor's bachelor quarters at the Anichkov Palace to make six rooms in all, and that the Dowager-Empress would continue to live at the palace, too.

Happily, love gilds everything, for anything less comfortable could scarcely be imagined. The rooms were small and not designed for a married couple, much less for an imperial one. Their Majesties shared one sitting room and consequently could not give audiences simultaneously. They had no proper dining room, which would have prevented their having any guests, had not deep mourning made this impossible in any case, and from the very first day the young Emperor and Empress took their meals with the Dowager-Empress. Indeed, so dutiful was the Emperor to his mother, and so fearful of hurting her by introducing any change, that at first the Emperor and Empress even went to her apartments for breakfast, although this was later given up.

Alexandra Feodorovna sat all day in these small rooms, moving into her bedroom when the Emperor gave audience in the sitting room, but she was entirely happy. Her husband was near her and he came to her room for a cigarette and a few words whenever his work allowed and always found her waiting for him.

Sovereigns have no holidays – Nicholas II, whose wedding took place on November 26, resumed his work on the 29th, receiving his ministers in the morning and working with them exactly as Alexander III had done – and there was no proper honeymoon. Sovereigns are not allowed such things and princes are never alone. It was very, very seldom that Their Majesties could sit *en famille*, as the Russian court servant language had it.

The Emperor's day was divided according to strict unvarying rules from the day of his accession until 1914 and the Empress had to fit in her day accordingly. There were small variations to suit special places of residence, but in the main the arrangements were the same. Breakfast was about nine a.m., then followed interviews with ministers until eleven, a short turn in the garden for half-an-hour or so, and audiences and guests for luncheon. In such cases Their Majesties made a *cercle* after luncheon, which lasted till a quarter to three. Then there would be a drive with the Empress, or in later years when her health failed, a solitary walk for the Emperor, and then more work from four until tea time, to which meal some member of the Imperial Family was generally invited. At a quarter to six, the Emperor retired to work with his ministers again until eight. In those early days the Emperor and Empress then went to dinner with the Dowager-Empress, after which the Emperor retired once more to his study and the Empress sat with her mother-in-law.

Sometimes in the evening the Emperor would find an hour to take his young wife out on a sledge ride far out on "the Islands," a favorite promenade of the people of St. Petersburg. This was a delight for both of them. The rapid pace of the horses, the crisp snow flying under their feet, and the quiet, snowy, winter landscape were all new and fascinating to the Empress and these were almost the only hours they had alone together.

Having devoted herself whole-heartedly first to her father and then to her brother, the Empress now centered her whole life on her husband and her days were mapped out so as to seize any chance moment that the Emperor could give her. She was an ideal wife and always true to her childhood nickname of "Sunny," the name by which Nicholas II nearly always called her. She was bright and cheerful and entered into all of her husband's interests, never letting him see that she was tired or worried.

More and more she came to appreciate her husband's inherently chivalrous nature, his equable temper, his great sense of duty, and his patience. More and more, too, she realized how conscientiously he set about the work that had come to him so suddenly and for which he felt himself so insufficiently prepared, but on the whole she knew very little about the Emperor's working life. He never spoke to her about political issues during that first year, nor indeed for some time later, and it was not until her son was born that she took any interest in the political life of the country. She did not think that politics were a suitable occupation for a woman, but rather that a woman's duty was to make a home, and she made a real home for her husband and their children.

The young Empress' household had been appointed by the Dowager-Empress and its members were all total strangers to her. Her Grande Maîtresse (Mistress of the Robes), Princess Marie Mikhailovna Galitzin, was a wonderful old Russian type, belonging by birth and marriage to some of the greatest families in the country. She was a *grande dame* of the old school and even her outward appearance was reminiscent of a bygone age. She wore the poke-bonnet and caps of her youth and always dressed in a style peculiarly her own. On State occasions this poke-bonnet was ornamented with all the feathers and flowers that Victorian millinery loved. This gave rise to an amusing incident during the imperial visit to France when a member of the press came up to a gentleman-in-waiting, Count Hendrikov, and asked him about the headdress Princess Galitzin was wearing, believing the poke-bonnet was part of a kind of national costume.

Notwithstanding her intimidatingly brusque manner – Princess Galitzin struck terror into the hearts of all the debutantes, glaring at them through her horn rim glasses – she was kind and straightforward and courteous, but she was no diplomat and could not do much to help the young Empress to whom she became deeply attached. Inversely, although the Empress was rather afraid of Princess Galitzin to begin with, she afterward loved her dearly, too. When Princess Galitzin died in 1910, the Empress felt her loss greatly and said to Princess E.N. Obolensky, *"J'ai perdu la plus grande amie que j'avais en Russie. Même dans toute la famille, personne ne m'était aussi proche."* (I have lost the best friend I ever had in Russia. Even within the family, no one was as close to me as she was.)

The male household was headed by Count Paul Constantinovich Benckendorff but the Emperor's suite did not come into contact very often with the Empress during the year of mourning.

Mlle. Schneider came daily to read or to go for a drive with the Empress to help her with her Russian studies which had been resumed. From the Empress' notes in her husband's diaries, it can be

52

seen that she worked hard at the Russian language, even in the early days after her marriage. The Empress later gained great proficiency in Russian, which she spoke without any foreign accent, but for many years she was nervous of starting a conversation in it, fearing she might make mistakes.

Living as she did under the same roof as her mother-in-law, the Empress saw much of the Empress Marie Feodorovna. She was full of sympathy for her, but as the Dowager-Empress had her own much-loved sister, the Princess of Wales, staying with her at the time, she naturally needed no other consolation. In her letters of this time the young Empress speaks with tenderness of the Dowager-Empress, however the temperaments and tastes of mother-in-law and daughter-in-law were so dissimilar that, without actually clashing, they seemed fundamentally unable to understand each other. Later, as is natural in such cases, people of the "old court" became critical of the doings of the "young court," and the idea arose that such criticisms were echoes of the Dowager-Empress' personal opinions, leading to gossip that was mostly unfounded. When, once or twice, slight friction did arise between the two Courts, society made the most of it, but the two Empresses always met on friendly terms.

According to a Ukase of the Emperor Paul I, the Dowager-Empress in Russia always had precedence over the reigning Empress. On ceremonial occasions, therefore, Empress Marie Feodorovna preceded the young Empress on the Emperor's arm, the Empress Alexandra Feodorovna following behind them on the arm of the senior prince.

During the first years of the Emperor's reign the Dowager-Empress' influence on her son was undoubtedly considerable. If the Emperor ever spoke of the political situation and of the difficulties of government, it was not to his young and inexperienced wife but to his mother, whose advice on general questions he had always been accustomed to seek.

The young Emperor and Empress never failed to be attentive to the Dowager-Empress and when they first moved into the Winter Palace they visited her nearly every day. As the years went by and the imperial couple gave up coming to St. Petersburg for the winter, the exchange of visits grew less frequent. Still, at every family fête, either the young Emperor and Empress went to the Dowager-Empress or the Dowager-Empress went to Tsarskoe Selo, while Christmas always united the whole Imperial Family at the Dowager-Empress' palace.

Ten days after the wedding, the Emperor and Empress went to Tsarskoe Selo to see for themselves what alterations should be made in that old palace that they meant to make their home. This was their real honeymoon. Their dutiful sentiments with regard to Empress Marie can be judged by the grateful tone in which the Emperor remarks in his diary that his mother has allowed them to stay for a few days longer at Tsarskoe Selo. As for the young Empress, her feelings at this time can be seen from this note she made in the Emperor's diary on November 26, 1894:

> *Never did I believe there could be such utter happiness in the world – such a feeling of unity between two mortal beings. No more separations. At last united, bound for life, and when this life is ended we meet again in the other world and remain together for Eternity.*

The same feelings are echoed in a Christmas letter to her eldest sister, then in Malta, on December 15, 1894.

> *I wish I could slip over and peep into your rooms and little garden – how glad I am that I know the dear place, so can picture you to myself there. Do give Mr. Kerr my very best wishes for the New Year and kind messages. Are there still so many snails on the bushes which you*

*used to have to pick off with the little gardener boy?
And have you taken Spiridon without moustache?*

*I long to know everything you are doing. It was too hard
you could not be here for our wedding. But how utterly
contented and happy I am with my beloved Nicky you
can well imagine, and that helped me over my sad
feeling being absent from my old home for Xmas and
beginning the New Year in another country. Our Xmas
will, of course, be a perfectly quiet one, which is in
every way pleasanter.*

The remainder of the year was spent partly at the Anichkov Palace
and partly at Tsarskoe Selo. Both of them were delighted with
Tsarskoe. The Emperor's recollections of childhood were linked with
it and he had been born in the very bedroom they occupied during
their first stay.

Life in town was very irksome to the Emperor, an outdoorsman to
whom exercise was a necessity. Happily the Anichkov Palace had a
garden and an ice hill, and whenever he could leave his audiences and
papers, the Emperor and Empress would join the young Grand Duke
Michael Alexandrovich and the Grand Duchess Olga Alexandrovna –
then sixteen and thirteen – in climbing and descending the ice hill or
walking around the garden.

The Empress, meanwhile, was busy with plans for the renovation
and decoration of the Winter Palace and Tsarskoe Selo, where she
hoped to have her own home and to have the Emperor completely to
herself. The young Empress planned changes to the old palace with
Grand Duchess Ella, who had come from Moscow, and enjoyed
creating her own individual setting. The *Jugendstil* [art nouveau] had
made its appearance in Darmstadt and Alexandra Feodorovna's taste
at that time was undoubtedly influenced by it. Her mauve boudoir, her
large, pale-green sitting room, connected by a private passage in an

overhanging gallery with the Emperor's study, were distinctly art nouveau.

The Empress' own personality was, however, clearly seen in her rooms, in the beautiful collections of ancient crosses, in the pictures on the walls, including a lovely 'Annunciation' by Nesterov in the mauve room, exquisite in coloring, and watercolors of Hessian and English scenes that she had known and loved, and beautiful knick-knacks and china on the tables, all chosen by her or gifts from those she loved and who knew her taste. Her friends could always guess which ones were the Empress' things. Pale mauve enamels (mauve was her favorite color), transparent green nephrite cups, crystal inlaid with amethysts, bookmarks and small objects decorated with edelweiss in baroque pearls, or bearing the emblem of the Swastika, a symbol of eternity, these were all stamped with the Empress' individuality, although these things did not always harmonize with one another or even with the setting. She liked a thing often more for its associations than for its beauty, for hers was a sentimental rather than an aesthetic nature.

She was not a collector of antiques. She loved a homely house, with children and dogs around it. She did not like to be constantly afraid for the safety of some priceless object and the atmosphere of her private rooms in the Palace was, above all, one of comfort.

The official reception rooms were, of course, more stately. She was a lover of flowers and nature, and her rooms were always a mass of white lilac and every kind of beautiful orchid. These throve, for the Empress' rooms were always extremely cold, a trial to those unaccustomed to them. Like her grandmother, Queen Victoria, she could not stand a temperature that was even moderately warm. It sent all the blood to her head, even when she was young, and in later years, with the onset of her heart trouble, she found too much warmth even more trying.

The bedrooms and nurseries were all simply upholstered in bright chintzes, The Empress kept faithfully to the English ideas that had been her mother's and these rooms were just like those of a comfortable English house. There was no wondrous luxury, but real comfort, for the Empress was eminently practical, and in planning her house she saw to all the details herself and in her home were to be found mementoes of all her past life.

Chapter 6

The Empress in her New Home: 1895

The winter of 1895 was spent by the imperial couple removed from the world. Mourning was somewhat relaxed for Christmas. There was the traditional Christmas tree for the Cossacks of the Emperor's escort, and on New Year's Day the Empress held her first *sortie*, the equivalent of a drawing room occasion, which took place in the afternoon. After a solemn Mass in the chapel of the Winter Palace, which the whole Imperial Family and the Court attended in gala dress, the ladies of St. Petersburg society were presented in turn to the Empress, who described the ceremony in a letter to Princess Victoria of Battenberg, dated February 4, 1895:

> *Yesterday was a baise-main for all the ladies; it was rather amusing, especially seeing those I knew in 1889, but when Madame Narishkin, Papa's friend, whom we also saw at Illinskoe and who was photoed on the group came I could scarcely swallow my tears, it made me think so awfully of him. The deputations from the whole country came twice last week, and were interesting in their different picturesque costumes. They brought most beautiful plates and images. Another day, three Tartar ladies came and brought me a costume. It was the first time their husbands allowed them to come from Orenburg. They need not be veiled before the Russian men, which is odd ...*
>
> *My two ladies at present are Princess Galitsyn, sister of Madame Ozeroff at Frankfort (who will be, probably,*

*appointed at Darmstadt instead of 0. Sacken), then
Countess Lamsdorff, the sister of Stuttgart Lamsdorff.
They are both charming and I like them exceedingly. I
see them rarely, they live in the Winter palace,
"Schneiderlein" – my lectrice, now, please – too. She
was 38 or 39 the other day. She comes every morning
for a good lesson, and reads an hour to me before
supper, whilst Nicky is occupied with papers; he has a
fearful amount to do, so that we are scarcely ever to
ourselves ...*

*The news from Georgie is good again, after he has had
a bad cough again. End of February or beginning of
March, this style here, he will go on the Derjava or
Polar Star for a cruise perhaps, he may pass Malta.*

*Do let me hear from you soon again, dear, as your dear
letters are a great joy to me. I am sure fat little Georgie
must be a great joy to you and now that he can walk
more. The tiny frames are for Alice and Louise. No more
today, else I shall bore you with this long rigmarole.*

It was a very beautiful and picturesque scene. All the ladies wore
the traditional dress of the Russian Court. The *dames à portrait*
(Women of the Bedchamber) and maids-of-honor were obliged to
wear certain colors and forms of headdress. The rest of the company
wore Court dress, in which the wearer's imagination had been allowed
full play. The result was a gorgeous picture. The young Empress at
her first *sortie* wore a dress of heavy fabric of silver, fur-edged, with
magnificent diamonds and pearls. The long ceremony must have been
very tiring. Hundreds of wedding presents had been showered on the
new sovereign and his bride, and many deputations came to give them
in person.

The young Empress found interest in everything Russian; she read and translated from Russian authors and studied the music of the country, which had at once appealed to her. Whenever they had an evening alone, the Emperor read aloud, a habit to which he always adhered. At first the readings were mostly in French, as the Empress wanted to improve her knowledge of the Russian court language.

They read no light literature. The Empress, in one of her first letters to her sister, mentions the titles of the books they were then reading: 'Le Roman du Prince Eugène;' Nolhac's 'Duchesse d'Angoulême;' 'Napoléon à Ste. Hélène,' etc. Later, when the Empress could understand Russian sufficiently, the Emperor read his favorite authors to her, and in this way she gained a considerable knowledge of Russian literature.

It was from these readings that she formed her own idea of the Russian peasant. Though not in sympathy with all of Tolstoy's philosophy, she accepted his ideal view of peasant life without being able to judge for herself and realize the whole complexity of the Russian nature, including its weaknesses and its defects of character. She saw these distinctly in the members of the upper classes with whom she came into contact, but she imagined the peasant to be different. He seemed to her a simple, innocent child with all the artlessness of childhood and a childlike faith. She was an inveterate idealist. Although she had many disillusions, as all princes must have, she continued to believe in the inherent good of all humanity. The future of Russia lay, she thought, with the peasants, with the classes that were still untainted by the poison of civilization.

She became more and more attached to the Russian Church, throwing herself into the practice of its religion with all the fervor of her nature. In this she was encouraged by the Emperor. He was the official Head of the Church, far from narrow in his views, but deeply religious by nature. Those who saw him in church could tell by the expression in his eyes how sincere he was in his faith.

The Empress had come to Russia imbued with the feeling that she must do her duty to her husband's country. This duty seemed to her above all to consist of social work. In her very first letter to her sister, in January 1895, she noted that she had not yet seen any hospitals, although she could not do much that year, for she was expecting a baby in the autumn, and spent a quiet spring and summer at the little seaside villa at Peterhof. This hope made the Empress' happiness complete and all her thoughts were full of the coming child. Motherliness was essential to her character and every pleasure was sacrificed that might possibly endanger her health. The coming event seemed to her to be so sacred and so wonderful that she scarcely wanted to speak of it to anyone except her sisters and her old friend Toni Becker.

In the autumn, the imperial couple moved to the now refurnished Tsarskoe Selo Palace, and there on November 15 the Grand Duchess Olga Nicholaevna was born. The Grand Duchess Ella came from Moscow to be with her sister and the Dowager-Empress hurried to the Palace as soon as she heard that the event was imminent. The guns of the old fortress of SS. Peter and Paul thundered out the announcement of the birth and the population of St. Petersburg eagerly counted the shots: 300 would mean an heir, 101 a Grand Duchess. The number of shots seemed endless - 99 - 100 - 101. People broke into wild cheering in clubs and regimental messes, but the firing stopped. It was only a Grand Duchess after all!

Whether it was a boy or a girl was all the same to the proud parents, the father noting in his diary that "the baby weighed 10 lb. and is 55 cent. long."

"It is a radiantly happy mother who is writing to you," the Empress wrote to her sister, Princess Victoria, on December 13, 1895. "You can imagine our intense happiness now that we have such a precious little being of our own to care for and look after." She nursed her little daughter herself, with an official wet-nurse in attendance in case of unexpected complications.

The christening in the Big (or Catherine) Palace church was a splendid event. The baby was taken to church in a gold coach like a fairy princess, a mantle of cloth-of-gold covering her little body, and carried in state by aged Princess Galitzin on a golden cushion. The Dowager-Empress and Queen Olga of Greece were her godmothers, and it was Empress Marie, wonderfully young-looking for the grandmother's role, who held the baby during the ceremony.

The Grand Duchess Olga was a fair, fat baby, not yet showing as a tiny child the good looks that were to be hers when she grew up. The Empress had the cradle placed in her boudoir, as she had those of all her subsequent babies, and there the little girl spent most of her days. An English nurse, sent out by Queen Victoria, had a Russian nurse under her, and old "Orchie" had the general supervision of the nurseries. It must be said that she often clashed with the others and caused great trouble to the Empress by contemptuously sweeping aside her inexperienced suggestions. The Empress fed and bathed her baby herself, knitted endless jackets and socks for her, and enjoyed her even more than most young mothers enjoy their first-born. She was devoted to children and had often been lonely in her first year in Russia, as the Emperor's work kept him very busy.

This was the Empress' first St. Petersburg season since her marriage. After the Christmas celebrations, the New Year *sortie* and diplomatic reception, came a series of Court balls. Much has been written about the splendor of these occasions, the marvelous setting of the Winter Palace balls, and the beautiful uniforms and dresses. Every Guards regiment had a special gala uniform for Court. The servants and the members of the Emperor's private band wore gold and scarlet liveries, the picturesque "Runners" had quaint, be-feathered headgear – something like the ballet dress of the *"Roi Soleil"* [Sun King, Louis XIV of France] – and the negro servants, in Oriental costume, lent a touch of Eastern splendor.

Their Majesties' entrance was heralded by the tapping of the canes of the *Maîtres des Cérémonies*, tall ivory-topped canes decorated with eagles embossed in gold. The ball was opened by a stately polonaise in which the Emperor and Empress, the Princes and the ambassadors took part. Except in this polonaise, the Emperor did not dance, although before his accession he had been a good dancer. The Empress took part only in square dances with the partners that etiquette prescribed. During the round dances she held her *cercle* and the debutantes were presented to her.

The Empress did not relish attending these great functions. She had loved dancing as a girl but ordinary dancing was impossible for her now. If she had felt shy and frightened at Darmstadt parties, where all the people were her friends, here in unknown surroundings, facing hundreds of strangers – 2,000 people were asked to the big ball and 800 to the concert balls) – she felt absolutely lost. She used to say that during the *cercles* she longed to disappear under the ground. All her French evaporated and her conversation languished; she blushed and looked ill-at-ease. During the famous suppers under the palm-trees that followed the concert balls, her neighbor on every occasion for over ten years was the *doyen* of the Diplomatic Corps, the Turkish Ambassador, Husny Pasha. He was a heavy and uninteresting old gentleman, whom, it was said, the Ottoman Government only kept on at his post because he was the *doyen*, thus ensuring that the Turkish representative remained first in rank among the ambassadors.

In addition to presentations made at the balls, the Empress daily received large groups of ladies in audience. In this, too, she was greatly hampered by her shyness, and Princess Galitzin could not help her as much as she might have done had she been able to tell her who the people were and what topic of conversation would be most suited to each one. The Princess was a Muscovite and had tended to stay at home prior to her appointment, and so hardly knew any of the younger people. To her old-fashioned ideas, it was a sufficient honor for the ladies to be received by the Empress at all. What did it matter what she said to them? Why torment the poor soul with details and explanations? So the Empress had to speak in a general and non-committal manner to everyone who came, which did little to increase her circle of acquaintances in St. Petersburg society. Had she come to Russia as the Tsarevna (the wife of the heir), a position the Empress Marie Feodorovna had held for fourteen years, it would have been easier for her. The Dowager-Empress, with her knowledge of the world, her love of society and charm of manner, would have helped her young daughter-in-law to know people in the natural course of events. She would therefore have created a circle of friends for herself who would have supported her as Empress. Coming straight into an exalted position that would inevitably isolate a sovereign from the rest of the world, the Empress Alexandra Feodorovna could not easily make friends, and there was no possibility of her getting to know anyone better at the big functions and at the Russian Court, where everything was regulated by unshakeable tradition and any kind of small or informal entertainment was unheard of.

The result was that Society did not know her and her timidity was put down to haughtiness and her reserve to pride. Worse, there were no young women of Alexandra Feodorovna's age in the Imperial Family at the time of her marriage, except Grand Duchess Xenia Alexandrovna, the Emperor's eldest sister and herself a bride. She and her husband, Grand Duke Alexander Mikhailovich, and their baby daughter, Princess Irina (now Princess Irina Yusupova), were living temporarily at the Winter Palace. The two imperial children were about the same age and always together, and the young mothers engaged in baby worshipping for hours at a time. The Grand Duchess Ella, whose help would have been invaluable to her younger sister, was tied down in Moscow, where her husband was the Governor-General. The older generation – the Emperor's uncles and aunts – were outwardly friendly but, as they were accustomed to the Dowager-Empress' worldly *savoir-faire*, they didn't even attempt to help the newcomer to their family, who in her turn felt shy of them.

One of the aunts, Grand Duchess Marie Pavlovna, wife of Grand Duke Vladimir, was a brilliant Society leader, but much older than the Empress and very unlike her in character. There was a contingent of lively young bachelor cousins, who led their own merry life in St. Petersburg and Paris, but who could form no link between the young Empress and Society either. Alexander III had always held a big family dinner once a week, but this was discontinued in the new reign. The relatives had according to custom to ask permission to call on the Emperor and Empress, and were then generally invited to lunch or tea, but return visits were infrequent and always inevitably marked with a certain amount of formality.

So it was that Alexandra Feodorovna only succeeded in completely winning the hearts of the senior members of the family: the splendid looking old Field-Marshal Grand Duke Michael Nicholaevich – son of Nicholas I – and his equally handsome sister-in-law, the Grand Duchess Alexandra Iossiphovna, wife of Grand Duke Constantine. She paid them all the charming little attentions with which a bright young woman can cheer up the old people. Here she was in her element and she so much endeared herself to her old aunt that, although the Grand Duchess Alexandra Iossiphovna had withdrawn from the world many years earlier, she decided to attend the coronation in Moscow!

Alexandra Feodorovna's study of Russian charitable institutions continued and she accompanied the Emperor to visit the schools and hospitals in St. Petersburg. Official visits did not satisfy her, but she had to put off more thorough inspections until later. All this spring her thoughts and time were taken up with the preparations for the coronation to be held in Moscow, according to tradition, in May 1896. Throughout her busy winter, the Empress' thoughts were centered on this event and on the great mystical and religious importance attached to it by all of Russia. The Grand Duke Serge explained to her every detail of its complicated ceremonial and encouraged her to realize its deep religious significance.

The actual ceremony, the general atmosphere in Moscow at the time, the old rites and customs, made an indelible impression on the Empress. They turned her thoughts more and more towards the old traditions in religion and art that had always attracted her, and this, indirectly, had its influence on her growing political ideas.

Chapter 7

The Coronation: 1896

At the Coronation, the whole old-world pomp of the Russian Court was on display. It was a glorious pageant for the whole country, beyond the importance it held in the eyes of those who saw in the religious rites the real consecration of their sovereign, and everything was done to foster this feeling in the people who came to Moscow for the celebrations from every part of the vast Russian Empire. The Emperor granted amnesties to prisoners and gifts to all classes of his subjects; fines were remitted and accommodations were made for the payment of taxes.

In the run up to the actual Coronation, the Emperor and Empress stayed at the Petrovsky Palace, near Moscow, preparing themselves for the ceremony by retreat and fasting.

Princes representing nearly every sovereign state in Europe came to Moscow, although no reigning sovereigns were present (except Queen Olga of Greece, who was a Russian Grand Duchess), for on this occasion the Emperor and Empress had to play the primary role and could give precedence to no one. All the embassies migrated to the old capital and were lodged in different palaces belonging to the great families there.

On the day of the Coronation, the state entrance to the Kremlin was a marvelous sight. Tremendous crowds lined the streets and people of all classes were represented, so that well-dressed ladies could be found side-by-side with peasants in Sunday clothes, and everyone's enthusiasm was indescribable as they crossed themselves with emotion as the procession passed by.

The Emperor rode alone at the head of the procession, surrounded by all the Grand Dukes and foreign Princes. Then the Empresses followed in beautiful gilt state coaches which were real eighteenth century works of art with panels painted by Boucher. The Dowager-Empress went first, her coach surmounted by a crown, as she had already been crowned; Empress Alexandra Feodorovna drove alone and had no crown on her coach.

The long progress through the city lasted for several hours. When it reached the Iverskaya gates, all dismounted, the Empresses leaving their coaches to enter the Chapel of Our Lady which contained the celebrated Iverskaya, a greatly venerated icon, before which everyone who passed bared his head.

The procession entered the Kremlin through the Nicholsky gates and then vanished from the sight of the people, who stood gazing spellbound after it as if hoping that the brilliant vision would appear again.

The next day, heralds in medieval dress read out the proclamation announcing to "the good people of Our first capital" that the coronation was fixed for May 26 and was to be held in the old Cathedral of the Assumption, Uspensky Sobor. This was a fitting setting for so impressive a ceremony. Although the cathedral had suffered much at the time of the French invasion in 1812, when Napoleon's troops had stabled their horses there, its ancient splendor had long since been restored and all of its walls and pillars were covered with fifteenth century frescoes depicting the Saints and scenes from the Old and New Testaments. This brilliant background enhanced the beauty of the uniforms and robes. The jewels that were worn were wonderful, Grand Duchess Ella's famous emeralds and the old Grand Duchess Constantine's sapphires, every flawless stone of which was about two inches across, attracting everyone's attention. The *ikonostasis* (altar screen), containing some very old and venerated icons, glittered with gold and silver.

The ceremony began early in the morning and lasted for several hours. The Emperor and Empress arrived on foot in a state procession from the Kremlin. First came the Dowager-Empress alone, pale and serious-looking, with sad eyes that reminded the onlookers that her own coronation had been not many years before. After her, each walking under a separate canopy, came Nicholas II and Empress Alexandra Feodorovna, attended by numerous court officials in splendid uniforms. In contrast to the Dowager-Empress, who was blazing with diamonds and wearing an imperial crown, the young Empress had no jewels except a string of pearls around her neck. She wore a Russian court dress of silver tissue, her hair in two long "love-locks," and no ornaments on her head where the imperial crown was to rest. She looked lovely. At first she was a little flushed and nervous, but she regained her self-possession as the ceremony proceeded.

The Emperor wore the uniform of the Preobrajensky regiment, the oldest regiment in Russia. He had at first expressed the wish to wear the robes of the old tsars and their "Monomach" crown, as the newer "imperial" crown was very heavy (weighing nine pounds) and he had suffered from acute headaches ever since he had been wounded in the head by a Japanese fanatic in Otsu, but iron etiquette proclaimed that any change was impossible and the Emperor was condemned to suffer the considerable pain inflicted on him by the heavy crown.

The whole five-hour long ceremony was a time of intense emotion for Empress Alexandra, although she was not tired at all, she told her sisters, and found everything very beautiful. For her the Coronation represented a mystic marriage to Russia itself, whereby she became at one with the country, sealed forever as a Russian in her heart and in her soul, and remaining so from that day forth for the rest of her life. She saw the entire event – the long Mass, the robing of the Emperor, and his investiture with the imperial insignia – as if it were a dream.

It is easy to imagine how ardent her prayers were as she knelt alongside everyone else while the Metropolitan read the prayer for the Emperor, and how her heart went out to his when he knelt, this time all alone, the others standing, and prayed for Russia and his people. Then Their Majesties alone received the Holy Communion and the Metropolitan anointed the Emperor with the holy oils. On this one day, for the only time in his life, the Russian Emperor enters the sanctuary and receives the Blessed Sacrament like a priest.

Ominously, while Nicholas II ascended the altar steps, the chain of the order of St. Andrew fell to the ground, but the Empress was not troubled by this. She only saw the sunbeam that fell at that moment on his head to provide him with a halo.

The Metropolitan handed the Emperor the crown and he crowned himself. Then the Empress left her place and knelt before him. The Emperor took off his crown and touched her forehead with it. Then he took a smaller crown and with the utmost gentleness put it on her head for her ladies to affix. The Emperor kissed her, took her hand as she rose, and both of them went to their respective thrones.

The church ceremony ended with Empress Marie and all the Princes present doing homage to their crowned and anointed ruler. When his mother approached, pale with emotion, the Emperor's embrace seemed to everyone to be not that of a sovereign to his subject, but that of a dutiful son to his mother.

The whole procession left the Cathedral on foot and returned to the Kremlin, this time with the Emperor and Empress at its head dressed in full regalia. Bells rang in all the "forty times forty" Moscow churches, cannons thundered, and the countless multitudes in the streets shouted themselves hoarse.

The imperial couple turned at the top of the celebrated Red Staircase and bowed low to the crowd three times. This symbolized their greeting to the country. In the palace they passed the representatives of their Mohammedan subjects, whose religion did not allow them to enter a Christian church. These were certainly the most picturesque of all the guests; the splendor of their dress alone would take pages to describe.

In one room a group of people in ordinary clothes stood off by themselves. The foreign Princes inquired who these people were and were told that they were all descendants of people who had saved the lives of Russian sovereigns at different times. There were descendants of Ivan Sussanin, who had, by sacrificing his own life, saved the first Romanov from the hands of the Poles and others who had saved Alexander II from assassination. Their presence spoke of the constancy of imperial gratitude, but was also a cogent reminder of the perils that all tsars face.

The coronation banquet took place on the same day as the Coronation in the old Granovitaya Palata, the council chamber of former tsars, whose walls were painted with frescoes like those of the Cathedral of the Assumption. A special table was set for the Emperor and Empress under a baldachin. There they dined alone, wearing their robes and crowns, with high court officials waiting upon them. The head carver handed out the dishes and the *"grand échanson,"* the goblet, and when the foreign ambassadors came in, the Emperor drank a separate health with each of them.

The foreign Princes watched the scene from the windows of the upper gallery (Tainik), from which the old tsaritsas used to look down unseen at banquets and receptions, for only Russians could take part in the banquet in the hall.

In the evening, the illuminations made Moscow look like a town in a fairy tale. The young Empress started the illuminations from the Kremlin by pressing a button hidden in a bouquet of roses. She "looked blooming and radiant," wrote her sister Princess Victoria to Queen Victoria in a long account of the proceedings. The Empress' brother and sisters were present, Grand Duchess Ella looking especially magnificent in a court dress of cream velvet embroidered with gold fuchsias; the Duke of Connaught came with the Duchess to represent the Queen of England. An attraction for all eyes were the beautiful Crown Princess of Romania and her sister, the Grand Duchess Victoria Melita of Hesse, dressed in cloth-of-gold, the one embroidered with autumn leaves, the other with violet irises. The immense, bearded Emir of Bokhara, wearing a Russian General's epaulettes encrusted with diamonds on his Oriental khalat, shared the admiration of the crowds in the streets with the Emperor of China's envoy, the celebrated Li-Hung-Chang, an unforgettable sight in his yellow mandarin's robes and peacock feather.

The Empress, as a recent bride, took particular interest in an engagement that came about at the Coronation. The Prince of Naples (the present King of Italy), who was representing Italy at the festivities, met the Princess Helena of Montenegro at the house of Grand Duchess Ella and became privately engaged to her.

While no incident marred any of the first day's proceedings, nor the ball at the Kremlin or the gala performance at the opera (with a whole sequence of great fêtes planned for thereafter) a terrible, even ominous, accident then took place, casting a deep shadow over everything, instantly compared as it was with the disaster that marred the wedding ceremonies of King Louis XVI and Queen Marie-Antoinette of France.

A popular fête had been arranged at the Khodynskoe Pole, outside the town, during which small gifts and souvenirs were to be distributed to the people. Peasants from all parts of the Empire had come to Moscow for this. The authorities had counted upon the same numbers as had attended the last coronation, but in fact this time the numbers were vastly greater. Owing to mismanagement by the local authorities, who had not taken the necessary measures to prevent a crush, the fête ended in disaster. It was a crowd "as large as that of three Derby days," wrote Sir Francis Grenfell in his letters. Early in the morning, before the police had arrived or anyone was present to keep order, the crowd tried to get to the booths where the presents were to be given and a panic ensued when the whole surging mass of people collided, and thousands were killed and injured hours before the fête was even supposed to begin.

The extent of the disaster only gradually became evident. At first no one could tell even approximately how many people had suffered. The whole truth was indeed not told to the Emperor at all. He was informed that an accident had happened, but not its full extent, and there were still thousands of people who had travelled immense distances to see their Sovereign, perhaps for the only time in their lives. The Ministers thought that countermanding the planned entertainment would cause disappointment to the people who had not seen the accident and, in consequence, the Emperor and all his guests attended the fête at the appointed time in the afternoon.

The Emperor's horror knew no bounds when he heard later of the terrible disaster that had preceded it. Both he and the Empress wanted to cancel the French Ambassador's ball, arranged for that very night, but they were told that this was impossible, the French Government having made the most extravagant preparations for the ball. Beautiful tapestries and plate had been sent expressly, and at great expense, from the Garde-Meuble National in Paris, so the Emperor had to give in and go and the Empress had to control her tears, but it was with a face of utter misery that she attended the Marquis de Montebello's wonderful entertainment. She behaved like an automaton and all her thoughts were with the dead and dying. When the imperial couple visited the hospitals where the victims lay, the scenes they saw rent the Empress' heart. She would have given up all festivities on the spot and have nursed the people with her own hands, but official duties had to be fulfilled, private feelings being held to be of no account. The Emperor had large sums distributed to the relatives of the victims, but the sovereigns themselves had to continue to play their parts in the proceedings, whatever it might cost them. The Empress never forgot her feelings at a State luncheon, given just after their return from a hospital they had visited, at which she had surreptitiously to wipe her eyes with her napkin as she remembered the terrible things she had seen.

This tragic incident cast a gloom over all the remaining programmed activities, with too many balls, reviews and receptions to enumerate, until June 7, when the foreign Princes left and the Emperor and Empress went for a private visit to Grand Duke Serge's estate at Illinskoe. The Empress was still nursing her baby, and fatigue and emotion were beginning to take their toll upon her. The large party of

73

visitors included the Empress' sisters and her brother and his wife, members of their suites, and many of the usual friends of the Grand Ducal couple. The atmosphere was simple and sociable, and the Empress enjoyed her stay.

Grand Duke Serge provided theater and concerts for their entertainment, and the Empress and her sisters revisited the neighbors she had got to know in 1889. Among these, Prince and Princess Yusupov gave a wonderful theatrical performance in Their Majesties' honor in their own private theater at Arkhangelskoe, with a number of guests from Moscow arriving for the event. All the best singers and dancers took part in this performance and the scene was a marvelous sight, with the guests occupying the boxes while the whole pit had been turned into one huge bed of wonderful roses. It was an entertainment on the lavish old grand Russian scale and a worthy sequel to the coronation fêtes.

Though the Khodynka disaster had dimmed its radiance, the Coronation itself always remained a great and sacred memory to the Empress.

Chapter 8

Journeys in Russia and Abroad: 1896

That summer, the Emperor and the Empress undertook their first real journey through Russia and attended the opening of a great International Exhibition at Nijni-Novgorod. The three days spent there were at the time of the annual fair – the center of all commerce in Russia and the East – which interested them greatly. The Emperor, being young, believed that he would have time to see everything personally and in detail.

At Nijni, the imperial couple received deputations from peasant elders from the whole country. The Empress ever afterwards cherished a dream that someday they would be able to travel down the Volga, visiting all the towns on that great river's banks. This they did, but only partially, in 1913.

After a short stay at Tsarskoe Selo, the Emperor and Empress started out on a series of state visits to foreign courts, as is customary on accession to the Russian throne. On all subsequent journeys the baby accompanied her parents, as the Empress wanted to show her "precious treasure" to her great-grandmother, Queen Victoria, in England.

The first visit was to Vienna, where they stayed with the Emperor Franz Josef, arriving on August 27, 1896. Empress Elizabeth of Austria, who had retired from court life after the tragic death of her son Crown Prince Rudolph, came especially to Vienna to welcome the young Empress and was exceedingly kind to her. This was the only time they ever met. Both Emperor Nicholas and Empress Alexandra fell immediately under the spell of Empress Elizabeth's romantic personality and never forgot how magnificent she was at the State dinner at the Hofburg which took place, by the way, at five p.m., as

Emperor Franz Josef always followed the daily timetable set up for him in childhood.

Empress Elizabeth, all in black and with her glorious, thick, deep brown-colored hair, was still a great beauty and became very animated and charming when talking to Emperor Nicholas.

Then there was the usual succession of reviews and gala performances and Emperor Nicholas went shooting with the Austrian Emperor at Lainz while Empress Alexandra visited museums.

The imperial couple returned home through Kiev, and on their way had a great shock when the Minister for Foreign Affairs, Prince Lobanov-Rostovsky, who was travelling with them, suddenly died from heart failure after a walk at one of the stops on the journey. Prince Lobanov was an eminent statesman and a great loss to the country and his death robbed the young Emperor of one of his ablest ministers, a loss he felt most keenly.

In Kiev, the Emperor and Empress visited different institutions and were much fêted, as this was their first visit to the town. Among other places, they went to the celebrated Lavra Monastery of the Caves, a monastery where thousands of relics of saints are stored in catacombs like those in Rome. They were also present at the consecration of the Cathedral of St. Vladimir, where the Empress saw for the first time the work of the painter Vasnetzov. The adaptation of Byzantine art to modern taste – his particular style – greatly pleased her and she was ever afterward an admirer of this celebrated artist's work.

After attending maneuvers near Kiev, their journeys abroad were resumed. At the Emperor William's invitation, the imperial travelers went on to attend maneuvers in Germany. They were met by the German Emperor and Empress at Breslau, where they were also joined by Prince Henry and Princess Irene of Prussia. Empress Alexandra was delighted to be able to avoid an official visit to Berlin as she hated all formal receptions and the stay at Breslau was very short, although it included the inevitable round of reviews and banquets, with the usual exchange of speeches and a gala performance at the local opera.

Copenhagen was next on their list, after they spent a day on the way there with Princess Irene in Kiel. They then remained ten days in Denmark with the Emperor's grandparents, the King and Queen of Denmark, where a large family party had been gathered together to meet them.

Their new yacht The Standart, then making her maiden trip, took the Emperor and Empress from Copenhagen to St. Abb's Head where they were met on September 22 by the Prince of Wales and the Duke of Connaught on behalf of the Queen. From Aberdeen, where a naval review was held in their honor, Their Majesties went on to Balmoral with Lord Pembroke in attendance. They were also escorted from Ballater to Balmoral by a squadron of the Scots Greys, of which the Emperor had been appointed Colonel, and by Highlanders bearing torches.

The Empress was impatient to see Queen Victoria again and their meeting was very warm and affectionate one in the presence of Baron de Stael, the popular Russian Ambassador, and of members of the British Cabinet, including Lord Salisbury, the Duke of Devonshire, Lord Lansdowne, Mr. Arthur Balfour, and others.

A large party of relatives had gathered at Balmoral to meet the Russian sovereigns – including the Prince and Princess of Wales, the Duke and Duchess of Connaught, the aged Duke of Cambridge, Princess Louise, the Marchioness of Lorne, Princess Beatrice, and the Empress' special friend, the Princess Helena Victoria – and after the first solemn banquet, the ten day visit became quite informal and the Empress went about, as in the old days, with her cousins.

Queen Victoria expressed herself happy to see Empress Alexandra grown into so fine and flourishing a woman, for she had been thin and drooping and suffering from acute sciatica during her previous visit. The Queen had always approved of her granddaughter's match and personally liked the Emperor more and more with every meeting. This liking did not, however, influence her political attitude towards Russia, as she believed that "family ties don't count in politics," a sentiment repeated by Empress Alexandra in a letter she wrote to her sister Princess Victoria of Battenberg on March 3, 1897.

The Empress' feelings on leaving Balmoral may be seen in a letter to Miss Jackson:

BALMORAL CASTLE,
October 3rd, 96.

DEAREST MADGIE, - Just before leaving, I hasten to send you a few words of loving thanks for your dear letter. Not knowing your Eastbourne address, I send this epistle to London. Tho' I did not write to you for the 20th, my thoughts and best wishes were with you. I hope my Harrogate and the beautiful Yorkshire air did you good! Here we have not had the finest weather. My husband has not shot one stag, only a brace of grouse.

It has been such a very short stay and I leave dear kind Grandmama with a heavy heart. Who knows when we may meet again and where? Now I have made the acquaintance of Lord Pembroke about whom and whose sisters you used to tell me. He is charming and very good-looking. I have good news from Irene but, alas, we shall not see her.

We had a good passage from Denmark. Next Saturday morning, God grant, we shall be at dear Darmstadt. Goodbye, Darling, and God bless you.

Yr. old P.Q. No. III,
ALIX.

The Emperor and Empress embarked from Portsmouth for France. Great importance had been attached to this visit by politicians both in Russia and in France. No Russian Emperor had been to France since the Franco-Russian entente, and Emperor Nicholas' visit was taken as proclaiming to the world his willingness to continue his father's policy of friendship with France. In consequence, the French Government did all in its power to give its imperial guests a splendid reception.

Apart from the political motives that dictated the visit, the Empress was keenly looking forward to seeing Paris, which she had never visited. She may even have had ideas of going about privately to see the scenes of the Empress Eugénie's splendor, of which she had heard so much from the Empress herself.

From the moment they set foot on French soil, the Russian sovereigns were the objects of unceasing ovation and when they reached Paris, their reception became positively delirious, the enthusiastic Paris public cheering them on every occasion. Even the baby Grand Duchess, now ten months old and arriving quietly at another station in her nurse's arms, had her own private reception amid cries of *"Vive le bébé et la nounou!"* The press was full of nothing but France's guests and every detail of their way of life was accounted for. Reams of poetry were written and the town was wonderfully decorated. In order to show Paris at its very best, the chestnut trees had been covered with artificial blooms, which, if unseasonal, were still effective. Popular opinion, as reported in the newspapers, considered that *"la dame du Tsar est bien belle."* (The Tsar's wife is very beautiful.)

However, the program of official functions and sight-seeing was much greater than the allotted time would allow, so, to the Empress' secret disappointment, there could be no private excursions and they could only hurry around the places of interest she had so much longed to visit. When they rushed through the Louvre, she was unable to view a single gallery, and there was no question of her going out shopping at all, which, as a woman, she would certainly have wished to do.

The newspapers reported that, dressed in an exquisite blue satin, she was present with President Fauré and the Emperor at the laying of the foundation stone for the Alexander III Bridge; that she accompanied the Emperor to Notre Dame, where the organ played the Russian anthem during an otherwise religious ceremony; that they visited the Pantheon and also Les Invalides, where they stood before the tomb of Moscow's invader, the great Napoleon. They also went to the Mint and paid a visit to Sèvres on their way to Versailles, where, at the china factory, they were presented with a bust of Empress Catherine the Great.

To the Empress, the most interesting day was the one at Versailles, where she was thrilled by the palace, its artistic beauties and its historical associations. The rooms placed at her disposal were those of Queen Marie-Antoinette, to the suppressed horror of her suite who superstitiously found the associations ominous.

A marvelous theatrical performance in the Salon d'Hercule was arranged after the state dinner. During the performance the great Sarah Bernhardt recited verses by Sully Prudhomme, a favorite poet of the Empress'. Here the "Divine Sarah," in the guise of a wood nymph of Versailles, welcomed the imperial couple, addressing a few special sentences to the Empress. Coquelin followed in the 'Sous-Préfêt aux Champs' and Réjane in another small piece. The best singers of the day appeared in the 'Seasons of Haydn,' a small ballet closing a really wonderful performance.

The last event of their stay was a review at Chalons on October 9.

They left Versailles in the Napoleon III's private train which was being used for the first time since the fall of the Empire. It had been the zenith of comfort and luxury when it was used by the French Emperor, but in 1896 it seemed strangely out-of-date in its old-fashioned elegance, and small in comparison with modern Pullman cars.

Their stay in France and the warmth of the welcome they received remained an unforgettable memory for both the Emperor and Empress, and often in later years the Empress delighted the small Grand Duchesses with stories of Paris and Versailles.

From France, the Emperor and Empress went on to Darmstadt. This was a short visit, but a great pleasure to the Empress, who longed to be with her brother again after the first long separation of their lives. She had left Darmstadt not knowing what the future had in store for her and now returned as Empress of Russia.

She went about very little as she wanted to spend as much time as possible with her family, but Hesse gave its Princess a splendid welcome.

Chapter 9

First Charities and Life: 1896 to 1901

On the advice of Grand Duchess Ella, the Empress had planned a little informal entertaining for the following winter that would help her to get to know St. Petersburg society better. Nothing could come of this plan, however, as another baby was expected and the Empress was far from well, having to lie up for months and spending seven weeks actually in bed. Even when she was up, she was again a martyr to sciatica and had to be wheeled about in a chair. (The Emperor's diaries make frequent mention of this.)

The Empress was always very unwell before her confinements, although the general public did not know this as it was contrary to Russian Court etiquette even to mention the health of the sovereign or his wife, and the Empress herself was always shy of letting anyone know of her condition and hid it as long as she could. All of her children, with the exception of her eldest daughter, were born in the spring or early summer so that she was generally incapacitated in the winter at the time of the St. Petersburg season, without its being known that it was her health alone that kept her so much in retirement. Further, she insisted on nursing her babies, which was an additional tie. She considered this to be a mother's sacred duty, although it probably exhausted her physically far more than she realized, given that she tried to continue carrying out her official duties at the same time.

The Empress certainly had bad luck where her health was concerned. In the years when she was neither expecting nor nursing a baby, she invariably fell ill. One winter she had influenza three times; another year she had measles; then the children were ill. There seemed to be always something that at the last moment prevented the Empress from giving the smaller receptions through which she would have known society better and have become better known herself, although she could, left to herself, have done very well without fêtes and amusements. These "meant nothing to her," as she wrote to Princess Victoria. Her home life was idyllically happy and she begrudged every moment away from the Emperor and her children, but the Emperor was a very busy man and she could never be alone with him for very long. Every party he attended, every hour he spent with her, was paid for by long hours reading his papers late into the night, and so, as time went by, and her growing family took up more and more of her attention, the Empress gave up the struggle to contrive opportunities to see people outside her immediate and easily accessible entourage.

During the long weeks of enforced quiet before the birth of her second daughter the Grand Duchess Tatiana on June 10, 1897, the Empress planned many of her future charities. From her very first letters from Russia, written just after her marriage, in which she lamented the fact that she had not yet seen any hospitals, she was intent on developing philanthropic activities. When she came to Russia, all the existing charitable institutions – the Red Cross and the girls' schools – were under the patronage of the Dowager-Empress, who was also the head of the vast organization called The Establishment of Empress Marie after its founder, Emperor Paul's wife, so it was suggested that the young Empress should identify herself with some new foundation which should bear her name. Her choice fell upon workhouses for the poor, to be set up all over the country, and to be managed by a committee called the Help by Work Committee.

The Empress, being a really enthusiastic philanthropist, took a great interest in the development of this work. She loved to think up fresh schemes and put them into action. She was practical and gave minute attention to every detail; she had a broad vision and brought a personal element to everything she did. She always plunged straight into the subject under discussion and generally provided most practical suggestions for whatever would enlarge and improve upon the original project. All those who came into contact with this side of her character speak with the same admiration of her clear head and her sound common sense. She lost all self-consciousness when she was speaking on subjects that interested her, and she at once put her fellow-workers on an easy footing. In particular, everything to do with infant welfare was of interest to her. There was much to be done in that line of work in Russia and the Empress was very anxious to take this up actively.

Another favorite scheme of hers was a school for nurses and housemaids. She speaks of having written to England for "rules to try and go by a little," and modelled her school on Princess Helena's School for Nurses in London. This was also carried through by her and the school was opened at Tsarskoe Selo in 1905 after considerable difficulty. She visited it regularly and planned improvements and enlargements there until the last.

Speaking of these projects, the Empress wrote to Princess Victoria on June 17, 1902, that, "All new things are difficult, but awfully interesting when one takes them into one's hands – the only way to make things progress quickly." In all her charity work the Empress had to fight not only against inertia but often against great opposition to the introduction of new ideas. The difficulty of providing funds for her schemes was generally used as an argument against them, for in Russia there was not that ready response from private charity that is usual in England, and nearly all the charities had to be supported by the Government. When she managed to surmount this obstacle, she had always to take precautions that her ideas should not be shelved, but actually carried out. She often had to fight hard to carry out her plans, and although she succeeded in doing much, there were a great many projects that she was never able to get off the ground.

The Empress often had to draw heavily on her own purse for her charities. Strange as it may seem, the Empress' private fortune was not very large and she had to curtail her personal expenses to meet the expenses of her charities. She was very generous in her donations and it is not generally known that the Empress provided for the upkeep of her school for nurses out of her own pocket. In October 1915, during the war, an unheard of thing occurred: New petitioners were told in her secretary's office that they would have to wait until January 1916 to get their remittances, as the Empress had spent all her yearly income in giving generously right and left to war charities, widows and orphans. During the famine year of 1898, for instance, she gave 50,000 rubles out of her privy purse to relieve distress in the districts ravaged by famine.

She realized the need for professional schools for girls and wanted to transform the so-called 'Patriotic Schools' into more modern establishments. This, however, proved beyond her power. Innumerable objections were raised and the officials responsible for these schools could not see the need for any alterations and Empress Alexandra only made enemies for herself among the great ladies who were the patronesses of the schools that she had denounced as being out of date and impractical. She took this idea up again in 1915-16, during the war, but ran out of time when she was forcibly sent to Tobolsk by the Government.

During the spring of 1897, Princess Irene of Prussia took the opportunity to come and stay with her, leaving some little time before the Grand Duchess Tatiana was born. In the spring and summer of this year, all the sovereigns to whom state visits had been paid came in their turn to Russia. The Emperor Franz Josef was the first, accompanied by the Archduke Otto, but the Empress' health precluded any public appearances on her part. This visit was followed later in the summer by one from the German Emperor and Empress, and in the autumn the French President Felix Fauré came, accompanied by Admiral Gervais, General de Boisdeffre and M. Gabriel Hanotaux.

All these receptions were arranged on much the same lines. The magnificent palace at Peterhof (the Imperial Family did not reside in it themselves), with the park that surrounded it, gave the festivities a more effective setting than did the stiff Winter Palace in St. Petersburg and the command performances given in their honor were always greatly appreciated by the foreign guests. The ballet and the opera singers from the Imperial Theatre generally appeared in one of the small court theatres at Peterhof or at the camp at Krasnoe. A particularly good ballet was given on a beautiful summer evening on one of the islands on the lake in the Peterhof Park, on the occasion of the visit of the German Emperor.

When the Court was at Peterhof, the Empress often went with the Emperor to the camp at Krasnoe Selo, and during maneuvers they sometimes stayed there for several days, living in small wooden datchas. She was a true soldier's daughter and enjoyed these expeditions, military pageants and reviews, and camp life with bands playing, bugles sounding and regiments marching. The Emperor, too, was happy to revive the old associations of his soldiering days. The Empress was appointed honorary Colonel of the Guard Lancers and was very proud of her regiment, taking great interest in all the officers and men. In May 1903, the jubilee of the regiment, she was present at the review in Lancer's uniform and rode at the regiment's head.

Every autumn during these first years – up until 1905 – the Imperial Family went to the Emperor's Polish shooting lodges, Skierniewice, Spala and Belovege. Sometimes the Empress walked with the Emperor for hours while he shot, for she always entered into all her husband's interests, although she never handled a gun herself as she shared Queen Victoria's opinion that this was "a mannish pastime." When she was not walking with the Emperor, she would ride or drive her four-in-hand through the vast forests in which the lodges stood. These country sojourns, away from towns, noise, bustle and state entertaining, were a delight to her.

The Emperor was a great walker and whenever they were together in the country his wife accompanied him on his longest walks. He went at a terrific pace and even his gentlemen in attendance had the greatest difficulty in keeping up with him, but the Empress would never admit fatigue. The long walks she took with the Emperor in the early days almost certainly laid the foundations of the heart trouble from which she suffered so badly in later years. The Emperor never realized how tired she must have been, for she was always game to the end.

She described one of these shooting visits to her sister, Princess Victoria in 1897. "Generally out for ten hours – bisons, roebucks, stags, elks, wild bear, capercailzies." These were "their" holidays. There were no ministers in attendance except Baron Fredericks whose papers followed the Emperor wherever he was.

After one of these visits, in 1897, the Emperor and Empress went to Warsaw to see the capital of their Kingdom of Poland. They spent three days at the Lazenki Palace and were very well received by the Poles, the nobility giving the Emperor a million rubles for charities. All the Polish ladies came to the Empress' reception at the Palace and the young men of the aristocracy, of their own initiative, kept order in the streets during the imperial visit.

In 1897 and 1899, the shooting in Poland was followed by visits to Darmstadt. On the first visit, the imperial couple laid the foundation stone of the Russian church that was built in Darmstadt in memory of the Empress Marie Alexandrovna, the Emperor Nicholas' grandmother, who, it will be remembered, had also been a Hessian Princess. The Emperor entrusted the paintings and mosaics for this church to Vasnetzov, the artist whose paintings had so charmed the Empress at Kiev, and it was consecrated in 1899. It is the only specimen outside Russia of this great Russian painter's work. Who knows what has been the fate of the churches in Russia that were decorated by him?

During this journey abroad, both the Emperor and the Empress came into contact with wider ideas, and heard freer and more varied opinions on political and general questions than they could do in Russia within the limited circle from which all sovereigns find it so difficult to escape. In Darmstadt, the imperial couple went about a great deal with their hosts and met all kinds of people, for the Grand Duke of Hesse was a liberal and intellectual man and liked to hear and discuss every kind of general question, and they always returned with a store of new ideas. In later years these trips abroad became rarer as the Emperor was more and more tied down and the Empress never even contemplated the possibility of going anywhere without him. One day of separation was a wrench to her and for the first ten years of their married life the imperial couple never parted.

In 1899, on June 26, a third daughter was born, the Grand Duchess Marie Nicholaevna. For the last months before her birth, the Empress was again very unwell. Indeed, brave though she always was, she wrote to her eldest sister on April 4, 1899, "I never like making plans … God knows how it will all end." There was great anxiety for her when the baby was born, but both were saved, and the little Grand Duchess was strong and healthy, as were all her sisters.

A fortnight after the birth of the Grand Duchess Marie, on July 11, 1899, the Tsarevich George, the Emperor's brother and heir apparent, died in his villa in the Caucasus. He had long suffered from lung trouble and had not lived in St. Petersburg for years. The Emperor's second brother, the Grand Duke Michael Alexandrovich, was proclaimed heir to the throne.

The last years of the century passed without bringing any great outward change in the Empress' life. Her private life was always growing fuller, her happiness greater, and the winter of 1897-8 was a brilliant one. The Empress' cousin, Princess Helena Victoria, the daughter of Princess Helena, came on a visit, and on her account the Empress went about far more than ever before to balls and dinners at the foreign embassies and private houses in St. Petersburg. Her young cousin's presence seemed to give her support, and the more she got into the spirit of society life, the more she enjoyed it. However, the ill luck that seemed to dog her met her again now, for, just as she seemed to be getting into the swing of society life, she developed a case of measles, caught in one of the St. Petersburg schools that she visited twice daily with the Emperor to give the growing generation a chance to see their sovereigns.

In 1900, the imperial couple revived the ancient custom of spending Easter in Moscow in order to get to know the old capital and its people, and at the beginning of Holy Week the whole Court migrated to Moscow. Easter is the greatest Church festival in Russia. All the most impressive ceremonies of the Orthodox Church are centered around this season. The old-world atmosphere of the Kremlin, and of the beautiful churches, both within the palace itself and inside the Kremlin walls, added to the splendor of every ceremony. The Emperor and Empress were present at the elaborate rites of brewing the Holy Chrism at the Metropolitan's palace, which took place every two years, with much ancient and symbolic ceremonial. Night and day for several days the oils were stirred by a succession of priests, while others read the Holy Scriptures aloud to them. The beautiful silver cauldrons and the vast apartments, lit at night by innumerable wax candles and scented by the boiling spices, made a picture that seemed to belong to the earliest Byzantine times.

The Empress loved to explore every church and every cranny of the Kremlin with her brother-in-law, the Grand Duke Serge, as her guide. He knew all the history and all the art treasures of the ancient city. The Empress always fell under the spell of old Russia in Moscow. Although in other countries she could be modern and a believer in the new, here the gorgeous treasures and the religious ceremonies reawakened her admiration for the old. Moscow at Easter seemed to her to breathe the real spirit of Russia and involuntarily she fashioned her mind to suit it. She used to say that she felt like an ancient Tsaritsa as she sat in her rooms in the Kremlin with her sister and their ladies, embroidering velvet hangings for their church. This particular work took more time than had been anticipated and finally the Empress had to call in some nuns from a neighboring convent to help her. One morning, when she came into the room where they were working, the Empress felt her heart stand still an instant in fear, for all the nuns together fell prone on the ground at her feet! A terrible picture arose in her mind of their having worked so hard through the whole night that they were suddenly overcome by fatigue. To her relief, they rose as suddenly as they had fallen, their pink countenances perfectly unruffled. They had not worked through the night and indeed had only just arrived. They were simply greeting the Empress in the way that convent rules directed that they should greet their Abbess, by prostrating themselves before her.

During the week before Easter, the Empress accompanied the Emperor to the traditional ceremonies. They assisted at midnight Mass at the church in the Kremlin, curiously called 'Of the Savior Behind the Golden Gate,' and on the night of Good Friday they unexpectedly mingled with the crowd at the night Procession of the Winding Sheet at the Cathedral of the Assumption. Here Russia's Emperor and Empress stood beside their humblest subjects, holding lighted tapers in their hands.

The Good Friday night procession in the Kremlin is an unforgettable scene. Only those who have seen it can realize the poetry of the huge and reverent crowds, of the lighted tapers, and of the procession wending its slow way to the cathedral looming majestic and mysterious in the darkness. The whole scene, the whole atmosphere, entranced the Empress. Here she felt that she was at one with Holy Russia and at one with the Russian people in their simple and fervent faith.

Altogether Moscow seemed delightful to her. The Emperor and Empress went to all the schools, to the Assemblée de la Noblesse, and carried out an extensive official program. Grand Duke Serge and Grand Duchess Ella went with them. Supported by them, the Empress felt at her ease; she found Moscow charming and the people of Moscow were delighted with her.

That autumn, the Imperial Family went to Livadia in the Crimea for the first time since the Emperor's accession. Now everything was steeped in sunshine for Empress Alexandra. She was a happy wife, the mother of three fine children, and the Crimea appeared to her to be an earthly paradise indeed.

The big palace was too full of the sad memories of 1894, but the little old palace in which they lived proved very damp and unhealthy, delightful as it was outside. At first they were perfectly happy and enjoyed their stay, but soon the Emperor fell ill with what proved to be a rather serious form of typhoid. The Empress had a great horror of the illness that had carried off her grandfather, the Prince Consort, and had so nearly been fatal to King Edward VII, but a crisis always found her self-possessed and resourceful. She nursed the Emperor herself, even doing the night nursing, and acted as his private secretary when he was able to attend to papers, transmitting his decisions to his Ministers. Her link with the outside world was her former lady-in-waiting – now her friend – Princess Marie Bariatinsky, who was on a visit and with whom she shared her anxieties.

The Empress wrote to her sister, Princess Victoria, at the time:

> *Nicky was really an angel of patience during his wearisome illness, never complaining, always ready to do all one bid him. His old valet and I nursed him. The shock of his illness and feeling myself necessary gave me new strength, as I had been very wretched before. I rebelled at a nurse being taken and we managed perfectly ourselves. Orchie would wash his face and hands in the morning, and bring my meals in always. I*

took them on the sofa still for some time. Now I suffer from head and heartache, the latter from nerves and many sleepless nights. When he was getting better I read to him, almost all day long.

In remembrance of these anxious days, Princess Bariatinsky and her two colleagues presented the Empress with a small icon. In the evening the Empress wrote to her as follows:

LIVADIA
Dec- 31St, 1900

DEAREST MARY, - I feel I cannot go to bed without having once more thanked you from the bottom of my heart for the Image. It touched me deeply, and tears were not far off when you three gave it me. Bless you for your kind thought. I shall always take it with me everywhere as a remembrance of that anxious time and Xmastide and the beginning of the new century. What sorrows this last year brought us, what endless anxieties, what worries and losses – God grant the new year may be a calmer and happier one for the whole of dear Russia. Sleep well and peacefully ...

The Emperor's strong and wiry constitution triumphed – he was scarcely ever ill in his life – but the Court could not return to St. Petersburg until January when they expected a visit from the Grand Duke and Grand Duchess of Hesse. They had been there only a few days when the news came for which her last letters from England had prepared her.

Queen Victoria died on January 22, 1901.

Chapter 10

The Empress and Queen Victoria – New Friendships

Her grandmother's death caused the Empress great sorrow. Queen Victoria had been a special link with the mother she dimly remembered, as well as a very loving grandmother, and had been particularly fond of her Hessian grandchildren, of whom Princess Alix was considered by the family to be her favorite.

The Queen's feelings were probably influenced first of all by sympathy for the little motherless girl, but the Queen and the Empress had many points in common, which Queen Victoria herself was quick to recognize. The Empress Alexandra had the Queen's warm heart, her capacity for great enthusiasms – both for ideas and for people – the same intense sense of duty, and the same fidelity in friendship.

Queen Victoria had always given tangible proof of her interest in her grandchildren, keeping in touch with their goings-on and participating personally in important events in their lives. When she went to Coburg for the wedding of her grandson the Grand Duke of Hesse, the idea of coincidentally arranging the engagement of Princess Alix may have been on her mind. In any case, the Queen was there, at that important moment, ready to give the Princess the sympathy and good counsel that she might have sought from her mother at such a time, had she been alive.

Indeed, much as she liked Emperor Nicholas, the Queen had many personal regrets that "her darling Alicky" lived too far away to be able to pay her yearly visits to England. "I have a right to her," the Queen used to say poignantly.

For her part, the Empress wrote to Princess Bariatinsky on July 16, 1900, and spoke of the Queen.

My grandmother invites us to come to England, but now is certainly not the moment to be out of the country. How intensely I long to see her dear old face, you can imagine; never have we been separated so long, 4 whole years, and I have the feeling as tho' I should never see her any more. Were it not so far away, I should have gone off all alone for a few days to see her and left the children and my husband, as she has been as a mother to me, ever since Mama's death 22 years ago.

To-morrow is the Christening ...

She, who never left her husband, even thought of going "all alone for a few days to see her," but some ailments among the children finally prevented the Empress from putting her plan into action.

When she heard of the Queen's death, the Empress wanted to start immediately for Windsor with her brother. She was dissuaded from this notion, however, as she was pregnant at the time – the fourth Grand Duchess, Anastasia, was born in the early summer – but she quite broke down at the funeral service in the English church at St. Petersburg.

Writing to her sister Princess Victoria on January 28, 1901, she said:

How I envy you being able to see beloved Grandmama being taken to her last rest. I cannot believe she is really gone, that we shall never see her any more. It seems impossible. Since one can remember, she was in our life, and a dearer kinder being never was. The whole world sorrows over her. England without the Queen seems impossible. How thankful, that she was spared all physical suffering. Morally, she had too much to bear this year.

"She was in our life" explains the great void that the Queen's death meant for the Empress. There was now no older authority to whom she could turn for counsel. She was thrown on her own judgment and had to travel by her own light.

Ever since her marriage, the Empress had corresponded regularly with her grandmother, and Queen Victoria had always feared that the Empress' great reserve and shyness would hamper her and make her misunderstood. It is probable that, in addition to her grandmotherly interest in the Empress' family life, the Queen sometimes gave her favorite grandchild the benefit of her wide experience. All of the Queen's letters and the Empress' answers, which were returned to Her Majesty after Queen Victoria's death, were destroyed in March 1917 by the Empress, who did not want things so precious to her to fall into the hands of the Bolsheviks.

The Empress' mourning and general state of health obliged her once more to lead a very secluded life that winter, but she had now found congenial friends within the Imperial Family in Grand Duchess Militza Nikolaevna (who was married to Grand Duke Peter) and her sister Anastasia, familiarly known as 'Stana' (who was married to George, the Duke of Leuchtenberg), the daughters of King Nicholas of Montenegro. Their sister, Princess Anna, had just married the Empress' cousin, Prince Francis Joseph of Battenberg, and had gone to live in Darmstadt. This was a link between them, and the anxieties caused by the Emperor's illness had drawn them all together.

Grand Duchess Militza was a clever woman, with wide intellectual interests and with a real knowledge of the East and of Eastern things. She could speak Persian, was an authority on ancient Persian literature, and had read and translated books on the philosophies and religions of Persia, India and China. She had also made a study of theological questions connected with the Orthodox Church.

The sisters were devoted to each other and had delightfully warm and attractive manners, and the Empress soon became really intimate with them, while the Emperor found a friend in Grand Duke Peter Nikolaevich, an intellectual and artistic man, and an architect of no mean ability, who had never taken any part in public affairs and who, on account of his health, had lived away from the capital. That year, however, the "Montenegrin Grand Duchesses," as they were called, came to St. Petersburg, and the Empress saw them nearly every day.

Stana, the Duchess of Leuchtenberg, married Grand Duke Nicholas Nikolaevich (Grand Duke Peter's brother) in 1901, after her divorce from the Duke of Leuchtenberg, and Grand Duke Peter spent the summer close to Peterhof so that the Empress could often see her friends. They read together and talked over books and the abstract subjects that the Empress loved.

The Grand Duchesses awakened in the Empress a real interest in theological questions. From the Lutheran creed of her girlhood, the Empress had come by now to the most rigid adherence to the Orthodox Church. She held views that were considered unduly strict by many modern Russians and zealously studied the intricate works of the old Fathers of the Church. Besides these, she read many French and English philosophical books.

Empress Alexandra's fourth daughter, Grand Duchess Anastasia Nikolaevna, was born at Peterhof on June 18, 1901. However well the Emperor might have hidden his feelings, and although he never showed any visible regret when the sex of his successive babies was announced, the Empress knew how intensely he longed for a son. When Grand Duchess Marie was born, it was noticed that he set off on a long solitary walk but that he came back as outwardly unruffled as ever.

Among the upper classes of the country, however, there was much disappointment at the births of so many daughters. It was felt that the Empress was failing to do her duty by the state. The country people, on the other hand, did not care much if it were a Grand Duke or a Grand Duchess who was born: Every imperial baby meant that amnesties were granted, that jails were opened, and that criminals saw their terms of imprisonment cut short. They heard Grand Duke Michael prayed for in church and did not trouble their heads much if the heir were the Emperor's brother or his son.

It was the Empress herself who longed most of all for a son. Under her new friends' influence, her whole heart went out in prayers that she might give Russia an heir, and in July 1903 an eighteenth century monk named Seraphim was canonized by order of the Russian Holy Synod, and the Emperor and Empress went to the ceremony in the monastery of Sarov. To the Empress, this journey was a pilgrimage. Not only did the religious service impress and inspire her, but she was in close contact with the simple country people whom she loved during their whole journey and their stay in Sarov. The Empress was never shy with the peasants. She talked to them like children in her still indifferent Russian, and meeting her as they did without official pomp, the peasants loved her in return.

Grand Duchess Ella also fell under the Sarov's spell, as she wrote to Princess Victoria:

> *So many beautiful, healthy impressions. We drove six hours before arriving at the convent and in the village the pretty bright red costumes and pretty healthy people looked so picturesque. The convent is lovely, situated in a splendid colossal pine wood. The ceremony and prayers were very fine. Seraphim was a monk, who lived in the 18th century a very pure and holy life, cured many physically and morally, and after death the miracles continue. Thousands and thousands from the whole of Russia came for that day [i.e. the canonization] to pray and brought their sick from Siberia, from the Caucasus. Oh, what misery, what illnesses we saw, and what faith!*

It seemed as if we were living in Christ's time ... Oh how they prayed, how they cried, these poor mothers with their sick children, and thank God, how many were cured! We had the blessing of seeing a little dumb girl speak, but how her mother prayed for her!

These scenes made an immense impression on the Empress. It is difficult for practical Protestant minds to grasp the intensity of religious fervor that seizes an Orthodox or Catholic crowd. Only those people who have been on a pilgrimage to Lourdes or to Jerusalem can realize how, when the Russian pilgrims come to the Holy Week services, a crowd can be swayed with religious emotion.

It may be noted that in the beautiful church built at Tsarskoe Selo after the heir's birth, the upper church was dedicated to the Holy Virgin "Feodorovskaya" – a venerated Romanov icon – and the lower church to St. Seraphim of Sarov.

Chapter 11

Foreign Trips and Life from 1901 to 1904

In the friendship of Grand Duchesses Militza and Stana, the Empress found the one thing that had been missing from her life since her friend Princess Bariatinsky had left for Rome – congenial society during the hours that the Emperor was busy.

However, the Grand Duchesses were of no help to the Empress in enlarging her circle of acquaintanceship. They were not fond of society, their meetings were always *en famille*, and the abstract interests into which they initiated her did not change her mode of life, nor did they appear to influence her outwardly. She was always cheerful at home and full of interest in her family, and she was now beginning to think of her children's education – giving her eldest daughter her early lessons herself – and her charitable endeavors.

During the years 1897-1905, the Emperor and Empress went abroad nearly every second year or received State visits in Russia. The King of Italy came to Peterhof in 1901 and the visit was returned in 1911. The French President, M. Loubet, also came to Russia in 1901 and the Russian Sovereigns returned his visit in the autumn of that same year.

On their way to France, the Emperor and Empress once again stayed with old King Christian in Copenhagen. On this occasion, too, the Emperor met the German Emperor in Danzig, and the Empress paid a flying visit to Princess Irene of Prussia at Kiel, where she left her three small daughters during the State visit to France.

This French trip began most inauspiciously. The Standart, although she was wonderfully steady, had never met such a storm as that encountered between Germany and the French coast. The Emperor, who was an excellent sailor, saw his suite disappear one-by-one on different pretexts. The Empress was invisible, and soon the groans of the ladies and their maids began to resound throughout the ship, and loud supplications were heard that the ship should call into port, the supplicants not realizing that they were on the high seas and that there was no land in sight.

When they arrived in Dunkirk, the Empress still got no rest as she had to appear on deck to meet the French President, her ladies crawling up behind her like flies in autumn, although it was some slight consolation to Her Majesty to discover that that the French President also had no sea-legs and had to stay on board The Standart during the naval review, the weather being too bad for him to reach a French man-of-war.

An amusing picture in an illustration of the time shows the French members of parliament, who had come to see the review, all huddled together on deck, presenting the picture of abject misery often seen in a Channel crossing. This picture was accompanied by an extract from the telegram from the President of the Chamber to the Minister of Marine saying, possibly with sarcasm, *"C'était un spectacle reconfortant de voir, etc."* (It was a reassuring sight to see).

The unfriendly reception of the elements was forgotten at Compiègne on September 28, where the imperial couple spent a day as guests of the French President. They didn't go to Paris this time, to the great disappointment of the public, but the Emperor had come chiefly to be present at the great French maneuvers, which he and the Empress attended, together with President Loubet.

The visit to Compiègne was planned along much the same lines as that memorable day at Versailles in 1896, but here the setting was Napoleonic and the Empress enjoyed her day roaming around the park and visiting everything there was to see. In the evening there was a State banquet and theatricals, but the program was necessarily less full than it had been at Versailles. The Empress was also pleased to meet some people she knew, among them the Marquis and Marquise de Montebello – Nicholas de Montebello was the French Ambassador in

Russia at the time of their Coronation – and the Emperor agreed to act as Godfather to their first grandson.

In the course of the subsequent maneuvers, during which the review of the French army at Béthény was held, the imperial couple visited Rheims, where, for the first time since the fall of the Second Empire, the choir of the cathedral intoned 'Domine salvum fac imperatorem.' (God save the Emperor.) The Empress told me later that this served to reminder her that all earthly power is transitory. The scene was beautiful and she was sorry not to be able to linger and visit Rheims properly, but the official program had to be fulfilled.

Until 1905, the Emperor and Empress traveled every year to St. Petersburg for the winter season. In 1901-2 and 1902-3 a Grand Ball, two or three concert balls, and several balls at the Hermitage Palace were given, followed by the *Folle Journée* before Lent. The Diplomatic Corps was received on New Year's Day, and was entertained to luncheon after the ceremony of 'the blessing the waters,' which took place on the ice of the Neva during Epiphany.

The Empress was at this time at the full height of her beauty. The Emperor's favorite picture of her, the portrait by Kaulbach, was painted in 1903, and is an excellent likeness. Her well-cut features, upright figure, wonderful eyes, and golden hair made her the embodiment of what an Empress should be. Children and peasants did not need to see her wearing a crown or mantle to know she was the "Tsaritsa." Her face was generally sad – it was her standard expression for official occasions, the photographic face of her youth – and it seldom lighted up in public with the particularly charming smile that those who knew well saw in her private life.

The 1903 season was marked by an especially beautiful costume ball at which the Imperial Family and all the guests appeared in costumes of the time of Peter the Great's father, the Tsar Alexei. The Empress took the greatest interest in all the preparations for the ball and designed both her own and the Emperor's costumes with the help of the Director of the Hermitage Museum, Ivan Alexandrovich Vsevolojsky, who gave her the necessary historical information.

The Emperor wore a copy of a real dress worn by the Tsar of the time, "raspberry and white with gold embroideries," wrote the Empress. His staff and headdress were specially brought in for the occasion from the Granovitaya Palata at Moscow.

The Empress was dressed as the Tsar Alexei's consort, the Tsaritsa Maria Miloslavskaya. She described her attire as "gold brocade with silver design, emeralds, pearls and diamonds." On her head she had a kind of miter studded with jewels, with a thin white handkerchief under the miter and yet another quite thin one to cover her hair stuck into her collar. None of the photographs of the Empress in this dress does her justice. Those who saw her agree that she looked perfectly lovely and an ideal Empress, and her jewels were real, of course. The long and heavy earrings of the time were such a weight that they had to be fastened with gold wire round her ears and she told me that her headdress was so heavy that she discovered at supper that she could not bend her head to eat!

Men and women of society vied with one another at this ball, and the most gorgeous fabrics, jewels and furs were produced from private collections. Officers wore the uniforms of the time, courtiers the dress of Tsar Alexei's court. The Grand Duchesses wore dresses of the style of their ancestors, designed by the greatest modern artists. Grand Duchess Ella looked best of all. Old Russian dances, carefully rehearsed, were danced, and the whole effect was marvelous.

This was the last great festivity of the Russian Court. The season of 1903-4 was cut short by the outbreak of the Japanese War and no balls were ever held again.

The autumn of 1903 saw the imperial couple and their children in Darmstadt as half the royal families of Europe assembled there for the wedding of the Empress' niece, Princess Alice of Battenberg, to the King of Greece's son, Prince Andrew. This, like all family events, was a matter of great interest to the Empress. She wrote of this engagement to her sister, Princess Victoria, on August 16, 1902, "May she be as happy as we are, more one cannot wish." The young couple was securely married in the Orthodox Church, the Protestant Church, and at a civil wedding.

In the middle of the wedding festivities, the Empress' young lady-in-waiting, Princess Sonia Orbeliani, fell desperately ill. She was an orphan, and the Empress, notwithstanding all the ceremonies at which she had to appear and the claims of her family, nursed her like one of her own children. She spent every free hour with the semi-conscious invalid, and when the whole wedding patty moved to Schloss Wolfsgarten, the Empress motored up to Darmstadt sometimes three times a day to see Sonia, despite this being considered a breach of etiquette by the stricter courtiers.

After the wedding, the Grand Duke Ernest of Hesse and his little daughter Elizabeth went with the Imperial Family to their shooting box at Skietniewice in Poland. This stay was planned principally to give the Grand Duke a change of scenery. He led a solitary life in Darmstadt, having just separated from his first wife.

Little Princess Elizabeth was a singularly captivating and beautiful child, adored by both her parents, but she fell ill soon after arriving at Skierniewice, having probably brought typhoid with her to Poland, and she died a few days later from a virulent strain of ambulatory typhoid.

Wild stories were current at the time, but the post-mortem and the testimony of all the doctors leave no doubt as to the cause of her death, which was a terrible blow to Grand Duke Ernest and to the Empress, whose grief was increased by the fact that the tragedy happened under her roof. It was only thanks to her moral support in never leaving him alone that her brother got through that dreadful time. Then, after the Grand Duke had returned for his child's funeral in Darmstadt, the Empress fell ill in her turn and was confined to bed for some time. She was completely worn out, for she always felt the sorrows of those dear to her even more acutely than her own.

Chapter 12

The Russo-Japanese War and the Birth of the Heir: 1904

Clouds were gathering on the horizon as the tension between Russia and Japan grew ever more acute, although few people realized the imminent danger. The general public, and indeed many statesmen, treated the idea of a small Eastern power challenging Great Russia with contempt.

After a theatrical performance at the Hermitage Theater, the Japanese Minister made a particularly low bow on taking leave of the Emperor. Seasoned diplomats noticed this and felt uneasy: It looked as if the polite Japanese, who had always been personally friendly toward him, were taking their private farewell of the Emperor. Two days later the Japanese bombarded the harbor of Port Arthur and hostilities began.

For many years Russia had enjoyed the blessings of peace. Now St. Petersburg suddenly awoke in an atmosphere of war. It is true that the Russo-Japanese War did not touch the vital chords of the country in the way that the European conflict was to later – incomparably fewer men were mobilized; the loss of life was small when compared with the war of 1914-1918; there was no question of food restrictions or of changes in the everyday lives of the people; the great battles were fought so far away that the country had no feeling that an enemy was invading Russian soil – but it showed up grave defects in the governmental machinery of the country from which revolutionary elements profited, as they did from the ferment that often accompanies the prosecution of an unsuccessful war.

In St. Petersburg, the center of government, the war occupied the minds of all classes and Empress Alexandra began at once to take an active interest in war work. The Dowager-Empress headed the Red

Cross, while her daughter-in-law started an immense workshop – or *sklad* – in the Hermitage Palace to supply the ambulance trains with hospital garments, warm clothes, and medical materials. The Red Cross had insufficient resources to keep up with the needs of the military hospitals, as supplies in Siberia were very small, so the Empress sent warm clothing to the troops and the following Christmas sent thousands of presents at which she worked for whole days herself.

Hundreds of women of all classes were busy in her workshop. All those who came were welcome and the huge rooms were full. Every day the Empress went to her *sklad*. The doors leading to the Hermitage from the Winter Palace would open and the Empress would come in carrying her work, preceded by a negro attendant. She progressed through all the rooms, talking to first this person, then that, sitting first at one table, then at another, addressing even the humblest of workers, before going into the day's business with the ladies in charge. These were Princess M. M. Galitzin – the Grande Maîtresse – and Princess E. N. Obolensky – her maid-of-honor.

The Empress considered every detail herself. Her clear and practical mind noted everything, and when she made suggestions she saw that they were carried out. She was, however, again in a delicate state of health, and although she felt better than she usually did on such occasions, she had to give up active work over the summer as the time for her confinement neared.

In June 1904 she wrote to Princess Victoria:

There is no end of work to be done, but it is a great comfort to be able to help one's poor sufferers a little.

We have closed our work in the town now and re-open it in the English palace at Peterhof ... All work hard. Lilly [Princess E. N. Obolensky] manages it splendidly. She has such a clear, practical brain and good memory. We

work for the army hospitals (apart from the Red Cross)
and for the well who need clothes, tobacco ... and then
we furnish military trains.

I like following all and not to be a mere doll. Yes, it is a
trying time, but one must put all one's trust in God, who
gives strength and courage. Unluckily I cannot get
about at all and spend my days on the sofa ... walking
and standing causes me great pain ... I know I must lie,
it is the only remedy.

Up until the last days before her confinement, the Empress gave the audiences required of her, and only a few hours before the birth received a general who was leaving for the front. Then, on August 12, 1904, their longed-for son, the Tsarevich Alexei Nicholaevich, was born. Those who knew how the Empress had prayed and waited for this crowning happiness in her married life, and who understood the importance of direct succession in a country like Russia, can realize what this meant to her.

The boy was big and healthy, promised to be very handsome, and gave no signs of the hemophilia that was later to develop in him, and notwithstanding the stern atmosphere caused by the war, the baby's advent gave unmitigated joy to his parents. "My sunbeam," the Empress used to call him.

The whole country burst into frantic rejoicing. The news spread rapidly to every village in Russia and great demonstrations took place. The baby's christening was like a pageant. No heir to the crown had been born in Russia, as heir, since the seventeenth century, and the ceremony was surrounded with a splendor that matched the importance of the event. It took place in the Chapel of the big Peterhof Palace on August 24, 1904, and the future King George V of England (then the Prince of Wales) and the German Emperor were among the baby's godfathers. The Dowager-Empress Marie was his godmother.

The baby Tsarevich was appointed Colonel of many regiments and decorations were showered on him, and imperial bounty in every form – amnesties, remittances of sentences and gifts of money – were among the signs of the Emperor's joy at the birth of an heir.

The baby throve through it all. At the ceremony of his baptism, old Princess Galitzin once more carried an imperial infant in her arms to church, and this time her task was still more difficult as the result of a slip would have been even more terrible. Indeed, she was always in such terror of falling on these occasions that she had rubber soles put to her shoes, court floors being proverbially slippery.

The baby lay on a pillow of cloth-of-gold, slung to the Princess's shoulders by a broad gold band. He was covered with the heavy cloth-of-gold mantle, lined with ermine, worn by the heir to the crown. The mantle was supported on one side by Prince Alexander Sergeiovich Dolgorouky, the Grand Marshal of the Court, and on the other by Count P. Benckendorff, as decreed by custom and wise precaution. The baby wept loudly, as might any ordinary baby, when old Father Yanishev dipped him in the font. His four small sisters, in short Court dresses, gazed open-eyed at the ceremony, Olga Nikolaevna, then nine years old, playing the important role of one of his godmothers.

According to Russian custom, the Emperor and Empress were not present at the baptism, but directly after the ceremony the Emperor went to the church. Both he and the Empress always confessed to feeling very nervous on these occasions for fear that the Princess might slip or that Father Yanishev, who was very old, might drop the baby into the font.

All went off perfectly, however, although on another occasion – I think it was at the baptism of the Grand Duchess Anastasia – the singular family likeness of Princess Galitzin and her sisters caused the Emperor a moment of great uneasiness as she had three sisters (Mme. Ozeroff, Mme. Apraxin, and Mme. Boutourline) who all dressed in the same fashion as she did, and wore the same poke bonnets. On this occasion, the Emperor was driving to the palace where the christening, had, or so he was told, just taken place. On his way he passed Princess Galitzin's house and, to his horror and surprise, thought he saw her sitting in front of it when she ought at that moment to have been in church in full Court dress. Fearing that something had happened, the Emperor stopped his calèche and jumped out.

When he reached the deeply-curtseying lady, he saw that she was slightly younger than the Grande Maîtresse and that it was in fact someone else very like her. The Emperor said a few polite words to the old lady and never told her the fright she had given him, nor do I know if any but the members of the Tsar's family realized that his hurried stop was not due to a sudden desire to make Mme. Boutourline's acquaintance.

However, even at the time of his son's birth, affairs of State completely engrossed the Emperor. He was often absent, before and after the birth, travelling around Russia to review the troops that were to leave for the Far East. The Empress stayed with the baby and, as soon as she was well enough to travel, she went with the Emperor and all the children for a cruise on the Standart to Reval, where the Emperor reviewed Admiral Rodestvensky's ill-fated fleet before it left on its glorious, but disastrous, voyage to the Far East.

At Tsarskoe Selo, the Empress had her own little hospital which she visited daily, although she did no nursing herself, and she had a home for disabled soldiers, called the Invalidny Dom, built in the palace park, where the men were trained in all kinds of crafts. Some lived permanently in the home, while others only stayed just long enough to learn a trade that would enable them to supplement their pensions and to earn a living at home. This endeavor was the first of its kind ever done in Russia. The Empress put Count V. A. Schulenbourg at the head of this institution and continued to supervise it herself to the last.

The birth of the Tsarevich Alexei greatly increased the Empress' popularity so that she was no longer criticized for undue domesticity.

She had done her duty to the country and the knowledge of this gave her much more self-confidence.

There could be no question of great receptions in war time, but in the autumn of 1904 the Empress began to give dinners at Tsarskoe Selo for the young women of St. Petersburg society and their husbands. A whole series of these small dinners had been planned, and she had gone through long lists with Count Benckendorff, but only two dinners had been given when the news from the war became so bad that the Empress no longer had the heart to continue entertaining.

In 1904 the Russian armies had a few minor successes, but the fleet suffered serious losses during the bombardment of Port Arthur. Many vessels had struck mines, among them Admiral Makarov's flagship, the Petropavlovsk, which had been sunk, taking down with it the gallant Admiral and nearly all of his crew. Grand Duke Cyril was one of the few to escape after floating for hours among the debris. The Emperor balanced the successes against the disasters as chances of war, but in the country underground murmurings began to be heard. Revolutionary activity, which had not made itself felt since the beginning of the reign, emerged again, and Ministers whose policy was deemed too conservative were murdered in the streets.

The Emperor and Empress, although greatly shocked, always ascribed these attempts to the work of international anarchists and not to the home-grown revolutionary party, and it is true that the country as a whole was not revolutionary at this time. It was only among a small section of the working class and among the poorer peasants of some of the provinces that the revolutionary agents succeeded in spreading their teachings. Dissatisfaction at the mobilization and the unsettled minds of the people gave them fruitful ground in which to expand their influence.

Just before the Christmas of 1904, Port Arthur fell. This had been considered impregnable and its loss was a terrible blow to the national pride. Now all hopes were centered on the Baltic Fleet, but the conditions under which it had to fight were unfavorable. The enemy had every advantage and, on the anniversary of the Coronation – May 27, 1905, the fatal battle of Tsushima was fought, during which Russia lost nearly all its fleet and thousands of gallant seamen.

The horror of the moment when they heard the news of the disaster was never forgotten by the Emperor and Empress. The day of the Coronation was, after that time, a day not of rejoicing, but of prayer. It always meant Tsushima to them.

Chapter 13

Gathering Clouds: 1905

The winter of 1905 was a time of anxiety and trouble. On January 22, 1905, the St. Petersburg workmen, led by the priest Gapon, a political agitator, made a demonstration in front of the Winter Palace. The crowd had various elements in it: some were hostile and seditious, some had been deceived by their leaders. The crowd would not disperse at the summons of the police. Troops were called in and were obliged to fire, and many workmen were killed and wounded (this was the event called "Bloody Sunday.")

At this time the Emperor was inadequately supported by his Ministers. Prince Sviatopolk-Mirsky, the Liberal successor to the reactionary Plehve, had tried to promote reforms, but had difficulty in fulfilling the promises he made. The Empress was in despair at the state of the country and at the Emperor's embarrassments, although she could not grasp the situation properly as she had never before come face-to-face with Russian internal politics.

The state of her mind is shown in a letter of January 27, 1905, to Princess Victoria:

> *... You understand the crisis we are going through! It is a time full of trials indeed. My poor Nicky's cross is a heavy one to bear, all the more as he has nobody on whom he can thoroughly rely and who can be a real help to him.*
>
> *He has had so many bitter disappointments, but through it all he remains brave and full of faith in God's mercy. He tries so hard, works with such perseverance, but the*

lack of what I call "real" men is great. Of course they must exist somewhere, but it is difficult to get at them. The bad are always close at hand; others through false humility keep in the background.

We shall try to see more people, but it is difficult. On my knees I pray to God to give me wisdom to help him in his heavy task. I wrack my brain to pieces to find a man and cannot; it is a despairing feeling. One is too weak, the other too Liberal, the third too narrow-minded and so forth.

Two very clever men we have, and both are more than dangerous and unloyal. The Minister of the Interior is doing the greatest harm – he proclaims grand things without having prepared them. It's like a horse that has been held very tight in hand, and then suddenly one lets the reins go. It bolts, falls, and it is more than difficult to pull it up again before it has dragged others with it into the ditch. Reforms can only be made gently with the greatest care and forethought. Now we have precipitately been launched forth and cannot retrace our steps. All these disorders are thanks to his unpardonable folly and he won't believe what Nicky tells him, does not agree with his point of view.

Things are in a bad state and it's abominably unpatriotic at the time when we are plunged into war to break forth with revolutionary ideas. The poor workmen, who had been utterly misled, had to suffer, and the organizers have hidden as usual behind them. Don't believe all the horrors the foreign papers say. They make one's hair stand on end with foul exaggeration. Yes, the troops, alas, were obliged to fire. Repeatedly the crowd was told to retreat and that Nicky was not in town (as we are living here this winter) and that one would be forced to shoot, but they would not heed and so blood was shed. On the whole 92 killed and between 200-300 wounded. It is a ghastly thing, but had one not done it the crowd would have grown colossal and 1000 would have been crushed.

All over the country, of course, it is spreading. The Petition had only two questions concerning the workmen and all the rest was atrocious: separation of the Church from the Government, etc., etc. Had a small deputation brought, calmly, a real petition for the workmen's good, all would have been otherwise.

Many of the workmen were in despair when they heard later what the petition contained, and begged to work again under the protection of the troops. Petersburg is a rotten town, not an atom Russian. The Russian people are deeply and truly devoted to their Sovereign and the revolutionaries use his name for provoking them against landlords, etc., but I don't know how.

How I wish I were clever and could be of real use! I love my new country. It's so young, powerful, and has so much good in it, only utterly unbalanced and childlike. Poor Nicky, he has a bitter hard life to lead. Had his father seen more people, drawn them around him, we should have had lots to fill the necessary posts; now only old men or quite young ones, nobody to turn to. The uncles no good, Mischa, a darling child still ... [This was the Emperor's brother, the Grand Duke

Michael Alexandrovich, then heir-presumptive to the crown.]

Until the Great War, the Empress took no interest in political matters. The sudden events of 1905 had greatly upset her. In the following years, when things seemed to be going on as before, the Emperor continued his habitual policy of never discussing political questions at home. The Empress scarcely ever touched on political events in her letters. She had her own interests and exercised no influence whatever on public affairs during all those years.

The year 1905 saw the gradual spread of the revolutionary movement. On February 17, 1905, the Grand Duke Serge, the Emperor's uncle and brother-in-law, was murdered in Moscow. The assassin's bomb literally blew him to pieces. He was especially hated by the revolutionaries as he belonged to the extreme reactionary party. The Grand Duke was murdered just after he had tendered his resignation. A more liberal policy had been decided on and the Grand Duke had told the Emperor that, as this was not in accordance with his political views, he could not in the circumstances honestly carry on his work. The Grand Duke and Grand Duchess were only staying in Moscow until their St. Petersburg palace (across the bridge from the Anichkov Palace) was ready for them.

The unfortunate Grand Duchess was busy in her workroom at the Kremlin when the sound of the explosion reached her. She had an intuition that something had happened, rushed out, and saw the most terrible sight that a wife's eyes ever saw … She could never join in the life of the world again and afterwards lived only for the poor and suffering.

The Grand Duke of Hesse, with his young newly-married second wife and Princess Victoria, traveled at once to Moscow. The town was in a state of ferment and further political risings were feared. The funeral was accordingly quiet, only the Grand Duke's brother Paul and his cousin and friend, the Grand Duke Constantine, being present. The Emperor did not go to Moscow, but Empress Alexandra was prevented from going only by fear of the effect it might have on her son, whom she was still nursing. Grand Duchess Ella's first thought was for her sister and the effect the shock would have on her. She sent telegram after telegram imploring her to take no risks for the baby Tsarevich's sake.

"It is very hard," the Empress wrote to Princess Victoria on February 20, 1905, but Princess Victoria's presence in Moscow relieved a little of her anxiety and sorrow for Grand Duchess Ella, for the two elder sisters were particularly attached to each other.

In these troubled times, the Dowager-Empress joined the Emperor and Empress at Tsarskoe Selo and spent the winter with them. The news continued to be bad from all sides. The spring had brought the great naval disaster of Tsushima. Commanders-in-chief were changed in the army but still there were no significant successes. The country was weary of the war and, in the face of the complications in the internal political situation, it was thought inadvisable to persist in dragging on hostilities for another winter. The preliminaries for peace were discussed in America and peace with the Japanese was signed by Count Witte at Portsmouth, U.S.A., on September 5, 1905.

It is not generally known that in this matter the Emperor Nicholas II gave all the instructions to Count Witte himself. It was he who insisted that Count Witte should refuse the original conditions of the Japanese Government which he felt were incompatible with the honor of his country. He was determined that more favorable terms should be obtained and telegraphed orders to this effect to Count Witte, authorizing him to break off negotiations if the Japanese would not agree. This was disclosed by Count W. N. Kokovtzev, a former Russian Prime Minister, who was Minister of Finance at the time, in a lecture given in Paris in May 1927.

Summer saw an agrarian movement spread from the Baltic provinces to many of the provinces of Central Russia. This movement had begun in February. Strangely enough, in many of the provinces the agitators made use of the Emperor's name, persuading the peasants that the Emperor was granting them the estates of the landlords as a reward for having fought in the war. In some places the organizers of the rising actually read out forged manifestoes.

Many officials were murdered. There were naval mutinies in both the Black Sea and the Baltic Fleets. In the autumn, a general strike was proclaimed. Beginning with the railways, every pulse of Russia's life was paralyzed. The opinions of Ministers were at variance. At first it was hoped to remedy the situation by calling in a deliberative assembly, the Sobor, such as the old Tsars used to convene in times of great emergency.

After the general strike, the Emperor appointed S. J. Witte as Head of the Ministry, and on October 30, 1905, an imperial manifesto announced the institution of the Duma. The Duma's rights were wider than those of the Sobor and the manifesto granted liberty of speech, of meeting, and habeas corpus. This did not produce any immediate results, except the calling-off of the general strike, but gradually S. J. Witte's statesmanship led the country into quieter channels.

In St. Petersburg, there was considerable unrest encouraged by the Soviet of Workmen's Deputies, founded by Hrustalev Nossar. The Government succeeded in closing this down and had Hrustalev Nossar arrested. He had lost the full support of the workmen. Many were weary and returned to work, and when the Soviet was forcibly put down, it was already breaking up from within.

It took several years to quell the revolutionary waves. There were still Jewish pogroms in different places and the end of 1905 saw a violent uprising in Moscow which was put down by the Semenovsky regiment. The agrarian troubles in the Baltic provinces took some time to suppress. During the mutiny in the fleet lying at Kronstadt, the Empress distinctly heard the roar of cannon from her little sitting room in the seaside villa of Peterhof (the Nizhni Palace on the seashore in the Alexandria Park).

117

The imperial couple was not frightened. In the stream of calumny showered upon them by their detractors, no one has ever dared to accuse them of want of personal courage. The Emperor was a fatalist. He did not know fear. With his wonderful self-command, the result of years of schooling, he always seemed calm and collected under whatever circumstances. In 1905, at the ceremony of the Blessing of the Waters, a live shell was fired in the salute and flew over his head, crashing into one of the palace windows, but the Emperor scarcely moved, though eye-witnesses say that the sign of the cross he made at the moment was perhaps more devout than prescribed by ritual. The Empress was equally brave. She considered the possibility of attempts on their lives as inseparable from their position, and never referred to, or stopped to think about, the subject. It was just a chance that had to be faced, and with her deep faith she accepted the fact that all was in the hands of God. She was, of course, anxious sometimes in later years, though she never admitted it, when the Emperor was held up at some function. She gave no sign, but her anxiety could be seen in the relief with which her face lit up as she welcomed him. Before the real danger of the mutiny at Kronstadt she never trembled, and the Emperor and Empress remained at Peterhof with their children, though Kronstadt was nearly opposite.

The effect of character can be clearly seen in an incident that one of the Empress' ladies, Princess Obolensky, described to me. The imperial yacht, The Standart, struck a rock during a cruise in Finnish waters on September 11, 1907, happily in broad daylight. The extent of the damage could not be seen at once. The yacht was fast making water and listed more and more to leeward, and the convoy, which drew more water, had not been able to follow the imperial yacht into this particular channel. Sirens screeched and men ran about in obedience to commands from the officers. Boats were lowered. The Standart seemed to be sinking fast.

The Empress was always resourceful and full of energy, and never lost her head in face of danger. She arranged that the children and the ladies' maids should be first lowered into the boats. Then, with the help of her friend Mme. Vyrubova, she rushed into the cabins, tore the sheets off the beds, and tossed all valuables into them, making huge bundles of the most necessary and precious things. It was all done in about a quarter of an hour.

The Empress was the last woman to leave the yacht. The Emperor, through all the noise and rushing about, stood calmly on deck giving the necessary orders. Princess Obolensky, coming up to him, noticed he was holding his watch in his hand and bending down to look at the water-line. She asked him what he was doing. He said that he meant to remain on board to the last and was counting how many inches a minute the yacht was sinking in order to know how long she would stay afloat. He had calculated that there were still some twenty minutes.

Thanks to the watertight compartments and to the measures taken by the commander, the yacht did not sink, and a passing Finnish boat, the Ellekeinen, took the imperial party on board, whence they were moved to the cruiser Asia. Happily no one suffered from anything but great discomfort and agitation. But had the seas been high, the matter would have been serious, for the yacht would undoubtedly have sunk and the boats were very full.

The state of the country from 1905 to 1909 obliged the imperial couple to give up any journeys away from St. Petersburg because the Emperor had to be in daily communication with his ministers. The Duma was a new institution and many questions arose in connection with it. Shooting in Poland was given up and the Crimea was not visited. The ministers had great fears for the Emperor's life during these times of continual political murder. He was implored to give up his solitary rides in the Peterhof Park and his shooting. He submitted, very grudgingly, only when it was pointed out to him that it was his duty to the country. On one point, however, the Emperor was firm: he would not abandon his long walks, and every day he went out, whenever he possibly could, generally alone.

Both the Emperor and the Empress disliked the police measures that were taken on their account and dodged the detective in the parks. The Empress felt that she was being spied upon. The police who loitered around the palace in plain clothes greatly annoyed her. She enjoyed escaping from them and delighted in Haroun-al-Raschid expeditions.

She liked to drive without even a footman, with her children or her lady-in-waiting, and had her splendid Cossack placed on the box only on State occasions. She liked to stop during her drives to enter a church or a humble shop, or to admire a view. Often at Tsarskoe Selo she would drive slowly past some villa, for she liked to see into the houses unobserved. On her long drives in the woods around Tsarskoe and Pavlovsk a mounted Cossack of the Emperor's escort rode at some distance behind her carriage, but occasionally she dismissed even him.

This sometimes gave rise to complications, although the Empress would not admit it. On one occasion, an inexperienced cyclist collided with the Empress' carriage in one of the narrow lanes. The carriage had no room to swerve aside and was overturned into the ditch, although happily none of its occupants was hurt. The coachman was hampered by the long padded coat that Russian coachmen wear (the Empress always drove à la Russe, the Court people only having the red Louis XV liveries). Finally Her Majesty herself held the struggling horses while the young Grand Duchesses, the hapless cyclist and the coachman (when he had tucked up his robes) pulled the carriage out of the ditch by their joint efforts.

The Empress always made light of this matter, fearing that the youth who had been the cause of the accident might get into trouble, or that the coachman's feelings would be hurt by criticism of his driving skills. She said that no Cossack could have prevented this happening and continued her unattended drives.

Chapter 14

On The Standart: 1905-1912

After the agitation of 1905, the country readjusted its political balance very quickly. Still, during the sessions of the first Duma, subversive currents were very strong and the state of political tension remained great.

To the Emperor and Empress, the resumption of brilliant Court life seemed hardly suitable. They did not realize, of course, that the troubles of 1905 were only a general rehearsal for those of 1917, but they thought the times too grave for festivities.

The mistake they made was in not replacing these large functions by more informal receptions for prominent politicians and people of note. By this means they would have kept in touch with the general atmosphere of the country, for, by their position, they were cut off from direct contact with public opinion, and, owing to their mode of life, the opinions they heard were nearly always those of the same people. However, simpler intercourse was not customary at the Russian Court, and both the Emperor and Empress, after a few unavailing efforts to make other changes in Court routine at the beginning of their reign, found that even an autocrat's power was helpless against the set rules sanctified by custom.

They gave up attempts at innovations: the Emperor because he had no time; the Empress because any extra fatigue was already beginning to be too much for her strength, although she would never admit to this. So, except for two or three guests at luncheon – generally ministers or high military officials – their life within their household settled down into a quiet daily routine.

The Empress wrote to Princess Victoria on December 23, 1905:

Twice a week the regiments from town come out here. The officers dine with us (en famille, quite simply), spend the night in the Big Palace, and the next morning is a review out of doors or in the riding school ...

Further on one has a glimpse of her anxieties:

Don't expect a long letter, one is not in the letter-writing mood. Nicky slaves, many a day passes without his getting out, or if so, only in the dark. His poor head gets so tired, but he is brave and full of trust and hope in God's mercy.

There were a few indispensable official functions, but the Court no longer lived in St. Petersburg. All the winters were spent at Tsarskoe Selo, with occasional visits to the capital. This was no privation to the Empress, and the Emperor was so busy at that time that he would not, in any case, have been able to resume their former mode of life.

This retirement, mainly due to circumstances, had dire results in every way. The first was that the Empress gradually lost the popularity that she had begun to acquire after her son's birth. A very few people knew how charming she was; the rest did not know anything about her at all. Her circle narrowed more and more.

Her letters are full of her children, who took up an increasing amount of her time as they grew up. She wrote to Princess Victoria on June 13, 1905:

The children are getting on nicely with their lessons, they have English and French masters too; they ride much also, which they greatly enjoy.

Baby is getting on, thank God, splendidly. Do have Louise photographed, so as that I can get a good idea of

*her now, as a big girl; Marie P. also has her hair done
up now.*

*My Nurses' School has been opened now and makes a
nice impression. I only hope it will be a real success ...*

In summer the Court moved from Tsarskoe Selo to Peterhof. The Empress liked the small, unpretentious villa at the seaside (the Nizhni Palace), where all her children, except the eldest, had been born. She had loved the sea from childhood and the greatest pleasure she had was when the Imperial Family were on their yacht, cruising in Finnish waters.

This was the Emperor's only holiday, during which, for several weeks, his audiences and his work with the ministers were interrupted. Messengers came daily from the capital, bringing him ministerial reports, but his day was free for him to do as he liked – a rare treat for him. All possible formality was dispensed with and the Court led a simple life in which the officers of the yacht took part.

The Standart was fitted out with every comfort. The Imperial Family's cabins were nearly as large as their rooms in the Peterhof villa and were upholstered in pretty, light chintzes. The Empress spent most of her day lying on a couch on deck, one of her daughters always staying with her when she did not feel well enough to go ashore.

She was often joined by one or other of the officers, or by some of the Household, who sat and talked to her while she worked or drew. The Emperor would go on shore with the gentlemen of his suite to walk or play tennis on a rather primitive court, and in autumn there was generally some shooting in which the officers of the yacht joined.

The young Grand Duchesses now went about with their father, standing in for their mother, while the little Tsarevich played with the ship's boys on the rocky beach. It was a healthy life for the young people and the bracing air of Finland did them all good, particularly the delicate little boy, who, except on such occasions, never had real country air.

The stays on the yacht were sometimes prolonged until late in the autumn in the years when there were no visits to Poland or the Crimea, so loth were they all to return to the monotony of Tsarskoe Selo. Generally these cruises were limited to that part of the coast that lies between Kronstadt and Helsingfors, for the Emperor had to be within easy reach of his government. A favorite place of anchorage was the lonely bay of Pitkopas, near Biorke.

Here was typical Finnish scenery: rocky islands, with tall pines growing in the chinks of the grey granite, with no house in sight. Dark forests stretched far into the mainland, with a few lonely fishermen's huts hidden among them. The transparent waters were still and quiet in the wonderful "white nights" of May and June, when the light of one day lasted till the dawn of the next.

The Empress loved the long, still days, the bright moonlight nights on the water, and the evening prayer of the sailors on deck before the lowering of the flag, when the last rays of the setting sun rested on the sea, on the woods, and on the escorting ships, while the deep voices of the men, singing the Lord's Prayer, echoed far away into the silence.

The Emperor was asked by the ministers not to undertake any journeys by land in the years between 1905 and 1909. He therefore took advantage of these cruises to visit the naval bases in the Baltic – Baltisch Port, Reval, Libau and Riga. In the last-named town, the Imperial Family were present in 1910 at the inauguration of the monument to Peter the Great, when great festivities took place. The Empress was very ailing then and could only with difficulty manage essential public appearances. She was not well enough to go on shore and held receptions of the Baltic nobility on the yacht, while the Emperor and her daughters attended the functions on land.

Fewer foreign royalty came to Russia during these years, but in June 1908 there were some family visits. King Edward and Queen Alexandra came on The Victoria and Albert to Reval for two days on

June 9, the Imperial Family meeting them on The Standart, and, later in the summer, King Frederick and Queen Louise of Denmark came with their daughters to pay their accession visit. Their stay, which was at Peterhof, was more of a family meeting than an official visit, and the whole Imperial Family living in the neighborhood took part in entertaining them.

That same year a whole galaxy of princes came to Tsarskoe Selo for the wedding of the Emperor's cousin, the seventeen-year-old Grand Duchess Marie Pavlovna, with Prince William of Sweden on May 3, 1908, which was celebrated with much splendor. The Grand Duchess and her brother, Grand Duke Dmitry Pavlovich, were the children of Grand Duke Paul, who lived almost entirely abroad, and they had been brought up by their uncle and aunt, Grand Duke Serge and Grand Duchess Ella, who had no children of their own. After the terrible shock of her husband's murder, Grand Duchess Ella could not face a life in the world again, gave up all her palaces to her nephew and niece, and spent most of her fortune in establishing a religious nursing community in Moscow, The House of Martha and Mary, where she took up residence. From then on, the Empress and her sister saw even less of each other than formerly, and as the Grand Duchess became increasingly engrossed by her work, her influence with the Empress gradually declined.

The Grand Duke Dmitry became the Emperor's ward after the death of the Grand Duke Serge and for a time lived at Tsarskoe Selo, the Emperor and Empress treating him as a son of the house, to the great joy of his young cousins.

The King of Sweden was among the princes present at the marriage of the Grand Duchess Marie Pavlovna to his son at Tsarskoe Selo and members of the Swedish royal family were seen several times during these years. In June 1908, the Imperial Family went on a State visit to Stockholm. The visit was one of those that the Empress most enjoyed. She liked the Queen, was interested to see her niece in her new home, and glad to meet one of her English cousins again, Crown Princess Margaret (a daughter of the Duke of Connaught).

However, a shadow was cast on their stay by an attempt made at the time on the life of a prominent Swedish general. It was whispered that there were plots against Emperor Nicholas and that this attempt was connected with them. For a whole day the Imperial Family was asked to remain on their yacht, while members of the Swedish royal family visited them on board. Nevertheless, this scare passed and the Empress always looked back with pleasure to her stay in Sweden.

King Edward's visit was returned in 1909, the Imperial Family stopping at Cherbourg on the way to be present at the French naval maneuvers. President Fallières entertained his guests most splendidly on the Montcalm, but the visit was confined to Cherbourg, the Emperor and his family living on board The Standart on which they had come.

From Cherbourg they went to Cowes, where they were received by the King and Queen of England. It was just before the August Regatta Week, and Cowes was at its best and gayest. The stay was as unofficial as was possible under the circumstances, but was marked by a splendid naval review held in honor of the Emperor. It was an impressive sight, and the full significance of Great Britain's naval power was emphasized by the lines of mighty battleships and dreadnoughts, drawn up in three majestic rows, which thundered out a salute as King Edward and his imperial guest passed them on The Victoria and Albert.

The Empress wrote to Prince Victoria that "dear Uncle had been most kind and attentive." She saw all her relations and some old friends, went to Farnborough to see the aged Empress Eugénie – her mother's friend – and remembered the days of her own youth in the surroundings she loved. Naturally, she stayed with the older people, but in her heart of hearts she would have preferred going about "the Island," as her children did, deriving much enjoyment from their expeditions ashore. It was the first time they had been anywhere abroad, except to Wolfsgarten and once to Princess Henry's place near Kiel, and they were at heart regular tourists.

This was the last time the Empress saw her mother's family. King Edward died within a year and the Empress never came to England again.

On their return from abroad, the Imperial Family went to the Crimea for the first time for several years. The country had resumed its normal life outwardly, and an able Prime Minister, Piotr Arkadievich Stolypin, was leading the Government wisely and well. He sympathized with liberal ideas, without insisting on too sudden and radical reforms, and he took advantage of the momentary lull to start a vast plan of agrarian reforms which would enable the peasants to become small landowners and create an intermediate conservative class. It would have taken several years to bring this into force all over the country and long before that could happen Stolypin was dead. He was murdered in September 1911, shot by a revolutionary in the theater at Kiev during a gala performance given in honor of the Emperor's visit. The Emperor and his daughters were in the theater at the time, the Empress' health having prevented her from joining them that night, and they came back full of horror at what they had seen. It was hoped at first that the Prime Minister might recover, but he died four days later on September 18, 1911.

The loss of this great statesman was an irreparable one for the Emperor. Not only was he a great man, but he was loyal and faithful to his master, and had his full confidence. His murder seemed to thoughtful people an indication that the revolutionary organizations were active and ready to strike.

The Swedish return visit in 1912 was paid at Pitkopas, where country surroundings lessened the ceremony inseparable from an official visit which would have been fatiguing both to Queen Victoria of Sweden and to the Empress. For two days the Swedish and Russian anthems seemed never to cease being played, as members of the

Swedish and Russian royal families exchanged visits on their respective ships. Both the Russian Minister for Foreign Affairs and his Swedish colleague, Count Ehrenswaert, were present and took part in the State dinner on The Standart, and at the luncheon on The Manligheten.

Here again a sad incident occurred. During the salute on the Swedish man-of-war, a gun exploded and several men were killed and wounded. Such incidents always strengthened the Empress' belief that ill-luck attended them. The Emperor had been born on Job's Day and she could not escape from the feeling that something was against them.

During the summer cruise of 1912, in June, the Russian sovereigns had a brief meeting with the German Emperor, who came to Baltisch Port on his yacht, The Hohenzollern. Both imperial parties stayed on their yachts. Emperor Nicholas, as usual, was an amiable host, while the Empress took part in the entertainments only when it was absolutely necessary, and all present commented on her appearance of extreme fatigue. This was William II's last visit to Russia.

That same summer's stay at Pitkopas was enlivened by the visit of the Dowager-Empress, who came on The Polar Star on August 6 and gave a dance on board for her granddaughters. The Empresses sat side-by-side on deck, watching the dancing, the Emperor beside them, evidently deeply appreciative of his mother's visit. This was a real happy family meeting, without any untoward incident to spoil it.

Since 1905 the Empress had other troubles besides the political troubles of Russia to distress her, troubles that gnawed constantly at her heart and sapped her vitality. The apple of her eye was her boy, the child of so many prayers. She had waited for him for so long and had put her whole soul into her supplications for the granting of her heart's desire. Her overwhelming joy at his birth can only be understood by those who saw that outwardly reserved woman in church, pouring out her soul in intense prayer,

The baby was beautiful, developed rapidly and seemed a strong, fine child. His teething gave him no trouble and he was exceptionally bright and well developed. The proud parents exhibited the splendid little fellow to the public whenever they could. He was not a year old when, in his mother's arms, he was shown to the soldiers at a review, and "Baby behaved well."

When he started trotting about independently and had occasional tumbles, the Empress noticed that the boy seemed to suffer more from his bumps than a small accident warranted. In deadly terror, but without speaking of it to anyone, she watched her darling with a fear in her heart that she did not dare to put into words. As the child grew older and more active, he developed swellings typical of hemophilia, the dreadful disease from which one of her uncles had suffered, and the Empress realized that her only son, her beloved Sunbeam, had the same terrible weakness.

Doctors confirmed her fears, although they said that the Tsarevich was suffering from only a mild form of the disease. His mother's despair can be imagined at hearing her worse fears confirmed. Her agony was the more acute as she knew that it was through her that the boy had inherited the illness. She was in no way to blame, but this did not lessen her terrible feeling of responsibility. Both she and the Emperor hid their anxieties from the world, hoping against hope that there might be some mistake.

Alexei was perfectly well and strong between his attacks, which were caused only by some rash movement on his part, and the Empress always hoped that in the intervals a merciful Providence had wrought a miracle. Once, two whole years passed without a single hemorrhage. The mother revived, her health improved, she looked her former self. Alas, it proved to be a forlorn hope. The boy fell ill again, and although the cause was hidden from everyone and the parents still trusted that he might completely recover, the doctors had few illusions.

This grief destroyed the Empress' joy in life. The look of sadness that had always from time to time come over her face, now settled on it forever. For the sake of her boy's future, she hid her sorrow so well that in the country the nature of the Tsarevich's complaint was unknown. It was whispered about in the palace, but even there no one knew definitively the reason for his frequent sudden illnesses.

The strain under which she lived told gradually on the Empress' health and she was obliged to keep more and more to her sofa. Her heart began to trouble her in 1908. She never complained – it was even difficult to make her say how she really felt – but any exertion became such a visible effort that the doctors warned the Emperor about her health and a cure at Nauheim was prescribed.

The Empress disliked intensely the idea of making a fuss about herself. "It was despairing," she said to Princess Victoria. In a letter to her sister on June 5, 1910, she wrote:

Don't think my ill health depresses me personally. I don't care, except to see my dear ones suffer on my account, and that I cannot fulfill my duties.

But once God sends such a cross, it must be borne. Darling Mama also lost her health at an early age. I have had so much, that, willingly, I give up any pleasures – they mean so little to me, and my family life is such an ideal one, that it is a recompense for anything I cannot take part in.

Baby is growing a little companion to his father. They row together daily. All 5 lunch with him daily, even when I am laid up.

The whole family were to go with the Empress to Nauheim and it was arranged that they should be the guests of the Grand Duke of

Hesse at his castle of Friedberg, where the Empress could take advantage of her cure to see her brother and sisters, for Princess Victoria and her children, and Princess Irene were also at Friedberg.

The Empress' devotion to her family had not lessened in the years of separation and she continued to look up to her eldest sister, feeling in addition to her love a deep admiration for her clear and active mind. She was also on excellent terms with her brothers-in-law. With Princess Irene, a common sorrow knit her even closer, for each had a child for whose life she trembled and Princess Irene seized every opportunity to come to her youngest sister, understanding her anxiety as only another mother who knew the same grief could.

The Grand Duke of Hesse's lively temperament was outwardly just the opposite to the Empress', but there were traits in his character that were very like hers, and he always came first in her affections. He was now happy in his second marriage and his two small sons were the Tsarevich's constant playfellows at Friedberg.

During nearly all her stay, the Empress was so ailing and so much tired by her cure that she could not go about, and for the most part lay on a couch in her room or in the garden with one of her sisters or one of her old friends to keep her company. She was often not able even to come down for meals, but when she felt stronger she was wheeled in her bath-chair to shop with her sisters at Nauheim, an amusement which she enjoyed like a child.

The Emperor and his daughters motored a great deal with their host and were sometimes so badly mobbed, both at Homburg and at Frankfurt, when the public recognized them that they had to escape through back doors to their cars. The last three weeks of their stay were spent at Wolfsgarten, where the German Emperor came for a day on a surprise visit, arriving unexpectedly in shooting dress.

Though the Emperor was very fond of all of his wife's family, the long stay abroad in 1910 was a little trying for him. He was such a true Russian that he always became homesick after three or four weeks out of his own country. The Empress had undertaken this cure against her own wishes, agreeing to undergo the treatment for her family's sake, and she was glad when the cure was over, so the return to Tsarskoe Selo was hailed with joy by all, although the actual moment of parting from her own people was always hard for the Empress. Sadly, the cure had not done her very much good.

There is not much to note in the Empress' private life in 1911 and 1912. She was mostly ailing, going about for a short time and then paying for it by weeks spent on the sofa. Her letters to Miss Jackson give a glimpse of her life:

PETERHOF
May 31/June 13, 1911

DARLING MADGIE – Very tenderest thanks for your dear letter.

We came over here on Saturday and hope to go to sea on Saturday. We long for that rest, my husband has been working like a slave for 7 months and I have been ill nearly all the time. The quiet cozy life on board always does us good, so I hope to get a little better, so as not to be always lying.

Ernie and his wife will be over for the Coronation. May all go off well, and the heat not be too intense; here it is quite cold since a week, and even frost by night.

The children are growing up fast. In November Olga will be 16, Tatiana is almost her size 14 – Marie will be 12, Anastasia 10, Alexei 7. I send them to reviews with their Father, and once they went to a big military luncheon and made circle with the ladies, as I could not go – they must get accustomed to replace me, as I rarely can appear anywhere, and when I do, am afterwards long laid up – over-tired muscles of the heart.

Must end now. Good-bye – God bless you, darling. When do you go to Harrogate? Ella spent a week at Tsarskoe with us, looked well, pink and cheery.

A tender kiss from your old
P.Q. No. III,
ALIX.

DARLING MADGIE – Loving thanks for your last dear letter, forgive me for being such a shockingly bad correspondent.

I had Victoria's visit for a week, which was delightful, and Ella came also for 3 days, and I shall see her again in Moscow. Ernie and family we had in the Crimea, Waldemar came for 3 days on The Standart in Finland, and Irene will come at the end of September to us in Poland, Spala. She was there before, and so we thought she would like to come again after 11 years.

Next week we leave for Borodino and Moscow, terribly tiring festivities, don't know how I shall get through them. After Moscow in spring I was for a very long time quite done up – now I am, on the whole, better.

What terrible rains and storms you have in England – such a calamity. Here we had colossal heat and scarcely ever a drop of rain.

If you know of any interesting historical books for girls, could you tell me, as I read to them and they have begun reading English for themselves. They read a great deal of French and the 2 youngest acted out of the Bourgeois Gentilhomme and really so well, make Victoria tell you all about it. Four languages is a lot, but they need them absolutely, and this summer we had Germans and Swedes, and I made all 4 lunch and dine, as it is good practice for them.

I have begun painting flowers, as alas have had to leave singing and playing as too tiring.

Must end. Goodbye and God bless and keep you. A tender kiss from Your fondly

Loving old P.Q. No. III,
ALIX.

In 1912, all Russia celebrated the centenary of the French invasion and retreat. The Imperial Family went to Moscow for the inauguration of the monument to Alexander III, then to Smolensk, and to the battlefield of Borodino, September 8, where the monument commemorative of 1812 had been erected.

Here a score or so of old men (the oldest was said to be 122), who had been small children when the great battle was fought, were assembled for the Emperor to meet them. They all had the deep religious reverence of the old-time peasant for the Emperor, but some were getting a little childish and were not quite sure if they were in the presence of Nicholas II or of the *Blagoslovenny* – "The Blessed One," as the people called Alexander I – who had been Russia's Emperor in 1812. The expression of their faces when they talked to the Tsar was like what Simeon's must have been when he said his *Nunc Dimittis*. This whole ceremony made a great impression on the Empress and she left cheerfully, looking forward to a few weeks of quiet and her sister's visit.

Chapter 15

A Mother's Agony – Rasputin

After the Moscow centenary celebrations, the Imperial Family went to Poland for their first visit there for several years. At the shooting box at Belovege – their first stop – the little Tsarevich injured himself while jumping out of a boat and internal hemorrhaging set in, heralding the most severe and dangerous attack he had ever had.

His parents were greatly alarmed, but as usual his illness was at first made light of, and no one suspected that it was serious. Recovery was slow, but by early September Alexei was well enough for the family to go on to the other imperial shooting lodge at Spala. A further fall, however, caused a bad relapse, the inner bleeding began again, and a large tumor developed in Alexei's groin which caused him the most excruciating pain and the risk of blood poisoning and peritonitis. No operation was possible. His temperature rose alarmingly and the swelling pressed on all the inflamed nerves of his leg.

At first the poor child cried loudly, but as his strength gave out, this was followed by a constant wailing, which grew hoarser and hoarser. He could take no food and could find no restful position in bed. Sometimes his sailor servant, Derevenko, would carry the wasted little creature for hours in his strong arms when the child thought that movement might ease the pain. Sometimes he lay back on his pillows, growing thinner and more deathlike every day as the weakness increased, his great eyes looking like coals in his little, wan, drawn face.

Even now his condition was hidden from the public for fear that he might be considered a chronic invalid. His parents still hoped for an improvement, and to hide their anxiety and prevent gossip about the child's illness, they continued to lead their ordinary lives. Visitors were invited and the Emperor received the ministers, who came from St. Petersburg. Princess Irene was on a visit to her sister at this time and was a particular comfort to her as she had lost a son from the same dreadful illness.

The Empress was in agony, seeing him and being unable to relieve his intolerable suffering. The little boy cried for death to release him. Until then, no one had realized that the child, just eight years old and shielded from all sorrow, could know the real meaning of the word. He would beg to be buried "in the light" with the blue sky over him.

"When I am dead, it will not hurt any more, will it?" he would ask his mother. "Mamma, help me! " was his continual cry, for the Empress had always been able to soothe him and ease his pain during his earlier attacks, but now she was powerless. She could only hold him in her arms like a baby, caressing him, trying to find some position in which he could for a moment feel easier, while his terrible, heartbreaking wailing went on.

Celebrated doctors had been called in, but their science could do nothing, and Professor Fedorov warned the Emperor (through Count Fredericks) that the case seemed hopeless. Bulletins were issued and the Tsarevich was prayed for in church. A chapel was arranged in a tent in the grounds at Spala and the entire Household took part in daily prayers, with the Cossacks of the escort singing the service.

Throughout the whole country there was great alarm. The little boy had a winning personality and the country was proud of him. However, even the more guarded bulletins that were issued failed to conceal the danger he was in. Indeed, Professor Rauchfuss told me that the doctors worded the evening bulletin on the worst day in such a manner as to be able to follow it with an announcement of the child's death.

That same evening, Princess Irene asked the Household to disperse at an unusually early hour, saying that the news was bad. The Empress sat with her boy, stroking his forehead and pressing his hands. He was too weak to return her caresses. The Emperor went in and out, with a man's helplessness in illness, his face visibly ageing with anxiety.

It was at that moment that the Empress turned in despair to a wonder-worker, a faith-healer, whom she had seen before when she had been anxious about her son. He had prayed and his words had greatly impressed her, and it had seemed to her that there was an improvement in the boy when he came during her son's attacks.

The doctors had told her that they could do nothing more, so she telegraphed the healer to ask for his prayers.

His answer came that same evening and was consoling. He told her the child would not die, and the next morning, October 22, Alexei was better. From that day the improvement continued. The doctors pronounced him out of danger and in November he was moved to Tsarskoe Selo, where he ultimately completely recovered from the attack, although he had a contraction of the muscles of the leg that made him very lame for more than a year.

The Empress felt that she had witnessed a miracle. The child had been dying and Rasputin's prayers had called him back from death. She was too humble a Christian to attribute anything to her own supplications, so thereafter for her Rasputin was a saint, and she treated him accordingly. Indeed, she considered it almost a blasphemy to speak of him otherwise.

"Why should humanity nowadays," she said to me, "be deprived of the comfort and support given to former generations?" St. Seraphim of Sarov had not lived so very long ago and the Church had canonized him. Thus she reasoned in her conviction that to her, too, had been vouchsafed the blessing of seeing a wonder-working saint walk upon this earth.

The story of Rasputin and of the Empress' introduction to him has been told so often, and so inaccurately, that I think it right to give the correct version of the facts as I know them to have been. To those who say that it is incredible that the Empress of Russia could pin her faith to such a person, it is necessary to point to the followers of Mme. Blavatsky, Mrs. Besant, Dr. Steiger, and the many staunch believers in Christian Science. In the case of the Empress, mysticism was combined with a blind clinging to anything that might save her child, easily understood by some Russian minds in whom religion is curiously mixed with superstition. An English, German or French brain cannot quite understand her mentality, which was a mixture of Western mysticism and her newly-acquired, somewhat narrow, Orthodoxy, and like many converts, she surpassed even the usual Russian attitude to religion.

Her faith was pure and ingenuous. Coupled with this were her love, as a mother, for her child and her longing, as an Empress, to save the life of the heir to a vast empire. She had often previously begged for Father John of Kronstadt's prayers for herself and her child. When the Empress received Rasputin, she was convinced that the path she had chosen was the right one, and that the criticisms and obstacles were only those thorns thrown in the path of those who strive to follow righteousness.

When, through her friendship with the Grand Duchesses Militza and Stana, she became interested in mystical questions, she developed a belief in the existence of people in the world who by their saintly lives can become links between humanity and God. These beings are chosen by Providence to help and sustain their weaker brethren. Their prayers work miracles and the gift of knowing the future is vouchsafed to them. The Yogi of India are people of this kind. In Russia they were called the *Staretz* or *Stranniki*. A *Staretz* is a layman who has renounced the world and, without entering any special order, leads a monastic life. Some spend their time going from pilgrimage to pilgrimage, praying for the salvation of mankind; some live the lives of hermits. The ecclesiastical authorities look upon them most benevolently; educated Russians of the old-fashioned type treat them with respect; peasants go to them for help and advice. They admonish, pray and sometimes doctor, although as a rule they minister only to spiritual needs, exhorting those who come to them to penitence and confession, preparing them for absolution at the hands of a priest. Peasants believe these *Starzi* to have the gift of prophecy given them in compensation for their ascetic lives, and consider them almost saints and on the high road to canonization.

They are generally old men, as was the revered *Staretz* of Optina Poustin, to whom Leo Tolstoy went for counsel before his death. Many have been worldly in youth. As Count Keyserling says in his preface to 'Der Russische Christ,' to the average Russian mind, the just, the Blameless, do not seem so near in heart as those who have known human frailty and temptation, and have conquered and repented.

A venerated, saintly *Staretz* often has more influence with the people than a village priest. The *Starzi* have no official standing in the Church; they are a survival of the early apostolic teaching which still prevails in remote parts of Russia. They wander on foot through the country, speaking of the holy places they have seen – the Holy Land, Mount Athos or great Russian monasteries. They quote whole pages of Holy Scripture and prayers. The Russian peasant is too poor to own a Bible; he knows the prayers that he has learned in his childhood and those that he hears in church, but, except for this, his religious knowledge is small. He listens with delight to the pious talk of the pilgrims who recount the lives of saints and stories of marvelous healings and miracles – all the semi-mysticism that an uneducated Russian loves.

As early as 1901, the Empress had made the acquaintance of a French mystic, M. Philippe, a kind of clairvoyant as well as a faith-healer. He had preached to her that if she submitted to the decrees of Providence and strove for spirituality, she would always find teachers who would strengthen her faith. Philippe had studied medicine and had adapted theosophical ideas to his practice, treating his patients by prayer. He told the Empress in 1902 that she would have her longed-for son. This prediction was not fulfilled at that time, for in September

140

a bulletin was issued stating that the hopes of the Empress had suffered disappointment, but Philippe's teaching bore fruit and, when he left, the Empress was prepared for him to be replaced by another teacher.

Again the Grand Duchesses heard of a man with wonderful gifts of prayer and introduced him to the Empress. This was Gregori Rasputin. He was one of the wandering pilgrims who are often *Starzi* in the making, and some time beforehand his piety had attracted the notice of Hermogene, Archbishop of Saratov.

Rasputin was a Siberian peasant from the village of Pokrovskoe, in the faraway province of Tobolsk. In his youth he had been wild. There were stories of horse-stealing and of other unedifying things. He married, had children, and then, quite accidentally, fell under the influence of a priest who so much impressed him as to the error of his ways that he left his home and started on a pilgrimage, intending to devote his life to repentance and prayer. Thereafter he went from monastery to monastery with quotations from the Gospels on his lips, dressed as a pilgrim and loaded with the heavy iron chains of the penitent. He had the gift of sincere and impassioned prayer and his faith was increased by his pilgrimages. Soon he gained the reputation of being a saintly man and a healer among the Siberian people.

In 1905, he appeared in St. Petersburg, and was received with respect in pious circles and patronized by the Archbishop Theophane, Rector of the Ecclesiastical Academy, a universally revered prelate and at that time the imperial confessor. When the Empress heard of him, it is probable that her first idea was that he might do something for her boy, for she was just beginning to realize the nature of Alexei's illness. The Emperor asked his confessor's advice, and, according to M. Paléologue, the Archbishop even advised the imperial couple to receive the pilgrim.

Father Alexander Vassiliev, the Emperor's other confessor, also looked favorably on Rasputin at first. He thought him sincere and tried to gain an influence over him. Father Vassiliev was an honest man and when, in the course of time, he began to doubt whether Rasputin was, as he was said to be, "fighting the evil in him enough," he was much troubled about his own course of action. The opinion of a confessor is so important to a Catholic or an Orthodox mind that the judgment of mere laymen cannot compare with it.

In July 1906, the Emperor and Empress saw the healer for the first time. The Emperor mentions the date in his diary, simply noting, "Have seen *Boji Tcbelovek* – the man of God, Gregori."

He was "Gregori Effimovich" to the Emperor and Empress – "Father Gregori" to other believers – but in front of the imperial couple he had the respectful manner of the peasant before his sovereign. There was something in the Emperor, simple as he was, that made any familiarity in his presence unthinkable, but Rasputin kept his gruff way of speech and spoke as authoritatively to the Emperor as he would have spoken to a commoner. The Empress saw him solely through religious eyes, neither as an uncouth peasant nor as an ordinary man, but as a helping spirit sent to her in her hour of need. She trusted, from the first, that his prayers might cure her son.

She, who disliked all publicity, hid both the fact of the child's illness and of her meeting with the *Staretz*. She wanted the world to believe in the boy's health. She knew that Court circles had criticized her interest in Philippe, and she felt that a storm of talk and bitter comment would be aroused if it were known that she was interested in Rasputin. She knew the conservatism of the people around her and thought that class prejudice would make a *moujik* like Rasputin seem even more objectionable than Philippe as a visitor to the Palace. She did not realize that there were other reasons that alarmed her devoted entourage and that anything that might give rise to misinterpretation is dangerous to one in a high position.

Everything that concerned her religion – "her soul," as she expressed it – had been hidden jealously by the Empress since her childhood. She felt that in this, at least, she had a right to "privacy." Unfortunately, this word cannot exist for sovereigns. Every word, every gesture, is seen or heard and remarked upon, and the most insignificant details of their lives can take on a vast importance. The story that a wandering pilgrim, a faith healer, had been received by the sovereigns was therefore spread abroad and widely commented on.

Imagining that these visits of Rasputin were clandestine, the Empress forgot that every person who passed through the gates of the Palace had his name written down several times by the police and officials. Every step the Imperial Family took, every person they saw, was noted by the police and also in the minutely detailed Court Circular seen by the Master of the Household every evening. Leaf by leaf, this was eventually bound, to form large volumes, recording every single day of their lives, as the lives of all their predecessors had been recorded. Every visit of Rasputin to the Empress was known to dozens of people and the mystery which surrounded these audiences aroused much curiosity and gave rise to many tales.

At first Rasputin saw Their Majesties very seldom – not more than three or four times a year – but later the Empress saw him more often, but never more than once in a couple of months. Nevertheless, the appearance of such a personage within the precincts of the Palace was bound to cause a stir. The Emperor and Empress had by this time realized that anyone to whom they showed any special mark of favor would immediately be pecked at and intrigued against, and they imagined that this was the cause of the feeling against Rasputin, and when rumors against him were reported to the Empress, she supposed them to be due to jealousy and class prejudice.

By 1912, Rasputin had established himself in St. Petersburg, where he began to find many disciples. People of all sorts came to his modest apartment: mothers and wives asking for his prayers for their children and husbands, love-sick maidens seeking his advice in their love affairs, drunkards imploring him to cure them, and the sick, beggars and petitioners of every kind, ultra-pious people as well as those interested in mystic questions.

He was one of those men who inspire fanatical support. Knowing what sin was, he always preached repentance and always upbraided his hearers roughly in his imaginative peasant language for their sins and weaknesses. He gave advice to everyone and to the poor he gave all the money that his admirers gave him, keeping only enough for his simple needs. He remained a peasant with a peasant's tastes. To the last day of his life he wore peasant's clothes, dressing like the fashionable of his class in a silk shirt and fine glossy boots.

Women were his particular admirers. They came in great numbers and treated him almost as a god. This was his undoing as he gave up his pilgrimages through the country and stayed in St. Petersburg, going from house to house visiting his admirers. He was now a man of about fifty. Real *Starzi* were always very old men who had left worldly temptation far behind. With the opportunities he had for better living, he soon began to drink more than was good for him. This led him, it is said, to worse excesses in which the inborn coarseness of his nature made itself apparent. After each bout his contrition was equally extreme and was followed by a renewal of religious ardor.

His soul seemed to be divided into two parts: the one a kind of heaven and the other a kind of hell, in each of which he seemed to dwell in turn. His lapses caused his ecclesiastical patrons, the Archbishops Hermogene and Theophane, to renounce him. The Grand Duchesses Militza and Stana also gave up seeing him and warned the Empress of the rumors against him, but the only result of their intervention was their loss of the Empress as a friend.

The Empress believed that intriguers had influenced her cousins and the archbishops in a plot to rob her of the man who had given her peace of mind, repeating all the praise of Rasputin that she had heard from his early, and now disillusioned, admirers.

One must remember that, during his rare and brief appearances in the Palace, Rasputin never forgot that he was a peasant before the Tsar and Tsaritsa. He showed them only his good side, and that so convincingly that they would not believe that any other side existed.

He could always find the right word to allay their anxieties for their boy – apt quotations from the Gospels or from the lives of the saints, or a short, earnest prayer, whereupon the Empress would become tranquil again, with the conviction that all would be well. Had he only once tried to strike another note, he would not have kept his power, for the Empress was very easily shocked by human weaknesses.

It is perhaps worth noting that the Empress was always a believer in faith-healing. Once, in the course of conversation with her, I mentioned a case I had read about in the papers concerning some children who had died of diphtheria, and whose parents were prosecuted for not sending for a doctor, instead trusting to a faith-healer's prayers. I expressed my indignation at such folly being possible with all the resources of science within reach, but the Empress astonished me by saying, "My dear, they did not pray hard enough. Had their prayers been fervent, the children would have recovered."

The Empress was never a great believer in doctors, which is perhaps not surprising seeing how little is known of hemophilia or its cure. Rasputin was sent for only when the Tsarevich fell ill, and he always managed to arrive when the Tsarevich's health was on the threshold of recovery, which the Empress believed to be due to his intercessions. What probably happened was that he had his own sources of information and contrived to come in time for the recovery of the child to be attributed to him. By this means he kept the Empress' faith and she came to look upon him as a kind of guardian angel to her idolized boy.

Nonsense has been written about Rasputin's drugging the Tsarevich or hypnotizing the mother and son. Nothing of this kind ever happened. The story that Ania Vyroubova gave potions to the Tsarevich on the advice of a Tibetan doctor, Dr. Badmaiev, a friend of Rasputin, is also pure invention. Dr. Badmaiev never came to the Palace and the Empress would not have countenanced any such thing.

In 1911, Rasputin went on a pilgrimage to Jerusalem, from which he returned more deeply venerated than ever by his admirers. After 1912, when, as she believed, he had saved the Tsarevich's life at Spala, the Empress pinned all her faith upon him and would not entertain any doubt as to his sanctity. The Emperor was less credulous and had inquiries made by the police as a result of warnings from his ministers. Unfortunately, although the main charges against Rasputin, accusing him of immoral conduct with women, were probably true, he was able in one case to prove an alibi, having been at Tsarskoe Selo when he was supposed to have been in St. Petersburg. That was enough to discredit the whole report in the Emperor's eyes and to encourage him in the belief that Rasputin's enemies were simply conspiring to oust this man of the people from the Palace.

Still, in 1912, as a result of a direct appeal from Prime Minister Kokovtzev to the Emperor, Rasputin was told to go back to his native village when Kokovtzev pointed out to the Emperor that the stories of Rasputin's visits were damaging the imperial prestige.

At that time, Rasputin was much in the public eye. He had quarreled with a former friend of his, the monk Iliodor, who had broken his vows and gone abroad. Iliodor threatened to publish some letters belonging to Rasputin which had come into his possession. Among these were a few unimportant notes from the Empress to Rasputin. It was this threat that led to the Prime Minister's representations to the Emperor.

The book of letters was not published in Russia but the harm was done. Garbled accounts of the tenor of the Empress' letters were quoted on all sides and Rasputin was falsely believed to have great influence at Court. When he returned to St. Petersburg, his clientele increased among professional political intriguers and unscrupulous senior officials, who hoped that he might casually mention their names to the authorities, and junior officials, who hoped that he might speak of them to their bosses. They all came to Rasputin's apartment. Society women, as well as many of his own class, came to him, some from curiosity, others with the hope (which was not realized) that it might bring them into contact with the Court.

By the time the war broke out, Rasputin's unpopularity had become extreme. Notwithstanding this, many distracted mothers and wives came to ask for his prayers, hoping that he might enlighten them as to the future in store for their dear ones. Women were doing this in every country involved in the war in those dark years. If Rasputin had not been there, the wives and mothers of Petrograd would have gone to some other seer. In this case, the danger was that he gave all these people an impression that his influence in the Palace was far greater than it was.

I was told that he was a great boaster and would interrupt an interview in order to answer a pretended telephone call from the Palace. General Ressine, who had all the Palace telephone conversations noted down in his police reports, told me that Rasputin did call Tsarskoe Selo on occasion, but spoke to his private friends there, while his listeners believed him to be talking with some member of the Imperial Family.

The Empress' most intimate friend, Mme. Vyroubova, was a staunch believer in Rasputin. After disasters in her married life, she turned to religion. She had met Rasputin before, and now he found the right note with her and she became his devoted adherent. She was firmly convinced that Rasputin was the one person to give peace of mind to the Empress, whom she idolized, and so she became the willing and ever-ready link between the Empress and the healer. She carried messages from both sides and would always fan the flames of the Empress' faith when they seemed to be waning.

It was generally at Mme. Vyroubova's house that the Empress saw Rasputin. He seldom actually came to the Palace. I lived in the Alexander Palace from 1913 to 1917, my room being connected by a corridor to the apartments of the Imperial Family, and I never met Rasputin during all the time that I was constantly in the company of

147

the Grand Duchesses. M. Gilliard, who also lived there for several years, never saw him either.

Neither the Empress not her children ever spoke of Rasputin to those whom they knew to be disbelievers and, contrary to general opinion, the most in the Empress' household were indeed skeptical. The Empress was invariably kind in her manner to those who, like Countess Hendrikova and myself, did not share her beliefs. It did not influence her conduct towards us in the least; it was only a subject she thought we did not understand and she never tried to force her opinions on us.

Ania Vyroubova was the only one in the Empress' entourage who shared her opinions. This, naturally, strengthened her position with the Empress, for who else could be her messenger? Rasputin, moreover, was always ready to point out Mme. Vyroubova's devotion to the Empress, who was grateful to her friend for risking the world's censure by going to the persecuted saint to bring her his sustaining messages.

The Empress spoke of herself as a "great worrier," and this was true, but when her anxieties gained the upper hand, Rasputin's pious outpourings, and her faith in his prayers and prophecies, gave her confidence. The Emperor found a certain peace of mind in his hopeful assurances that in the end all would go well and was glad to see the comfort the Empress derived from her trust in Rasputin's healing powers.

Believing, as she did, in his heaven-sent powers of divination, the Empress passed on to the Emperor Rasputin's casual judgments of people. She also quoted everything he said about the needs of his own peasant class, to which he always remained true. It must be said that in such things his opinions were those of a very shrewd peasant and often quite sound, but they did not seem to have much effect on the Emperor, who generally passed them over or agreed with some small, unimportant thing so as not to hurt his wife's feelings by refusing what had transmuted into her own request.

148

Rasputin never had any influence in politics generally, and he was certainly too careful to start any political conversations himself. He believed that his pilgrimages had made him an authority on Church matters and he seems to have spoken on ecclesiastical affairs to the Empress, who listened to the authority of the "Saint," but even in this the Emperor does not seem entirely to have adopted her point of view.

What really happened was that Rasputin was spuriously transformed into someone with power and influence by the people who came to him in search of material advantages. These visits created in the public an ever-increasing idea of his importance. If a Cabinet Minister was said to have called on a man like Rasputin, as some are supposed to have done, even if it were only out of curiosity, Rasputin's position became stronger. The public did not believe in a personal or unofficial motive for such a visit. They imagined that Rasputin really had an influence on the affairs of State.

At the beginning of the war, when the Tsarevich was in good health and the Empress was wholly engrossed in her charities, she saw Rasputin very seldom. Mme. Dehn writes in her book that she was even commissioned by the Empress to suggest to Rasputin that he should return to his native village. This his female followers would not allow, and he did not carry out the Empress' wish.

Mme. Vyroubova's railway accident, which was followed by the serious illness of the Tsarevich in December 1915, again brought him to the fore. In that year, Mme. Vyroubova and Mme. Dehn went with Rasputin on a pilgrimage to the shrine of a newly-canonized saint at Tobolsk. They did this at the Empress' request as she had made a vow to go on that pilgrimage herself or to send a substitute. On the way, both ladies visited the village where Rasputin's family lived. Rasputin's wife received them and they were much impressed by everything they saw. Their account of the visit strengthened, if possible, the Empress' disbelief in all stories reflecting on the object of their veneration, although the testimony of these two ladies did not carry weight with anyone beyond the Empress.

Mme. Dehn, as the Empress' friend, was naturally shown only the spiritual side of Rasputin's character. Mme. Vyroubova knew him better, but his influence over her was so strong that she was not likely to look below the surface.

To sum up the question, Rasputin was not the political power pulling the strings of a political game in which ministers were his pawns, nor the dissolute "monk" that he was sometimes – mostly in novels – described as being, but he certainly was not anything like the saint that the Empress imagined him to be.

Had he remained in his native village, he would perhaps have kept his reputation as a pious man with weaknesses. His fellow-villagers would have condoned his sins. He had great faith and knew how to kindle faith in others. He was really indifferent about money. He honestly believed in himself, or so Father Vassiliev, the Emperor's confessor, told me. Rasputin thought it right that people should ask for his prayers, but his success in St. Petersburg was his undoing. Temptations were put in his way to which his weaker side surrendered. He revered his Tsar in his peasant-like fashion, but through his presumed political influence on the Empress he helped to bring about the sovereigns' unpopularity.

Contrary to general impressions, Rasputin did not wholly dominate the Empress' thoughts. He was but one of the many pages that formed the book of her life. When she wanted a fresh stimulus to her faith, when her son was ill and the doctors' help was unavailing, then she opened up the page of Rasputin.

Legends of Rasputin sprang up outside the Palace and grew and spread far beyond Russia, where a grossly distorted version of Rasputin's personality and the part played by him was generally accepted. Nothing is so hard to kill as a legend, but perhaps in time the truth will be realized and the whole pitiful drama understood.

Rasputin never had any official position at the Palace. He was never "lampadary," a nonexistent post, nor did he ever get any pecuniary assistance from either the Emperor or the Empress. Had he ever hinted at wishing help of this kind, his power with them would have gone, for they had the greatest contempt for mercenary motives, and, as regards money, he died in the same position as he had lived.

Chapter 16

The Empress and Her Family

The Emperor and Empress were everything to each other and their devotion lasted all their lives. Their natures were very different, but they had grown into harmony with each other until they had reached that perfection of mutual understanding in which the tastes and habits of the one are a development and continuation of those of the other.

The Empress had the stronger character, and in matters concerning the Household or the children's education – which the Emperor left in her hands – her wishes were law. If anyone referred such questions to the Emperor, he always said, "It is as Her Majesty desires." He believed in her intuitive good sense and depended on her judgment.

This trust in her opinion made the Empress more self-reliant than she had been in her youth. Once she had given her opinion, she stuck to it, as she did not like to bother the Emperor with changes of mind, but except in matters that were her regular province, she always quoted him as the one in authority, tactfully avoiding questions on which she knew he had definite prejudices, taking it as unalterable that "the Emperor dislikes [such and such a thing]," thereby avoiding direct opposition to him.

She was always ready with a welcoming smile whenever he came into the room. She loved him passionately, even fanatically, and had boundless admiration for his wonderful gentleness, self-denial, patience and sense of duty. She had adopted a semi-religious reverence for his rank, and although she was so modest about her own position, anything that seemed like the slightest disrespect to him made her flare up with indignation. The due respect she demanded for herself was for his sake, as the consort of the anointed Emperor. She would have preferred to be on more familiar terms with people but she felt that she owed it to the Emperor to endure a level of restraint and ceremony that was really distasteful to her. At the same time she was full of true dignity and on official occasions could be more impressive than Nicholas II, who had wonderful simplicity and an almost homely manner inherited from his mother, the Dowager-Empress Marie.

Perhaps it was the Empress' German blood that made her so devoted to her father, brother and husband. Her father and brother, stronger characters than Nicholas II, dominated her. The Emperor, chivalrous and gentle, full of pity for her in her agony over their boy, was, insofar as his home life was concerned, under the Empress' influence. She was the center of the life of her husband and children. All her thoughts were for them and they looked to her for sympathy in all their doings.

She was an ideal wife and an ideal mother. She shared her children's joys and sorrows, and entered into all their games and interests with real enthusiasm. She nursed all her children herself and the baby's cradle used always to stand in her boudoir during the daytime. When she had to give up nursing the little Grand Duchess Anastasia, she said in a letter to Princess Victoria, "It is very hard – she will be given over to the nurses, a moment that always makes me melancholy, as now she is always in my room or next door."

From an early age, the children came down to luncheon with their parents, even if there were guests present in addition to the members of the Household. While they were still babies, their table manners were very good and they talked quite easily to strangers. They changed into romping clothes for the afternoon, but appeared again at tea time in their best frocks with their toys. Later, the toys were replaced by needlework, for the Empress would never allow them to sit about idle. They were perfectly at ease with their parents, looking upon them not only as parents, but as delightful companions. When they grew up, they laughed and joked with them, the Empress joining in when the Emperor teased his daughters.

All four girls were remarkably healthy, although they had the usual children's complaints – croup, measles and chicken-pox. Anastasia had diphtheria also, and Olga and Tatiana typhoid. Their mother nursed them through all these illnesses, isolating herself with the sick child and sitting up for whole nights to soothe and comfort the restless little patient. They had, of course, a staff of nurses, with an English Head Nurse in charge, with Russians under her, while the Tsarevich had a Russian Head Nurse of his own.

The Empress' favorite child, the one on whom all her thoughts were centered, was her boy. His illness was the tragedy of her happy home life. She could never feel for an hour that he was safe. The little accidents that are bound to happen to a lively child were grave dangers in his case; just because a fall could have such serious consequences for him, he seemed always to be falling. When he hurt himself before any public function, the real reason was never given for his non-appearance. It was said that he had a cold or a sprained ankle. All he suffered in the course of his short life can scarcely be believed. It did not embitter him, rather it only seemed to give him a pity, unusual in a child, for the suffering of other people.

He was a pretty child, tall for his age, with regular features, splendid dark blue eyes with a spark of mischief in them, brown hair, and an upright figure. His frequent illnesses made him rather backward at his lessons, but he was very clever, with a good memory, and when he was well he worked hard to make up for lost time. He was full of spirit and had quick powers of observation, a generous nature and a very strong will. He had chosen as a motto the words of Peter the Great that he had found for himself in a book: "Prayer to God and service to the Tsar will not be lost [i.e. in vain]."

He knew the meaning of gratitude, a rare trait in the great, who are often too much inclined to take everything for granted. I gave him English lessons after the Revolution and it was pretty to see him get up ceremoniously when a lesson was over, give me his hand in an exact imitation of the Emperor's manner, and thank me with his own particularly sweet smile, even though he might have seen me several times before on that day and was likely to see me again. "It is really nice of you, you know," he would say. He felt he was under an obligation to me as I was not one of his regular teachers and he always tried to show me small attentions and chose little presents for me from among his own things because he could not buy anything as he was a prisoner. He was the most conscientious child I ever knew and always tried to learn his lessons well, "as a return for your trouble."

Nor was he impressed by his own importance and his simple courteous manner was like his father's. He knew and felt that he was the Tsarevich and from babyhood mechanically took his place in front of his elder sisters, but he took no pride in the position that he knew was his due, and after the Revolution gave it up without a word. His chief friend was the son of Dr. Derevenko, and as a small child he played with the sons of his sailor servant, whose name also, curiously enough, was Derevenko.

All the children adored their mother, but her constant caring of him made a particular bond of love between mother and son. When the Emperor left for General Headquarters in 1915, Alexei felt he was, as he once said to me, "the man of the house," and it was delightful to see the grown-up way in which he would look after the Empress when they went to church or to some function together. He would help her to rise, or would unobtrusively push a chair towards her, as the Emperor might have done.

From the very first, the Empress looked after her children's education herself. She gave them their first spelling lessons and taught them their prayers, going up each evening to pray with them – a custom she retained until the end, in the case of Alexei. As the children grew older, they had of course their own teachers. The Tsarevich had an excellent tutor in M. P. Gilliard, who was Swiss and who was assisted after 1915 by an English colleague, Mr. Sydney C. Gibbes.

For a long time the Empress did not want her daughters to have a regular governess. She did not like the idea of a stranger coming between herself and her children, but as the girls grew up, it became necessary to have someone to direct their education and go about with them, and the Empress appointed Mlle. Sophie Ivanovna Tioutchev as their lady-in-waiting and governess. Mlle. Tioutchev was a Muscovite and a relative of the poet Tioutchev. The Empress had heard of her from Grand Duchess Ella and at first liked her very much. She did not stay many years, however, as she and the Empress disagreed on the subject of Rasputin. Mlle. Tioutchev was deeply distressed at leaving, as she had got to love her charges, but she was the unconscious originator of many false rumors that spread around the Court. What she said carelessly was often twisted and turned into fabulous stories, which did the Empress a great deal of harm.

After her departure, the Grand Duchesses did not retain anyone to be especially attached to her daughters. Mlle. Schneider took the charge of the two youngest, Marie and Anastasia, while the elder ones went about with one or other of the Empress' ladies-in-waiting.

The Empress really brought up her daughters herself and her work was well done. It is not possible to imagine more charming, pure and high-minded girls. The Empress could exercise her authority when necessary, but not in such a way as to interfere with the perfect confidence that existed between mother and daughters. She understood the high spirits of youth and never put a check on their laughter or wild pranks. She liked, too, to be present at their lessons and to discuss with their teachers the line their studies should follow.

The girls were all very good-looking. The eldest, the Grand Duchess Olga, was fair and tall, with smiling blue eyes, a somewhat short nose, which she called "my humble snub," and lovely teeth. She had a remarkably graceful figure and was a beautiful rider and dancer. She was the cleverest of the sisters and was very musical, having, as her teachers said, an "absolutely correct ear." She could play by ear anything she had heard, could transpose complicated pieces of music, and play the most difficult accompaniments on sight. Her touch on the piano was delightful. She also sang prettily in a mezzosoprano. She was lazy at practicing, but when the spirit moved her she would play by the hour.

She was very straightforward, sometimes too outspoken, but always sincere. She had great charm and could be the merriest of the merry. When she was a schoolgirl, her unfortunate teachers had every possible practical joke played on them by her. When she grew up, she was always ready for any amusement. She was generous and an appeal to her met with the immediate response, "Oh, one must help poor [so-and-so]. I must do it somehow." Her more careful sister, Tatiana, would suggest practical solutions, would note names and details, and come back to the subject later out of a sense of duty.

Olga was devoted to her father. The horror of the Revolution told on her more keenly than on any of the others. She changed completely and all her bright spirits disappeared.

Tatiana was, to my mind, prettier than her sisters. She was taller even than the Empress, but she was so slight and well-proportioned that her great height was not remarkable. She had fine, regular features, recalling pictures of those of her ancestresses who had been universally recognized as famous beauties. She had dark hair, a rather pale complexion, and wide-apart, light-brown eyes that gave her a poetic faraway look, not at all in keeping with her character, which was a mixture of exactness, thoroughness and perseverance, with leanings towards poetic and abstract ideas. She was closest in sympathy to her mother, and was the definite favorite among the girls of both of her parents. She was completely unselfish and always ready to give up her own plans to go for a walk with her father, to read to her mother, or to do anything that was required of her. It was Tatiana who took care of the little ones and who was a constant help to the Household, always willing to assist them in arranging that their official duties should not clash with their private engagements.

She had the Empress' practical mind and love of detail, and planned and arranged everything in the "children's quarters," as they were called. She had less strength of character than Olga, whose lead she would always follow, but she could make up her mind in an emergency quicker than her elder sister and never lost her head.

When her brother was ill, Tatiana would take her mother's place, following the doctor's directions and playing with the sick boy for hours, and out of a sense of duty she undertook more than her share of public appearances. She was shy, like all her sisters, but her natural friendliness made her want to say pleasant things to people, and she became much better known than her cleverer elder sister as she took more trouble with the people she met.

Tatiana loved dressing up. Any frock, no matter how old, looked well on her. She knew how to assemble her clothes, and was admired and liked admiration. She was sociable, and friends would have been welcome, but no young girls were ever asked to the Palace. The Empress thought that the four sisters should be able to entertain one another and indeed they were close friends when they outgrew the squabbles of childhood. The two elder ones shared one bedroom, the two younger ones another, while their schoolrooms and dining room were in common. The little Tsarevich had his own rooms, over which M. Gilliard ruled.

Marie was like Olga in coloring and features, but on a more vivid scale. She had the same charming smile, the same shape of face, but her eyes – "Marie's saucers," as they were called by her cousins – were magnificent and of a deep dark blue. Her hair contained golden lights, and when it was cut after her illness in 1917, it curled naturally over her head. Marie, alone of the sisters, had a decided talent for drawing and sketched well, always with her left hand. "Mashka," as her sisters called her, was ruled entirely by her youngest sister, Anastasia Nicolaevna, nicknamed by her mother "the imp."

Perhaps Anastasia would have grown up to be the prettiest of the sisters: Her features were regular and finely cut; and she had fair hair, fine eyes with impish laughter in their depths, and dark eyebrows that nearly met. These combined to make the youngest Grand Duchess quite unlike any of her sisters. She was *sui generis* and was more like her mother's than her father's family. She was rather short, even at seventeen, and was by then decidedly fat, but it was the plumpness of youth and she would have outgrown it, as had her sister Marie.

Anastasia was the originator of all mischief and as witty and amusing as she was lazy at her lessons. She was quick and observant, with a keen sense of humor, and was the only one of the four who never knew the meaning of shyness. Even as a baby she had entertained grave old men who were her neighbors at table with her astonishing remarks.

All the Grand Duchesses were very Russian in their outlook and ideas. Their only experience of foreign countries had been in short visits to Darmstadt, and once to England, and they preferred life in their own country to anything else. They always spoke Russian among themselves and to the Emperor, English to their mother, and French to M. Gilliard. The two elder girls had a smattering of German, but spoke it with difficulty; the younger ones and the Tsarevich did not know it at all.

The Grand Duchesses' best and most intimate friend was their young aunt, the Grand Duchess Olga (sister to the Emperor). They looked on her as an elder sister and she was their ideal in everything. She had a delightful and cheerful personality, and was a great favorite with her sister-in-law, the Empress, and came constantly to Tsarskoe Selo before the war, and she had young people's parties for her nieces nearly every Sunday afternoon in her town house, at which they all enjoyed themselves immensely. No adults were invited to these parties, except the Grand Duchess' cousin, the Duchess Marie Leuchtenberg (née Countess Grabbe), who brought her own girls and acted as chaperone to all the others. These Sunday afternoons were great events in the girls' lives.

The two elder girls were to have made their official appearance in St. Petersburg society in 1914, when the Empress had meant to resume the giving of Court balls in their honor, and they were always present at the rare functions given at Court after 1915. They looked very attractive, the one fair and the other dark. The Empress dressed her daughters well. Sometimes all four were dressed alike; sometimes the two elder ones wore one color, the two younger ones another.

Though their outward surroundings had, naturally, to be luxurious, their private lives and tastes were very simple, simpler indeed in many ways than the lives led by many Russian girls of a lesser social position. The Empress would not allow them to be pampered. They dressed themselves, leaving their maids only to arrange their clothes. According to the tradition of Russian Court nurseries, dating from the time of Catherine II, when Rousseau's ideas on education had been followed, they slept on hard camp beds. They went on wearing their clothes until they were worn out, or they had outgrown them, at which point the dresses of the elder girls were altered for the younger ones.

The Empress did not like squandering money, even though she was so lavish in her charitable donations. The Grand Duchesses had large fortunes of their own, but they were each given as pocket money only two pounds a month with which to buy their notepaper, scent, small presents etc. Their dress bills were, of course, paid for them. In this way they learned to think before spending. Every present they gave was the result of some personal sacrifice; they had to go without something for themselves before they could buy anything for their parents, sisters and ladies-in-waiting out of their own pockets. In this way their mother hoped to make them realize the value of money, a thing that princes find it hard to understand, although etiquette prevented their going into any shops but those of the little stationers at Tsarskoe Selo and Yalta, and they never had any clear idea of the value and price of things.

Their rank meant very little to them and they felt ill-at-ease when they were treated ceremoniously. Once, at a committee where I had to address my President, Grand Duchess Tatiana, officially, I naturally began, "May it please Your Imperial Highness …" She looked at me with astonishment, and when I sat down again beside her I was rewarded with a violent kick under the table and a whispered "Are you crazy to speak to me like that?" In common with all of the Household, I called the Emperor's daughters in the Russian fashion, by their names and patronymic, and she thought it quite absurdly formal for me to have used her full title, and I had to appeal to the Empress to persuade her that, on official occasions, it was really necessary.

The Grand Duchesses very seldom saw other children, although sometimes their cousins, the children of Grand Duchess Xenia, came to see them. There was also an occasional tea party at Mme. Vyroubova's or a Sunday afternoon party at "Aunt Olga's." They were used to a quiet life and never grumbled or seemed bored with one another's company. They took the greatest interest in members of the Household from the highest to the lowest, and were considerate in little ways, often doing things for themselves so as to enable their maids to go out.

They knew the names and family histories of the officers and men of the yacht and of the Cossacks of the escort, and talked to them freely. I spent a great deal of time with the two elder Grand Duchesses, who had no lady-in-waiting of their own, and often went about with them. They were deeply interested in everything I did, and all four invariably came to help me to dress for a ball, somewhat to the consternation of my maid, who felt she could not do justice to my toilette with four lively Grand Duchesses in the room, each giving her own directions.

On one occasion they thought my dress needed a string of rubies to complete it. I said I had none and that my pearls would have to do, whereupon Tatiana rushed off and appeared with some brooches of hers which she wanted me to wear. I naturally refused, to her great astonishment. "We sisters always borrow from each other when we think the jewels of the one will suit the dress of the other," she said.

No appeal to them for help was ever ignored. They would ask over and over again if this or that person had been helped and what had been done for them. When Olga, at the age of twenty, began to have some of her own money, the first thing she did was to ask her mother to allow her to pay for a crippled child to be treated in a sanatorium. On her drives she had often seen this child hobbling about on crutches and had heard that the parents were poor and could not afford a long and costly treatment, so she had at once begun to put aside her small monthly allowance to pay for the treatment.

Family life at the Tsarskoe Palace had a special atmosphere of its own. The children were closely united, and, in spite of the differences in their characters, understood one another well. They could never have been happy apart. It would have been an unheard-of thing for one of the Grand Duchesses to go anywhere, even for a day, without her sisters. She would not have enjoyed it at all.

Of course, with such differences in their characters, there were bound also to be differences in points of view, leading to hot discussions. Marie was obstinate, Olga was hot-tempered and would sometimes turn suddenly cross when she was offended, but they never quarreled or wrangled, and with their parents they were on terms of fond familiarity and respect that were delightful to see.

Inevitably everyone wondered what would happen in so united a family when the question of marriage arose. The Emperor and Empress did not want their daughters to make marriages of convenience; they wanted them to marry for love, as they themselves had done. On the other hand, the Empress disliked the idea of marriage with commoners. She thought that it tended to weaken the prestige of the Imperial Family and that the Emperor's daughters had a duty to respect their father's position. She did not scheme for her daughters, nor would she have overridden their inclinations. There were discussions of a Romanian marriage for Grand Duchess Olga, which the families and ministers of both countries would have liked, but the young Grand Duchess was not attracted to the proposed bridegroom and told her mother so. In one or two other cases, Olga was equally firm. The Empress thought a loveless marriage impossible to deal with and was quite ready for her daughters to wait until the right man came along.

Chapter 17

The Empress at Her Home and With Her Friends

The Empress' life was made up of long and busy days. Most of her afternoons were spent in giving audiences, in going to schools, or in seeing people about her various charities. Her receptions took up a great deal of time, as she felt less shy when she saw each person separately.

Consequently, she was often quite worn out by the evening and to very little effect so far as her personal popularity was concerned. There was no one to arrange her work for her, to prioritize matters – those that the public at large would appreciate – and to omit those that were less important. The Empress wore herself out in doing kind things in individual cases in which she could have the satisfaction of knowing the pleasure she gave, but these things were neither known to, nor appreciated by, the public at large.

She always felt in a hurry, which is not to be wondered at, considering the great place her children filled in her life and the amount of work she got through. She often transacted her correspondence, both private and business, in bed, for she got up late in the morning according to doctors' orders and wrote her letters during long wakeful hours at night. Whenever she sat with her family she had some piece of fancy work in her hand, a habit acquired in childhood under the influence of Queen Victoria. She was a great reader. Her taste lay towards more serious books, although she enjoyed modern English novels and read them with her daughters as they grew up.

The Empress had never been a sportswoman and her sciatica prevented her from playing any games after her marriage. She loved riding and often rode with the Emperor in the early years – she even rode at the head of her Lancers at their jubilee review in 1903 – but she had to give up all forms of exercise shortly after the Tsarevich's birth. After 1905, when she had more time, she took up her music again, playing duets with Professor Kuendinger who came to her every week for some hours, and taking singing lessons with Mme. N. A. Iretskaya of the Conservatoire. The Empress had a fine contralto voice and looked forward to the time when she would be able to sing with her daughters. She sometimes invited other music lovers to sing duets with her: Baroness Mary Stackelberg (née Kaulbars), Ania and Alia Tanieva, Countess Emma Fredericks and Mesdames X- and X-, two well-known singers from the Opera. She was far too timid to sing in public and these few ladies were the only people who heard her.

Princess Sonya Orbeliani often arranged little musical parties to which the Empress came. Singers and pianists were invited, and a few of the Princess' personal friends made up the audience. Princess Orbeliani hoped this might lead to other parties of the same sort that the Empress could have given herself, however the Empress' heart trouble soon obliged her to give up her music altogether, which was a very real regret to her.

The Empress' personal tastes were simple, and in spite of the outward luxury and all the money spent by the Court, the Imperial Family had in reality fewer actual comforts than many private people, and they had to submit to old-fashioned rules and regulations which the Empress tried in vain to break through. Even an autocrat cannot alter established routine and she could change little even in her own household, except the dresses of her maids: For tea at the Palace, buns were served of the same kind as had been given to the Empress Catherine; scores of servants loitered about, when a quarter of the number could have done the work, had it been systematically arranged; and very often the Empress would do a thing herself rather than send for the special servant whose duty it was to do that special thing. There were also old-world traditions that hampered her movements. The Empress would have shocked the whole nation if she had ever dared to enter a shop in St. Petersburg (Yalta or Tsarskoe Selo were considered rural residences and shopping was possible). When she began to go to church alone with her daughters, people were astonished and dubious. It did not seem to be quite the thing for her to do. The Empress could not drive alone in an open carriage, except at Peterhof, where the Emperor's great-grandmother had occasionally driven a phaeton in the first quarter of the nineteenth century and, a precedent having been established, the Empress could drive alone in a victoria at Peterhof without being criticized. All these rules were irksome to the Empress, but when she disregarded them, she provoked excited comments.

The Empress was economical and knew the value of money. She dressed well but not extravagantly. She chose the clothes that suited her type and hated the extremes of fashion. She looked magnificent in full dress and was always beautiful. She never impoverished the Treasury by having costly jewels bought for her. She had many fine jewels that were family heirlooms – most of the Crown jewels were still worn by the Dowager-Empress – but as the big tiaras she wore on State occasions were Crown jewels put aside for the wife of the Tsarevich, she used to say laughingly that when Alexei married she would have to hand them over and shift for herself as best she could. The Emperor, of course, gave his wife many jewels, but they were things that were chosen in accordance with her own tastes and not on account of their value, so that she had many sets of her favorite stones, amethysts and aquamarines. She thriftily wore her gala dresses for years, and during the war made it a point not to get a single new dress for herself or for her daughters, using the whole of her dress allowance, and theirs, for charity. Blue and mauve were her favorite colors, and she loved the long sweeping fabrics of no particular shape in which she looked so well.

When the Empress found that she could not strike the right note with St. Petersburg society, she drew still more into herself. From the very beginning, she had thought it her duty to bring more serious

166

interests into the lives of society women and she tried to start a working guild – which continued to exist until 1917 – but it was looked upon as an educational measure, one of the conditions being that the work had to be done with your own hands, and all her schemes were scoffed at. She could never carry out the reforms she thought necessary in the Patriotic schools and changes in the lists of invitations to Court balls which were made at the beginning of the reign were ascribed to her personally and created bitterness. Her criticisms of outlandish fashions she came across were repeated and resented by those concerned.

The Empress felt that everything she did was criticized adversely by certain sections of society and, misled by the cheering that welcomed her on public appearances, she believed herself popular with the country at large, and this consoled her for her unpopularity in society. She disliked publicity, and by her special wish her charities and kindnesses were never spoken of outside a small circle, but family affection was the most important thing to her, and in this respect the Empress' life was full and happy.

She was devoted to the Emperor's two sisters, the Grand Duchesses Xenia and Olga, and she took an interest in the lives of all members of her Household, from the Grande Maîtresse down to the last little maid, often helping the humbler ones and their families in ways that no one knew about. She was democratic in the real Christian sense, and made no class distinctions. She would go to see a sick maid as readily as one of her ladies-in-waiting. During the terrible time of her captivity in Tobolsk, she remembered that her faithful maid Madeleine Zanotti had been with her for twenty-five years and contrived to have a little present made, and begged the Commander to send it to her on that anniversary.

Although she was naturally hot tempered, the Empress seldom gave way to irritation. When greatly provoked, she would flare up, but she would be much distressed at her hastiness and would worry for days about a small thing which had probably been forgotten about by the person who had incurred her displeasure. The forgiveness which, in accordance with the Russian custom, she begged of those around her before going to confession was really asked for from the heart.

The Empress found it inadvisable on principle to make friends of her ladies-in-waiting as she thought it might cause jealousy if she showed more sympathy to one than she did to the others, so she was kind and attentive to all. She gave us beautiful presents and she looked after us personally when we were ill, but there was a certain barrier that was never passed. Only when their official positions had ended – as, for instance, when Princess Bariatinsky left her post as lady-in-waiting or when Sonya Orbeliani became an invalid – did she show her ladies the personal friendship she felt for them, but if her ladies were not allowed the privilege of full intimacy during their time of service, she was always goodness itself to them, and all the members of the Household came to the Empress when they found themselves in any trouble or difficulty.

I shall never forget the kindness the Empress showed me at the time of my mother's death while I shared the Imperial Family's imprisonment at Tsarskoe Selo. It was a time of grave danger for the Emperor, a danger so great that I felt I could not leave them and go to my mother who was seriously ill in Kazan, as I had been told that, if I did, I should not be allowed to return. The Empress sympathized with my anxieties as if they had been her own and, although she had never asked a single favor for herself during all the time of her detention, she now begged the revolutionary Commander of the Palace as a personal favor to bring her the telegram about my mother at whatever hour it might come, as she wanted to prepare me herself for the news she feared it might hold. The telegram came on the night of the Empress' birthday and it was she who broke the news of my mother's death to me the next morning with a tenderness and love that no words can describe.

Having few friends in society, the Empress clung all the more to those she found. Motherliness lay at the root of her character and she was always particularly attracted to people she could help and guide. In her youth in Germany, and in her early years in Russia, she had two friends on whom she could lean in her turn. These were women slightly older than herself: Countess Julie Rantzau and Princess Marie Bariatinsky. It was to the latter that she wrote on November 23, 1905:

> *I must have a person to myself, if I want to be my real self. I am not made to shine before an assembly – I have not got the easy nor the witty talk one needs for that. I like the internal being, and that attracts me with great force.*

> *As you know, I am of the preacher type. I want to help others in life, to help them to fight their battles and bear their crosses ... What can I tell you in a letter? Things are more than serious and intricate, and all one's hope and trust must be placed in God. Serious times are yet ahead, and rough ones – One's heart is so full ...*

The Empress had a lofty ideal. She gave herself completely to those who were her friends. Differences of rank did not exist. She was ready to do literally anything for her friends; their interests became her own and their sorrows were hers. She would take up things and people with violent enthusiasm. The first enthusiasm might wane with time, but her friendships were lasting, even though she saw the objects of them as seldom as she did the friends of her youth, Frau Bracht (Toni Becker) and "Juju" Rantzau, whose death she mourned in 1901, or her old governess, Miss Jackson.

She wrote about Countess Rantzau to Princess M. Bariatinsky on February 24, 1901:

She was a rare flower, too delicate for this world, but rejoicing others with her fragrance and cheering them on the way.

She understood the difficulties of this world, and the different temptations, and always encouraged one in the right, and helped one to fight one's weaknesses. It came so naturally to speak about one's faith to her, that now I feel her loss greatly. Only her dear writings have remained to me. [The Empress and the Countess wrote a kind of diary to each other, which they exchanged every week.]

I pray to God to make me as worthy, as she was, of a new and more perfectly happy life in yonder world.

In a letter to Princess Bariatinsky from St. Petersburg on January 29, 1901, she says:

DEAREST MARY – I send you my most loving thanks for your dear letter from the frontier – it was great happiness hearing from you. I miss you and our cozy chats very much indeed, and since you left I have again had such a loss – it is very hard, but I cannot but be grateful, that God took her to Him and that her long and weary sufferings have come to an end. But to all that knew her it is a great loss, but she was well fit for Heaven – a pure, ideal Christian. Only an hour before the fatal news, I received her last letter, so you can imagine what a shock it was. But I must not write to you about sad things, though my heart is full of sorrow – and I am awfully anxious about Gretchen Fabrice – I hope the journey was not too tiring.

170

The Princess Marie Bariatinsky, to whom these letters were written, had been appointed the Empress' lady-in-waiting in November 1896 and had to resign her post in 1898 to be with her old parents, as her father's health was failing. She greatly endeared herself to the Empress and became one of her few friends after she gave up her official position. She had a fine and sensitive nature and great charm of manner, and her tact and worldly *savoir-faire* made her a great help to the Empress during her first years in Russia. After Princess Bariatinsky settled permanently in Rome with her parents, the Empress saw her only at rare intervals, but whenever she came to Russia, the Empress always had her friend visit with her for several weeks as a guest. She at first missed her companionship greatly: "I long for you," she wrote to her shortly after her friend had left, and in a letter to her on December 28, 1898, said, "To have such a true and devoted friend is indeed a gift of God and I thank Him for it daily."

The same feeling is echoed in another letter dated August 9, 1912:

Once more let me tell you bow very happy I was to have seen you again, dear, after 5 long years of separation. It is a joy to see a dear friend so unchanged again, and to feel as though we had never been separated at all, these years. But that is real friendship that remains the same though time and space may sever one. A warm heart is a treat, and I always deeply, gratefully, value it.

In another earlier letter, she said:

Separation makes no difference – friends remain the same, don't they, dear? And you will have a lot to tell me about your life and interests, and I shall have my little ones to show you.

171

Life brings us sorrows and trials without end, but all is for the best, and God gives one strength to bear one's heavy cross, and go on fighting ...

The simple, affectionate terms between the Empress and her friends are seen in these letters and in the following ones, which also show the interest she took in all those that belonged to them.

She wrote to Princess Bariatinsky on December 28, 1898, from Tsarskoe Selo:

Don't be anxious about me, I tell you openly all, so that you need not worry. I am careful, and rest all day and miss your dear company more than I can say. For your precious letter from the frontier a hearty kiss and many thanks. Your words of tender love did me much good.

And to Princess Bariatinsky on May 8, 1901:

Thank God that your dear father is a wee bit better. I can so well imagine your feelings and know well the anxiety you are going through. Only that he should not suffer. God give you all strength and comfort. If I could have a wee word from time to time with news of him, I should be most grateful.

The weather is glorious, so warm and nice. I sit working on the balcony. Anemones and blue flowers are out and the buds on the bushes are quite big, and the birds sing so sweetly.

But enough for to-day. Good-bye, and God bless you. Tenderest love from your devoted friend,
ALEXANDRA.

Protective feelings were at the bottom of the Empress' friendship for Sonya Orbeliani, another of her ladies. She was a Georgian, the daughter of Prince John Orbeliani and Princess M. D. Sviatopolk-Mirsky, and she was only twenty-three when she came to Court in 1898. Princess Orbeliani was very small and fair, with distinctive features, a good sportswoman, clever, amusing, and a very fine musician. She attracted the Empress by her frank, unaffected manners and high spirits, and in her turn formed an intense attachment to the Empress, which was, of course, increased by all the Empress did for her during her long illness as she suffered from a form of spinal disease that made her practically a cripple toward the end. The Empress had great moral influence over her and it was she who led the doomed woman, who knew what was awaiting her, to the attainment of that wonderful Christian submission with which she not only patiently bore her malady but managed to keep a cheerful spirit and keen interest in life.

For nine long years, whatever the state of her own health, the Empress never paid her daily visit to her children without going to Sonya's rooms, which adjoined those of the Grand Duchesses. When Sonya had an acute attack of the illness, which happened from time to time, the Empress went to her not only several times a day but often at night when the pain was at its worst. No mother could have been more loving. Special carriages and special appliances were made for Sonya so that she could share the general life of the Household as if she were well, and she followed the Empress everywhere. The Empress made her feel that she was a privileged person, so afraid was she that she might realize that she had become, instead of the help she had been, one more person more in need of the Empress' care.

The Empress' friendship with the Grand Duchesses Militza and Stana, which was at its height during the first years of the century, was more on the basis of intellectual affinity. When the Empress thought that her cousins had become the prey of intriguers who had prejudiced them against Rasputin, in whom they had at first believed, she turned from them in disappointment and bitterness.

The most intimate friend the Empress made in later years was Ania Alexandrovna Vyrubova (née Ania Tanieva). The Empress' interest in her was first awakened when Ania, as a girl of sixteen, was dangerously ill with typhoid. Her father was the Head of the Emperor's private chancellery and when the Empress heard of his daughter's dangerous illness, she showed the greatest sympathy and frequently visited the girl, who was not expected to recover. However, she did recover and the romantic young girl conceived a passionate admiration for the Empress in return for her kindness. There was more frequent intercourse in the next winter as the Empress had discovered Mlle. Tanieva's musical abilities, and she was often summoned to the Palace to play accompaniments or sing duets with Her Majesty. She was one of the numerous maids-of-honor, but never held the post of lady-in-waiting. Only once, in 1905, when there had been a suggestion that the maids-of-honor might occasionally come into waiting for a longer period than was customary, she was one of the three who were selected. The others were Mlle. Sophie Raievsky (now Princess Gagarine) and myself. This was, of course, before my appointment as lady-in-waiting.

Little by little a great friendship grew up between the Empress and Mlle. Tanieva. They had many tastes in common. Mlle. Tanieva was also of a deeply religious nature and the Empress had a motherly feeling towards the young girl, whose open adoration touched her greatly. She became a constant visitor to the Palace and was even invited to join the Imperial Family on their cruises on the yacht, which was an exceptional favor as only a few members of the Household were ever invited on these trips.

From the outset Mlle. Tanieva complained that the courtiers were less than amiable toward her and this aroused the Empress' protective feeling. This, in fact, was indeed the case, for Mlle. Tanieva had few friends at Court, except the family of Count Fredericks, the Court

174

Minister, which meant that her position was difficult. The Empress was mentally far superior to her, whom she regarded as a child whose mind she had to prepare for the struggle of life while Mlle. Tanieva poured out her whole heart to the Empress. At first these were the griefs of girlhood, but before long she had real sorrows to confide, for her unhappy marriage with Lieutenant Vyrubov was soon dissolved. After this the Empress devoted even more time to her childless and lonely young friend, and tried to introduce new interests into her life.

By this time Mlle. Tanieva (now Mme. Vyrubova) had made the acquaintance of Rasputin. Piety and great superstition were united in her nature, and she became a sincere believer, which was another link with the Empress, and Mme. Vyrubova now centered her whole life on the Empress, who would show her attentions and give her little presents in an informal way that was permissible in a friend but not in any member of the Household. The Empress thought her unpretentious and guileless, and felt happy in having again found a devoted friend, now that Princess Bariatinsky was away and Sonya Orbeliani could not be all that she had been, on account of her health.

Mme. Vyrubova was a handsome woman in the florid style, with small features and fine, child-like eyes. She was tender-hearted and generous to the poor to the point of recklessness, but not clever. She was genuinely devoted to the Empress, and yet, unwittingly, she harmed her in the latter years, for she did not realize how much she was in the public eye as the Empress' best friend, nor that her every word and gesture were watched and adversely commented upon. Her trustfulness often misled her into receiving everyone who came to her on one plea or another, believing that she was serving the Empress by keeping herself in touch with the world outside the precincts of the Court. She was far too inexperienced to distinguish between the people she thus received. She did not introduce them into the Palace, but the fact that she had even casually encountered them rebounded on the Empress, for in public opinion the French proverb, *"Les amis de nos amis sont nos amis,"* (Our friends' friends are our friends) is always believed.

The Empress' ill-health and consequent seclusion in her final years made it possible for Mme. Vyrubova's daily visit to the Palace to become an institution. The Emperor and the children liked her, and she was treated by each one of them as a member of the family. If, by chance, one day passed without her seeing the Empress, Mme. Vyrubova was thrown into childish despair. Her Majesty laughed at her but was always touched by her.

There were occasional clouds when Mme. Vyrubova became too gushing or demanding because, to her, the Empress was the meaning of her life, while, for the Empress, the Emperor and her children always came before everything, and she had also many other people to attend to when she would have preferred to be alone.

The Empress and Mme. vyrubova had a friend in common, Mme. "Lily" Dehn (née Smolsky). Mme. Dehn's husband had been one of the officers of the imperial yachts and the Empress was a godmother to their small son and had taken a great interest in the boy and his young mother. When the child was desperately ill, Mme. Dehn sent for Rasputin, and ever after believed that his prayers had saved her boy's life during that crisis. This created a bond between the two mothers, and during the war the Empress saw more and more of Mme. Dehn, comforting her in her anxieties for her husband who was fighting at the front.

Mme. Dehn often came to see the Empress, but never stayed at the Palace itself. She continued to live in their apartment in the officers' barracks of the Guard. She was a clever, pleasant woman, no intriguer, and she never forced herself into prominence on the strength of the Empress' friendship.

During the weeks that followed the Revolution, she offered to stay at the Palace and help the Empress to nurse the sick Grand Duchesses because she had been nursing Mme. Vyrubova, who was visiting the Palace and who had also developed measles at the time the Revolution broke out. For the three weeks Mme. Dehn remained with the Empress during that terrible time, she showed the Empress the greatest devotion and was of real help to her.

Sickness and suffering were always sure keys to the Empress' heart. She wrote to Marie Bariatinsky, speaking of Countess Hendrikova's mother, who was a confirmed invalid:

> *I thank God that He allows me to be the means of giving her a little comfort and brightness. After all, it is life's greatest consolation to feel that the sorrowing need one, and that is my daily prayer, for years already, that God should just send me the sorrowing, and give me the possibility to be a help to them, through His infinite mercy.*

Times without number, often weak and ailing herself, the Empress traveled from Tsarskoe Selo to St. Petersburg to see the sick woman, and when she was dying, she spent hours at her deathbed in fulfillment of a promise she had made to her.

She was herself such a devoted mother that she felt particular sympathy with other mothers' grief. The illness or loss of a child made an immediate appeal to her, were it the child of a great lady or that of some humbler person. It was with real understanding that she wrote in 1912 to the friend of her youth, Frau Erhardt, when she heard that Frau Erhardt's only daughter was slowly dying, and in all her letters she speaks with the warmest sympathy for sickness and grief.

For instance, of Princess Zenaida Yussoupova's grief over the loss of a promising young son, the Empress wrote to Princess Bariatinsky on March 21, 1905:

> *One's heart bleeds to see poor Zenaida in her terrible sorrow – she looks so wee and frail and lovely, tho' she*

177

sees people, and far more than she would like. Even out here they follow her.

Lily is again in sorrow ...

Young Mme. Balashov (who was mourning her baby), Princess Galitzine (who was mourning an idolized grandchild), people the Empress knew well, others that she knew but slightly, all were sure of finding warm, spontaneous sympathy in their troubles. Her first impulse was to go to them. When she could not do so, she poured out her warm heart in writing, accompanied by her favorite flowers and her best-loved books.

Many a time in Yalta I have seen her go unobtrusively and simply to visit some poor consumptive patient in his home and to talk with a mother's understanding to the youth's mother. During the war, many a poor widow and mother would be summoned to the Palace and be met with those words of human sympathy that came straight from the Empress' heart. Her ladies were often told not to remain in attendance during these visits because the Empress did not wish official ceremonial to intrude when she wanted her guest to feel that she was but a woman who understood the distress of another.

No one who saw this side of the Empress ever said that she was stiff and cold.

Chapter 18

Last Years of Peace: 1913-1914

The year 1913 was the jubilee of the Romanov dynasty, during which the completion of three hundred years of monarchy was celebrated with great rejoicing, and expressions of continuing loyalty reached the Imperial Family from every part of the country. It seemed scarcely possible that the people who hailed the Revolution with enthusiasm four years later could have shown so much loyalty to the Sovereign at the time and taken part in such celebrations.

During the winter of 1913, the Emperor and Empress spent some weeks in St. Petersburg, and the St. Petersburg nobility gave a splendid ball in their honor to which they invited all the members of the Imperial Family who were available to attend and hundreds of guests. The two elder Grand Duchesses even attended this ball with their parents, even though they were not yet officially "out" – as Olga was seventeen and Tatiana was not quite sixteen – but the importance of the occasion justified their appearance.

The Empress dragged herself with difficulty to all these functions despite being completely worn out by her son's illness. She felt so ill at the great ball in the Salle de la Noblesse that she could scarcely keep her feet and suffered from an overwhelming feeling of faintness until she was able to attract the attention of the Emperor who was talking at the other end of the room. He arrived just in time to lead her away and save her from the embarrassment of fainting in public.

The Emperor and Empress also held a reception at the Winter Palace, but their stay in town was cut short because Grand Duchess Tatiana fell ill with typhoid and had to be taken home to Tsarskoe Selo, where the Empress nursed her back to health, paying for her exertions with long weeks afterwards spent on her sofa.

Jubilee celebrations were held in the summer in Moscow and the Imperial Family had promised to go to all the various Russian towns associated with the first Romanovs. The Emperor and Empress and their children left Tsarskoe Selo on May 28 and went first, via Moscow, to Vladimir and Bogolioubov on May 30, then to Nijni Novgorod, where they embarked on a river boat and sailed up the Volga, as the Empress had wished to do for twenty years. On June 3, they went to Kostroma, where the first Romanov Tsar had received the offer of the Russian crown from the Boyars, and were met by the entire Imperial Family, except the Dowager-Empress. As the small flotilla sailed up the river – the Imperial Family in one boat, the Court suite in another – the banks were crowded with people, and at every village the peasants waded into the stream in their eagerness to see the Tsar's boat and perhaps to catch a glimpse of him.

The Ipatiev Convent was the goal of their journey to Kostroma. It was there that Tsar Michael had received the deputation of the Boyars. People from all the surrounding provinces had assembled, dozens of icons were presented, and loyal speeches were made and answered. It was a triumphal progress. Everyone seemed enthusiastic and full of loyalty.

From Kostroma, the Imperial Family sailed up the river to Jaroslav, where they left their boat and went by rail to Pereieslav and Rostov Veliki, although the exhausted Empress did not visit these towns but rather stayed aboard the train to save up her strength for Moscow. Here the festivities were on a grand scale, for the ancient capital was always anxious to out-do St. Petersburg in hospitality.

In the autumn of 1913, the Imperial Family went to Livadia where the old Palace had been pulled down and a beautiful new one had been built in the Italian style on its site. The Empress had taken the keenest interest in planning it, remembering and reproducing many things that she had seen in Italy. All assembled after lunch in the central courtyard that was modeled on the cloisters of San Marco in Florence, and there were many beautiful antiques in the reception rooms and ancient Greek marbles, found in excavations in the Crimea, in the gardens.

The Empress was especially interested in the gardens and spent hours driving about in her pony carriage, planning improvements. The scenery was lovely. Livadia was situated halfway up a mountainside, with the majestic Ai-Petri as a background and the rocky beach below. The wide expanse of the Black Sea was visible from nearly every one of the Palace windows. The Crimea lies far to the south and the vegetation is like that of the Riviera. There were wonderful groves of olive trees, cypresses among the rose gardens, and luxuriant southern creepers.

The whole Imperial Family loved Livadia. They went there chiefly on account of the health of the Empress and the Tsarevich, but the beauty of the surroundings and the free life were a delight to them all. The Empress really rested there, lying much on her balcony and avoiding fatigue, joining the family party in the cloistered courtyard after luncheon. When they weren't doing their lessons, the Grand Duchesses bathed, and rode, and played tennis with their father.

Nearly all the other members of the Imperial Family had villas dotted along the coast. Balls were given for the young people by Grand Duchess Stana, by the Grand Duchess Marie (née Princess Marie of Greece), by Princess Bariatinsky (sister-in-law to the Empress' friend), and sometimes by the officers of the one or two regiments stationed in the Crimea. Dances were also given by the Empress at Livadia. These were delightfully informal gatherings to which not more than one hundred and fifty guests – mostly young people – were invited.

There were many villas round Yalta, for this was a favorite resort of Russian society in the fall, and at Livadia the Empress' daughters had a glimpse of the life led by young girls of their own age, and enjoyed it to the full. They rarely had any opportunities for dancing elsewhere.

Many excursions were arranged when the Grand Duke of Hesse paid a visit to Livadia in the May and June of 1912. The Empress could not get about much, as motoring tired her, but she took part in an excursion by sea to Novy Sviet during her brother's visit.

Novy Sviet was a beautiful place with celebrated vineyards, which an eccentric old Prince Galitzine had given to the Emperor. Prince Galitzine loved the Crimea and the Tartar people, and he had settled down on his immense Crimean property after having spent the best part of his life in Paris. Then, as he had no son, he handed over half his estate to the Emperor. His two modes of life were shown in his costume, a combination between a Tartar merchant's full dress and that of an old-fashioned Parisian artist – a frock coat, long hair under a high sheepskin hat, and a flowing, gaudy tie. He received the imperial party with quasi-Oriental hospitality, with wonderful food, and with the choicest wine from his celebrated cellars. There was, however, a certain amount of discomfort, for Novy Sviet was miles away from anywhere, but perhaps the unconventional things were those that pleased his imperial guests the most.

After the Grand Duke of Hesse had left, the Imperial Family sailed to the Caucasian coast and paid a flying visit to Gagry. Here a popular fête was organized in their honor, but the weather was bad and the Empress had to stay on board.

Although Their Majesties seldom gave formal audiences at Livadia, in point of fact they saw more people there than they did at Tsarskoe Selo. Everyone living in the Palace was asked to luncheon, even the children's teachers and the priest, as well as four or five of the officers of The Standart, which was anchored at Yalta during the imperial sojourn in the Crimea. In addition to these, three or four people – local residents or visitors – were invited every day, as well as the ministers who came from St. Petersburg to report to the Emperor. After luncheon, conversation would last much longer than at Tsarskoe Selo, where every hour was accounted for in advance.

Once or twice a week the whole Household dined with the Imperial Family, and after dinner either the Balalaika orchestra of the yacht would play or the Cossacks of the escort would sing.

During the visit of the Grand Duke of Hesse there were some special command performances given by singers and musicians who happened to be passing through Yalta. Among the occasional guests was the Emir of Bokhara – the son of the previous Emir who had attended the Coronation – who owned a villa near Livadia to which he came every year. The Empress used to be much amused at the solemn conversations the Emperor carried on with him through an interpreter. The Emir could speak Russian perfectly, having been educated at the Corps des Pages, but Oriental etiquette forbade him from speaking anything but his own language on such an occasion. Two of his ministers were always present at these interviews. These were immense Orientals with long beards dyed bright red and the most gorgeous silver and gold embroidered *khalats*. They were real figures out of the 'Arabian Nights' and looked as if any of the 'Arabian Nights' adventures might have been theirs.

On one occasion, the Dalai Lama of Tibet sent envoys bringing gifts to the whole family, although Tibetan custom prevented the Empress and her daughters from being present at the reception.

Sometimes foreign ships came to Yalta – French torpedo boats or Turkish cruisers with a Pasha on board sent by the Sultan to greet the Emperor – but there were very few official functions at Livadia. Indeed, when the Spanish Ambassador, Count de la Vinaza, came to present his letters of recall, there was great difficulty in organizing the reception suitably. Finally all ceremony was abandoned and the Ambassador was simply received before the dinner given in his honor, for there were neither State carriages nor gala liveries at Livadia.

The Empress took an active part in all the charities of the area. She organized bazaars every year in Yalta, working on them for weeks beforehand, while she and her daughters sold items at their own stall for several days. Needless to say, these were successful bazaars. There was a sad side to the Crimea, as there is to the sunny Riviera, for it was full of sanatoria for consumptives seeking sun and warmth, and these sufferers were always on the Empress' mind. It was in her nature, amid the sunniest moments and on the brightest days, to remember sad things, and here too often they were forcibly brought to her notice.

She took part personally in a Flower Day in aid of the Anti-Tuberculosis League, both she and her daughters selling marguerites. She visited the hospitals and started two new sanatoria – a naval and a military one – on the imperial property of Massandra. She visited many individual cases, going unobtrusively to pay unexpected visits, and when she could not go herself, she sent her daughters. It was often pointed out to her that it might be dangerous for the girls to sit at the bedsides of tuberculosis patients, but she swept these objections aside and the Grand Duchesses visited many of the worst cases. "They should realize the sadness underneath all this beauty," she once said to me.

The Imperial Family stayed only a short time at Tsarskoe Selo in the winter of 1913-1914, returning from the Crimea on January 3, 1914, and leaving again for Livadia on April 5, 1914.

During the winter, the Empress was present at a ball that the Dowager-Empress gave at her Anitchkov palace in honor of her granddaughters. This was the event of the season and was one of the few public appearances that the Empress made with her daughters. The Emperor took them to the theater and to one or two afternoon dances. At the Anitchkov ball, whereas the Empress went home at midnight, he had to stay until 4.30 in the morning as the Grand Duchesses refused to be torn away any earlier. When we were all having a late cup of tea in the train that took us back to Tsarskoe Selo, I said to the Emperor that I was glad Her Majesty had no receptions before luncheon, which would have meant early rising for me. "Yes," he said, "you can sleep. As for me, I have X. at 9:30, and as I did no work tonight, I must look through some reports from the ministers before that. So I shall have to get up at 7!" Every late outing with his daughters meant so many hours taken from his rest. It is not surprising that the Grand Duchesses were taken to very few balls by their father.

On June 13, 1914, the Imperial Family went from Livadia to Constanza to return a visit paid by King Carol of Rumania many years before, and also a visit paid by the Crown Prince Ferdinand of Rumania and his wife, and Prince Carol, who had spent a couple of weeks at Tsarskoe Selo in the winter of 1913. The setting of that State visit gave it a special place among the many journeys that the Russian Imperial Family had taken to foreign courts. The details of the reception had been arranged by the Crown Princess Marie. The whole Rumanian Royal Family stood on the landing stage at Constanza as The Standart slowly approached. The lovely Rumanian children were in a group around their mother, the Crown Princess and Queen Elizabeth – "Carmen Sylva" – with her white hair and long white robes, looking like a priestess of ancient Greece.

She was charming to her guests and welcomed them warmly. She had spent some time in Russia during her youth and had always been very enthusiastic about the country. The one-day stay was too short for all that had been planned, and the Empress was almost in a state of collapse when the visit was over. After a State drive through the town, there was a service at the Cathedral. Then came a family luncheon party, to the accompaniment of appropriate airs played by a Rumanian band. The ministers and Court suite were entertained to another sumptuous luncheon at the same time by the Rumanian Prime Minister, M. Bratiano.

After lunch, the Emperor and the King visited the Russian and Rumanian ships, while the Empress rested before the tea party she was giving on The Standart for members of the Rumanian Royal Family and officials. About twice the number of guests as expected came to the party – I believe that there were several hundred – and the Empress was confronted with the worry, usual to most housewives but

185

most unusual for her, of wondering if there would be enough to eat. Count Benckendorff had not accompanied Their Majesties on this trip and his absence was much felt.

After the tea party, all the members of both Royal Families, with the exception of the Empress and Queen Elizabeth, went to a review of the Rumanian troops, Grand Duchess Olga driving with the Crown Princess. The young Grand Duchess was the center of all eyes, for it was much hoped that a marriage would be arranged between her and Prince Carol.

The day closed with a State dinner at the Palace, at which the King and the Emperor exchanged speeches. The Emperor's clear elocution made his speech much more impressive than King Carol's, which was spoilt by the strong German accent with which he spoke French.

A special hall designed by the Crown Princess in the Byzantine style in green and gold had been built onto the small Palace expressly for this dinner. The lovely room, the flowers and the wonderful Hohenzollern plate, brought specially from Bucharest, took away the formal impression usual at such State banquets. The Empress was dressed in flowing classic fabrics with a diamond bandeau in her hair. Queen Elizabeth had forgotten her Orders, and the Empress took off hers to be in keeping with her hostess. The Crown Princess Marie alone wore her Orders, and her only other ornament was a large diamond cross on a long chain. It was amusing to note that this fashion had been copied by all her fellow countrywomen. Most of the ladies present wore huge crosses – some in diamonds, some in gold – which dangled about their persons, but they didn't always look as good on them as they did on the Crown Princess.

The Empress could scarcely get through the conversation after dinner, and from sheer exhaustion could take but little interest in the fireworks and torchlight procession, which was the students' contribution to the entertainment and which the Emperor and his daughters watched from the balcony of the Palace with members of the Rumanian Royal Family.

It was about midnight when the last adieux were said on board The Standart and the yacht weighed anchor. The Empress had only strength to wave a limp hand to the people on the landing stage. Fortunately the journey back was not as tough as the original journey had been, for the next day there was a visit to Odessa. The Empress just managed to get through a large reception of ladies and a service in the Cathedral before she had to retire, leaving the Emperor and the children to carry out the rest of the program alone. The stay at Odessa was followed by a journey to Kischinev for the unveiling of a monument to Alexander I.

A few days after the return to Tsarskoe Selo, the King of Saxony came on a State visit and the usual ceremonial of dinners and reviews took place, but as this was a visit of a "Queenless" King, it was far less fatiguing than such visits usually were for the Empress.

After the King left, the British Fleet under the command of Admiral Beatty arrived at Kronstadt, and the Emperor and Empress went on board ship with their children. Admiral Beatty and his wife, and members of his staff, were also entertained at lunch by Their Majesties at Tsarskoe Selo. After this, the Court went to Peterhof, and there, soon after their arrival, they heard the news of the Archduke Franz Ferdinand's murder at Sarajevo.

This news greatly shocked and horrified the Imperial Family, but at first it was not even suspected that this tragic event would be followed by such terrible consequences. Preparations were being made for the visit of President Poincaré and everyone believed that the Balkan question could be settled without Russia being involved. The Empress was making plans for spending the autumn in the Crimea and had already invited her guests.

Before the Presidential visit, the whole family went for a few days' cruise in the Finnish waters. The President arrived at Peterhof on July 19 and was met on the landing stage by the Emperor, the Empress receiving him later in full state at the Palace. He lunched privately with Their Majesties, and delighted the Tsarevich and the Grand

Duchesses with the presents he had brought them. A big official dinner was given in his honor in the Peterhof Palace, which was an eighteenth-century building, kept unchanged since the days of Peter the Great, even as to the wax candles that lit up the halls. Then the whole Court and the President and his suite attended the tattoo at the camp of Krasnoe Selo. At this great review President Poincaré saw the élite of the Russian army, so many of whom were soon to lay down their lives for their country. The review was followed by a command performance at the local theater, and the French President gave a return entertainment on board the battleship France, which the Empress and her elder daughters attended with the Emperor.

The political future was uncertain, the horizon was dark, but no one imagined that these were the last days before the outbreak of war.

Chapter 19

Wartime: 1914

The outbreak of the world war came as a terrible blow to the Empress. She seemed to have a presentiment of coming events, for she was most depressed when they left The Standart on which she had gone with the Emperor to recover from the fatigues of the Presidential visit, and said to some of those with her that she knew it would be the last cruise they would all take together.

She had a horror of war. The memories of the Russo-Japanese War and of the troubles that had followed were still too fresh in her mind. The Emperor and she hoped to the last that some agreement might be reached. Although the Emperor did not distress her by giving her all the details of the Governmental discussions, she felt very anxious, but she still did not realize how tense the situation had become.

On the first of August, the Empress and her daughters waited a long time for the Emperor to come down to dinner. As a rule he was very punctual and the Empress felt that something serious must have happened. He was receiving the Minister for Foreign Affairs, M. Sazonov, and the audience seemed to last inordinately long. When the Emperor came, it was with the news that Germany had declared war.

At first the Empress could not grasp it. War! Her nightmare! She knew efficiency of German organization, and she knew that Russia was not prepared for war at that moment, and that England had not yet joined Russia and France. She was in despair, but, then and always, she had the conviction that Russia would win in the end.

The declaration of war made her set up a wall in her heart between Germany and Russia. She was the Empress of Russia – Russian always in heart and soul.

"Twenty years have I spent in Russia, half my life, and the happiest, fullest part of it. It is the country of my husband and son. I have lived the life of a happy wife and mother in Russia. All my heart is bound to this country I love," she once said to me during the war.

People in Germany do not understand how the Empress came to adopt the Russian standpoint so completely and to become so thoroughly Russian in her views. The reason for this was her intense, passionate love for the Emperor. She considered herself as wholly belonging to him. His country was her country, as also his religion had completely become hers. She always gave herself up entirely to those she loved and identified herself with them.

The thought of her brother and of his feelings at having to take part in a war where he would be in the other camp gave her acute pain, but she brought her will-power to bear to face the inevitable. She regarded the inexplicable telegram sent by Emperor Wilhelm, after his ambassador Count Pourtales had already handed the declaration of war to the Russian Foreign Minister, as an attempt to shift the responsibility for the outbreak of war onto Emperor Nicholas, and was very indignant. The mystery of that telegram has never been explained. She expressed her opinion on the matter to the Tsarevich's Swiss tutor, M. Pierre Gilliard, who quotes the conversation fully in his book, 'Thirteen Years at the Russian Court.'

According to her wont, the Empress did not remain content with lamentations. At ten o'clock at night on the day of the declaration of war, I came back from a drive, not knowing what had happened. My maid told me that a woman's voice from the imperial villa had rung me up three times during the last hour and that it was either one of the Grand Duchesses or the Empress herself.

I immediately rang up 'Alexandria,' the Emperor's villa, and found the Empress sitting in readiness by the telephone. In a voice broken by suppressed sobs, she told me of the event.

"War is declared," she said.

"Good Heavens, so Austria has done it!" I exclaimed.

"No, no," she said, "Germany. It is ghastly, terrible, but God will help and will save Russia ... But we must work ... Go at once to Mme. E. and speak to her about opening the workshop at the Hermitage. Then talk to my secretary and ring me up, no matter how late, or come round."

She entered into details, growing calmer as she spoke, and giving me minute instructions.

I spoke to the Empress again later. She was perfectly calm, having got over her momentary weakness.

The next day, August 2, the Emperor and Empress, with their daughters – the little Tsarevich was ill – went to St. Petersburg to attend a solemn *Te Deum* at the Winter Palace. This was an old custom that had been followed at the outbreak of the Japanese War. Crowds of people thronged the Winter Palace in a very frenzy of patriotism. Ladies clung to the Emperor, kissing his hands. No one alive had seen such enthusiasm, which was reminiscent of 1812. At the outbreak of the Japanese War there had been some street demonstrations of students in the early days, but now the whole country was roused.

The climax was reached when the Emperor, addressing the officers present, repeated Alexander I's promise of 1812 not to conclude peace while a single enemy still remained on Russian soil. Sir George Buchanan, in his book, 'My Mission to Russia,' quotes the words, "I solemnly swear not to make peace as long as there is a single enemy on Russia's soil."

Multitudes cheered in the streets, and when the Emperor and Empress appeared at the Palace windows, the whole crowd that packed the huge square spontaneously knelt down and sang the National Anthem.

The Duma, in a memorable sitting, expressed its loyal sentiments in words of ardent patriotism, so that the Emperor felt that the whole country was behind him.

On board the yacht that took them to Peterhof, the Emperor and Empress spoke optimistically to their Court suite of the turn events were taking and of their admiration for the spirit of the people. Telegrams were brought in just then, describing the plucky conduct of the young Grand Duchess of Luxemburg, and the Empress was full of admiration for her.

When the mobilization was announced in the St. Petersburg military district, the Guards were the first to go. The Empress went to a *Te Deum* before her Lancer regiment left for the front, and said goodbye in person to all the officers and men. All through the war she followed the actions of this regiment, and after every battle in which the Lancers took part she helped all the families to get news.

The Dowager-Empress was in England, on a visit to Queen Alexandra, when war became imminent. She tried to cross Germany on her way from London to St. Petersburg, but war was declared midway and she was not allowed to go farther than Berlin, being redirected from there to Copenhagen, so she had to travel a roundabout way via Sweden and Haparanda in the extreme North. On her way through Germany she was treated with great hostility and greeted with insults by the German crowd. In a conversation she had later with M. Gilliard, the Empress said very strongly what she felt about her mother-in-law's treatment.

When the Dowager-Empress returned to Peterhof after her long journey, she was met with unwonted ceremony by the Emperor and Empress as an expression of their affectionate and dutiful regard for her. The Empress also spoke to M. Gilliard of her own little Darmstadt, which, as she had often said to me, she always completely separated from the rest of Germany in her mind

"Whatever has happened to the Germany of my childhood? I have such happy and poetic memories of my early years at Darmstadt and the good friends I had there. But on my later visits, Germany seemed to me a changed country, a country I did not know and have never known … I had no community of thought or feeling with anyone, except the old friends of days gone by. Prussia has meant Germany's ruin. The German people have been deceived. Feelings of hatred and revenge, which are quite foreign to their nature, have been instilled into them. It will be a terrible, monstrous struggle. Humanity is about to pass through ghastly sufferings."

The Imperial Family had been prevented by the Tsarevich's health from leaving for Moscow, where, according to old custom, they had to announce the war to the inhabitants of the ancient capital. The child had hurt his leg and was again laid up. By ill luck, these accidents always happened before some public function, at which, if he appeared at all, he had to be carried in the arms of a stalwart Cossack. The Empress was in despair, as she feared that the idea would get about that the Tsarevich was permanently lame. However, it was decided that the ceremony could not be delayed until he recovered as his leg was stiff and would take some time to heal.

The Sovereigns arrived in Moscow on August 17 and found a great welcome awaiting them. If any place could have shown more enthusiasm than St. Petersburg, it was Moscow. The crowds in the streets, the nobility and the *Zemstvos*, all showed the greatest patriotic excitement.

The Emperor's informal drive through the city was an occasion for great demonstrations of loyalty, such as had only been seen at the State entrance at the Coronation. At the solemn service in the Cathedral of the Assumption, the Allied Ambassadors, Sir George Buchanan and M. Paléologue, were present, and when the imperial procession returned from the cathedral to the Kremlin in a scene of delirious enthusiasm, the Emperor asked the ambassadors to walk closer to him, saying, "These acclamations are addressed to you as well as to me."

Moscow was in a frenzy of activity. Things were being hastily organized. The Emperor and Empress went everywhere, and all day long saw various people in connection with war work. The Empress sat until late in her small dressing room, the room she generally used, discussing war charities with Grand Duchess Ella who had at once begun to take an active part in everything as well as doing her usual work at the Obitel.

The imperial party inspected the *Zemstvo* relief organizations, those of the nobility, and of the merchants, and the hospitals that had just been opened, and many others. The Empress never thought of her health and she braced herself to do more than ordinary human strength could manage. She seemed indefatigable and her suite could scarcely keep up with her.

She wrote to Princess Victoria on August 21, 1914, describing her work in her haste in telegraphic style.

> *Awfully busy. Have seen splendid sklad of merchants nobility, Zemstvos and mine. Blessed two hundred sisters, going to the war. Saw my train well arranged. Fastening images on to strings, whenever free. Returning over St. Serge and there part from Ella.*
>
> *Have no news from many people who could not return or be found and return in an awful plight, bruised, ill-treated. Such horrors they have gone through, it's inconceivable, simply twentieth-century culture.*
>
> *Saw a few wounded, happily nothing serious. Shall get my hospitals in order at Tsarskoe and then set Olga and Tatiana to work.*
>
> *Having bad health makes all more difficult and stops me from doing many things one would have wished to. Glad for dear Ella's sake, that we have been here to cheer her up.*

She has any amount to do, is energetic, here there and everywhere. All help as they only can. It is right one prints no news [from the front], but it is anguishing.

At one time there was a suggestion that the Imperial Family should transfer their residence to Moscow while the war lasted, living at the Neskoutchnoe Palace, a little way out of town. It was even inspected for the purpose by officials of the Court, but the idea came to nothing.

The visit to St. Serge, one of the oldest sanctuaries in Russia, took place on August 21, and the Abbot blessed an antique icon that had always accompanied the Russian Tsars in their war campaigns and gave it to the Emperor.

At Tsarskoe Selo the Empress continued to work with the same feverish energy. She thought out a whole program of work based on her experiences during the previous war, greatly changing and improving what had been done before. She desired to adapt as many palaces as possible for hospital work, feeling that all available space was likely to be needed. The Petrovsky Palace at Moscow had already been turned into a hospital, the Poteshny was soon to follow. The Nicholas Palace, the former home of Grand Duchess Ella, was a *sklad*. At Tsarskoe Selo, the Catherine Palace, where all the fêtes used to be given, was to be a hospital for officers. In the existing Court hospital, headed by Princess Hedroits, a renowned surgeon, the Empress and her daughters began their practical training. The Empress thought her daughters too young to nurse and agreed to their request only on the understanding that they and she should be trained together. All three went through the usual probationers' course and could be seen every morning working at the hospital.

Her Majesty was deft and very quick-handed, and brought to the work something that was most precious to the patient, her understanding of suffering and her capacity for comfort. Neither mother nor daughters ever shirked the most fatiguing and difficult task

195

and Grand Duchess Tatiana showed especial aptitude for the work as she enjoyed both its scientific and human aspects.

Both young girls were very enthusiastic and insisted on carrying on with their hospital duties when they had passed their examinations. The Empress did the same. It gave her moral satisfaction to feel that she was really working for the wounded and her work made her forget the anxieties and sorrows that pressed on her.

Writing at this time, she said:

> *To some it may seem unnecessary my doing this, but I can much better then look after my hospital here, and help is much needed, and every hand is useful, and it does one good, and draws one's thought away from much sorrow.*

Her soothing influence helped many a wounded man through the agonizing moments before an operation and many a dying soldier passed away happier for her presence. The humblest patient in her hospital would see her at his side when he called for the Tsaritsa.

This was a great physical, and still greater mental, strain. Sometimes she had only just come home when a message from her hospital would tell her that an especially bad case had called for her, and she would seize the first free moment to rush back to the hospital in her car. She visited the other hospitals at Tsarskoe Selo constantly and those in St. Petersburg about once a week during that year.

Her letters to Princess Victoria are almost all full of her hospital work. On November 25, 1914, she wrote:

> *With my big girls I went to Pskov one day, privately, as sisters, to see Marie. Then we went out to meet Nicky at Grodno, visited hospitals also there and at Dvinsk together. When he goes off again, shall go to more towns.*

196

It's shy work, but the sisters' dresses help one. We wear it on such inspection on journeys without Nicky.

We passed our exams and received the Red Cross on our aprons and got the certificates of sisters of the war time. It was an emotion putting them on, and appearing with the other sisters – 40 – who had finished their course. We had a Moleben [Te Deum] in my Red Cross Church.

We are continuing lectures about illnesses, medicaments, anatomy, etc. to have a fuller course and we all enjoy it. Our mornings at the hospital continue, and weekly a train arrives with fresh wounded. Three thousand places at Tsarskoe and Pavlovsk.

In the Big Palace we have officers and I go there every afternoon to see one who is specially suffering. He is contusioned, and in the last week always unconscious, recognizing nobody. When I come, he regularly recognizes me, and then remains with a clear head all the night. He thinks he sleeps all day, suffers hideously – such cramps in the head and whole body-nerves too shattered, poor soul.

He is touching with me, I remind him of his mother's kindness and as soon as I come, takes me at first for her (she is dead). When I call him and talk, he stares, then recognizes me, clasps my hands to his breast, says he now feels warm and happy. His children are in Siberia and his wife (that has not made him happy) too.

Such sad cases always awakened the Empress' sympathy. There were several such unknown, solitary men, from obscure line regiments, who died in her hospital whose last hours were comforted by the Empress. She lost her shyness in her nurses' dress. She felt she was one of many, and she showed herself to all in the hospital in her true light and as her home circle knew her.

Many princesses wore nurses' dress during the war, and in many cases the feeling that dictated this was admired and understood. To the general public in Russia, however, and particularly to the uneducated mind, this was not the case. The Empress was advised not to wear nurses' dress when she went about the country during the war. She was unknown in the towns and the people did not recognize her when she came without the usual apparel, and so the effect on the public of the imperial visit was lost.

At the close of the year the Empress wrote to her old governess.

Tsarskoe Selo,
January 8th, 1915.

DARLING MADGIE – I cannot tell you how deeply touched I was that you sent Ella and me those charming books and we thank you heartily, as also for your dear letter. We did not send you any present, not being sure with these abominable times whether a parcel would ever reach you.

During your Xmas we were at Moscow – he [the Emperor] was away a month from here and the children and I two weeks. I visited hospitals in 8 towns with my big girls and in Moscow he joined us from the Caucasus and the 3 little ones from Tsarskoe.

The result has been that my heart has been so bad again and such weakness – I utterly overtired myself. Nothing is more tiring than visiting heaps of hospitals and speaking by the hour to the poor wounded. So I have not been able to work in the hospital now, which is a great grief to me, as I love the work and find consolation in nursing the sick and binding up their wounds however terrible they may be. And we assist at operations and I always gave the instruments.

We have many hospitals at Tsarskoe and now Xmas trees everywhere and the children go instead of us. He has also been in bed with a chill and cough – overtired, but now almost well again.

The children are all right, thank God. Winter has been mild here in the North, but now severe cold has set in, but not much snow.

Such a sad Xmas, one's thoughts are all at the war. Will send this off now and hope it will reach you safely.

Very tenderest blessings and kisses,

From your fondly loving

P.Q. No. III
ALIX.

Chapter 20

The Empress' War Work: 1915

At the end of 1914 and the beginning of the following year, the Empress again enjoyed a moment of great popularity. Even people who were not in sympathy with her admitted this. For instance, the Minister for Foreign Affairs, S. D. Sazonov, spoke of it to me on one occasion when I was lunching at the Foreign Office in 1915. The Empress travelled about, she was seen in public, her work became known. "One must take things personally in hand," she had written to Princess Victoria on March 23, 1915.

Neither the Red Cross nor the Commissariat could cope with the ever-growing demands of the hospitals for linen and supplies. The Empress arranged for her *sklads* to co-operate with these institutions, particularly in helping small military hospitals close to the fighting line. She had *sklads* in Petrograd, Moscow, Odessa, and Vinnitza, and a whole line of lesser *sklads* in small towns near the front. Their sphere of activity became very wide. Supply trains and single carriages attached to empty ambulance trains took hospital material from the main *sklads* up to the front line. Automobile squads had been formed in Poland in connection with these trains, most of them being run by members of the great Polish families who put their private cars at the disposal of the *sklads*. They did excellent work all through the war.

The needs of the moment were what guided the Empress and her assistants. At the head of the Moscow *sklad*, which directed the whole work, was M. Nicholas de Meck, always called by the Empress "Uncle Meck," and his nephew V. V. Meck. The Petrograd *sklads* were organized by Princess E. N. Obolensky. Count Apraxin, the

Empress' gentleman-in-waiting, was continually going with the trains to the front to see how everything was working.

To villages where there were no baths, the Empress had bath cars sent out, attached to the supply trains. The soldiers greatly appreciated them, called them "disinfection cars," an apt mispronunciation of the Russian word. In the winter, warm clothing was supplied, as well as linen. In 1915, when the armies were more stationary, she arranged to send field churches, as the country in which the fighting was taking place was Catholic and there were few Orthodox churches. Priests accompanied these portable churches and were a great comfort to many dying men unable to get into touch with the regimental priests.

New ideas were always working themselves out in the Empress' brain and the days were too short for her.

On March 23, 1915, she wrote to Princess Victoria:

My heart got so bad again, there was lots of work, and it helps me when the heart is heavy and, knowing you bring happiness, how not go to the poor wounded? and forget yourself?

My day was like that: at 9:30, a second into the Znamenya church to get my blessing for the day's work, then with Olga to the Big Palace to see a very seriously wounded officer (through the lungs). At 10 Tatiana fetched us (after her lesson) and they dropped me at Ania's. At 10.30 – we worked at our hospital, with officers and men, and operations, rather often appendicitis, etc., too. Then I would go and sit with that poor officer again, for an hour or more, then pass through the other wards. After tea rested, if did not have audiences or officers to bid goodbye, before returning to the war. After dinner, off to Ania or to the hospital, or to both according to necessity.

*Now my poor officer died, and that finished me off,
besides had to go to town to a hospital, and so on.*

The Empress does not say that, besides all this, she looked through
the papers her secretary sent her until late at night, and began to work
on them again early in the morning before going to her hospital. There
was sometimes no chance for the members of the Household to see
her except at lunch, and she usually saw her ladies on business then.

It was evident that such feverish activity could not be kept up long
by so delicate a woman as the Empress. Only sheer will-power kept
her going during the first five months of the war. Then she fell ill in
December 1914, when her heart trouble reappeared, caused by the
long standing and the real, hard physical work to which she was
naturally unaccustomed, and by the motoring, which had always
disagreed with her. Added to this was the mental strain of continual
contact with suffering, in which she was always expending herself
wholeheartedly in helping and comforting others.

She roused herself at the time of her friend Mme. Ania Vyrubova's
illness in January 1915, but afterward had a serious setback and could
not leave the Palace for several weeks. She went on intermittently
with her hospital work, being loth to give it up entirely, but she could
stand it less and less. She hated to admit that she was beaten by her
health, but in 1916 she was completely worn out.

The Empress had written to her sister during the Russo-Japanese
War that she was determined not to be "a mere doll." Every official in
her trains near the fighting line could telegraph to her personally,
reporting his movements and appealing to her in cases of difficulty. If
action had to be taken promptly, the Empress telegraphed herself,
stating the case and asking for the necessary measures to be taken as
soon as possible. She hated formality and red tape, and she felt that
the interests of the wounded should always come before everything

202

else. Personal sympathies or antipathies did not influence her in her work.

The heart trouble that at first had been only a nervous affection then became really serious. She had constant pain and a feeling of suffocation, while chronic facial neuralgia had taken the place of the sciatica from which she used to suffer so badly. On account of her heart trouble she had to submit reluctantly to being carried upstairs in the hospitals she visited, while loathing "making a spectacle of myself."

The organization known as the 'Union of Towns' did very useful work with the assistance of the *Zemstvos*, but the Empress was rather distrustful of them as she had heard that much political propaganda was carried on under cover of their war activities. One of their main leaders was Purishkevitch, the future murderer of Rasputin.

The Empress referred to him in a letter to me:

Please let X know that Purishkevitch asks for ten thousand pieces of body linen for the Dvinsk, Riga and Minsk front. Have arranged baths and that linen is urgently needed. Have arrived today, leaving tomorrow. It's good to give Purishkevitch as much as one can, as he really works well. I several times helped him. Tell them to answer at once – he is in town.

Although, naturally, she did not correspond with her relatives in Germany, the Empress thought of them often with sadness. It was a great comfort to her to know that the Grand Duke of Hesse and his armies were not fighting on the Russian front.

She wrote to Princess Victoria on November 25, 1914:

Today is our Ernie's birthday, the first time in his life that three sisters can give him no news. How lonely he must be away from his dear ones, in a foreign country and hating the war ... One's heart bleeds, thinking of all the misery everywhere and what will be afterwards! The amount of lies, printed in the German papers (and in Turkey), is sickening. The fright of the German prisoners that they were going to be shot, and noses and ears chopped off, and their surprise and contentment, when they are well treated and fed, are great. Ella will return in a few days from Lvov.

She wired that she was in the Carpathian, that there was snow in Lvov, and that it was bitterly cold, but that she was content with what she saw, and with her *sklad* there, and to see that her four *sklad* trains were working.

Nearly all the male members of the Russian Imperial Family were with the army. All the Grand Duchesses either had *sklads* or worked in the hospitals. The whole Court lived in an atmosphere of war, colored by the news from the front.

The disaster of Seldau was a terrible blow, relieved to some extent by the Marne victory.

The Empress wrote on October 21, 1914:

One's heart bleeds, such misery, such losses. The worst is, when one cannot get the news about the losses for ages.

From home, no news, of course. Mavra returns tomorrow, after burying her poor son, Oleg.

It's one's consolation to be with the wounded and dress their wounds and look after them.

All are well here. Ducky is out with Miechen's sanitary
train, not as a nurse but to look after all, and works
well. Olga and Marie are still out in the hospitals.

When the Emperor was away reviewing troops and visiting
munition factories, as he frequently was, the Empress went on tours of
inspection to provincial hospitals with her daughters and a lady-in-
waiting. These were often long journeys, and although the imperial
train was very comfortably fitted up, it was no small undertaking.
During 1914 and 1915 the Empress visited more towns than ever
before during all her years in Russia. She wanted to see for herself
how things could best be improved and to show her personal interest
in as many wounded as possible.

She would have liked these to be surprise visits in which she could
dispense with ceremony and see things thoroughly, and this was
managed several times in Petrograd. However, on longer journeys, it
was pointed out to the Empress that it would not be fair for some
people who might have worked untiringly in the hospitals not to know
of her visit, as they might perhaps just happen to be away on the day
she came if her visit was a surprise one.

The thing that the Empress hated most of all was to feel something
was being hidden from her, that she was being shown some
'Potemkin' villages. On one occasion it was evident that the officials
did not want her to see a particular hospital in one of the towns she
visited. She was told that the hospital was too far away, that the road
was impossible, and that there were scarcely any patients in it. The
Empress replied that a few would be as much pleased to see her as a
number. At last she was told that the bridge on the river was
impassable, and as this excuse was corroborated, she had to give in.
She sent her gentleman to ford the river, should this prove necessary.
The bridge was under repair, but this was the only story that proved
true and the hospital was not one of the glories of the town.

The Empress went with the Emperor to Dvinsk and Grodno, and they also made a tour of the central towns, the Empress meeting the Emperor, who had been inspecting some troops, on the way. In every town they made a tour of the hospitals to see the wounded and the Empress often used to linger near especially bad cases. Sometimes they saw as many as 3,000 men in a day.

Even when she was without the Emperor, the Empress received great ovations in nearly every town. At Kharkov, for example, the students gave her a rousing welcome and her car could scarcely move through the wildly cheering crowd. Later in the war, the welcome was more stilted and formal, but the Empress did not seem to notice this. Only once did she feel some coldness in her reception and this was in Moscow the first time she went alone there in 1914. She told the Governor that the visit was to be a private one and that she wanted to visit the hospitals under Grand Duchess Ella's guidance. The Empress and her daughters wore nurses' dresses, and the Governor let it be known that the Empress had come incognito. No one in the town knew of her arrival, the streets were mostly empty, and those who met Her Majesty did not recognize her. She felt hurt and thought that it was the result of some intrigue against her.

The pleasure she believed she was giving kept the Empress going all the time, but she would come back to the train so tired that she could only sink down on the first chair in utter exhaustion, unable even to go to her own compartment. She allowed herself no respite and, even when ostensibly resting, she would be looking through the innumerable petitions she received in every town until her daughters would entreat her to stop.

When she saw an ambulance train at any station, she would throw a coat over her rest gown and rush out to inspect it. She thought that people would feel slighted if they saw the imperial train and she did not go and see them.

She never shrank from the overcrowded carriages or the saddest sights, and would stand in the close atmosphere, her face on a level with the upper rows of bunks, while the doctors gave her a detailed account of their work.

She drove in some curious and impromptu vehicles in many of the towns. Sometimes a car was placed at her disposal, sometimes the antique coach of an archbishop, sometimes even a homely *isvoztchik* (cab).

Outward displays seemed needless to her, and even wrong at such a time. However, her desire to pass unnoticed was sometimes disappointed. I remember a case in point when the Empress stopped for a couple of hours at Bielgorod on her way from Kharkov. There was a monastery there, a well-known place of pilgrimage, which she wished to visit and she wanted no one disturbed on her account as the train passed Bielgorod in the evening. No one in the town knew of her arrival, and with her daughters, General Ressine, Mme. Vyrubova and myself, she set off in the very worst possible *isvoztchik* over muddy, bumpy roads in the pitch darkness to the monastery. Great was the Empress' disappointment to find the whole monastery brilliantly lit and the sleepy Archbishop in full vestments, preceded by equally sleepy monks bearing lighted tapers. Someone had evidently tipped them off.

The Empress was led in procession from her humble conveyance, the Archbishop respectfully holding her arm, to the church, where a solemn *Te Deum* was chanted. Her mischievous daughters were much amused at their mother's 'unobtrusive' visit, but most of all at the appearance of the conveyance, drawn up with great dignity for our departure.

There were no German prisoners at any of the hospitals Their Majesties ever visited, as there were hospitals set apart especially for them, but at Dvinsk they saw some German civilians who had been taken prisoner by the advancing armies. Among them was a man of about eighty who threw himself on his knees before the Emperor and begged for his liberty. The old man looked like an ancient patriarch with a long flowing beard, and the people with him, women and children, were all his family. The Emperor at once gave the order for his release and he was sent back to the German lines.

All the winter of 1914-1915 there was little movement on the Russian front, but the Empress personally had a strenuous time, for Ania Vyrubova was the victim of a terrible railway accident which left her lame for life. Both her legs were broken, her spine was injured and her skull fractured. The Empress scarcely left her side for the first three days after the accident, despite being in a very poor state of health herself. She was torn at this time in many directions as there were serious cases in her hospitals who were also calling for her, and she was continually on the road from one sick bed to the other, but she wrote on March 23 to Princess Victoria that "the wounded's grateful smiles are a recompense for every fatigue."

In March 1915, Lvov was taken by the Russian army and the Austrian fortress at Przemysl fell. This was hailed with delirious joy by the country.

In the same letter of March 23 to Princess Victoria, the Empress wrote:

Such gratitude fills one's heart, that Peremyschel [sic] has fallen at last. Now one can breathe freer, as it kept many troops, which we needed to send elsewhere.

Thank God, on all sides the news is better and in France too.

One's heart suffers for the ships in the Dardanelles – such an ignoble way of fighting. I loathe these mines. Three minutes and all over – brave souls.

How glorious, when St. Sophia will be again a Christian church, if we live to see it.

To Miss Jackson she wrote:

TSARSKOE SELO
March 26, 1915

MY DARLING MADGIE – I hope this letter will reach you by Easter, it is to bring you my tender love and blessings. We feast it the same time this year, I am glad to say – I do hope there will be no fighting for a few days then, it would be hard.

There is so much to do, tho' I am lying since a week again overtired my heart and strength – so despairing when one wants to be useful, not only with the brain.

We have cold sunny days, masses of snow. The fall of Peremishel was such a Godsend, as it kept so many of our troops occupied which will now be free to throw elsewhere. It is interesting to have that old Russian town back again ...

All are busy sending off Easter parcels with linen, eggs, Kulich (bread one specially bakes for Easter), tobacco, sweets, writing paper, candles, etc., and a little Image always for them to wear. I have several 100 of letters of thanks for our presents all these months.

Must end now.

A tender kiss for your loving old
P.Q. No. III

Ella is well – have not met since Dec.

ALIX.

The Emperor went to the two Galician towns very soon after their capture. The Empress was at first a little dubious about this, although she would not admit that she had tried to dissuade him from going there so soon. And when she wrote to Princess Victoria on April 30, she said:

> *Nicky was at Lvov and Peremyschel – most interesting. He has not yet returned as he went to Odessa, Sebastopol to see the troops, dockyards, etc. We expect him back in about 5 days.*
>
> *But spies are everywhere. Going to Bielostock, one threw masses of bombs from the aeroplanes on that town – railway – on Olga's sanitary train too. In time Nicky turned off – so filthy!*

She also wrote in May 1915 to Princess Victoria:

> *I would to God, that this hideous bloodshed would end – but it is too early. The work is not yet done, and they still underrate us. One day they advance, the next we, and on the other side too.*

And a week later, on May 11, 1915:

> *How too outrageous the sinking of the Lusitania. There are things one cannot understand.*

210

During the war, the Empress and her children stayed the whole year round at Tsarskoe Selo, as a change of residence would have interrupted the hospital work. The Empress spent few hours actually nursing, but still went to her hospital.

One hears an echo of the operating theater in a letter to her sister on May 11, 1915:

> *An officer died on the table. A very difficult operation succeeded, then the heart gave way. Hard such moments, but my girlies must know life, and we go through all together.*

She wanted to arrange sanatoria for the wounded in the Russian spas, which were splendid "but primitively arranged." She was tied to her sofa mostly now, but new ideas were always taking shape, and her old charities had to be attended to as well. She was keenly interested in the development of the School of Popular Art she had started, and the newly-founded Society for the Protection of Mothers and Infants, which united all infant welfare work in the country.

In the summer of 1915, the Empress had a call on her sympathy from within the Imperial Family, for Grand Duke Constantine died on June 18. The Grand Duke was a man of great culture and a well-known poet. He had been very hard-hit by the war, as he had lost a promising young son and his daughter a very gallant husband. The Grand Duke's death came at a time when events on the Russian front had taken a serious turn and the Empress' letters show her anxiety.

After the Galician successes of the winter and spring, the Germans came to the assistance of their allies when General von Mackensen attacked the Russian armies, which had to retreat all along the line it had cost such efforts to take. The shortage of munitions and the rapidity of the Russian advance in the winter were largely responsible for this.

211

On all sides the news was bad. The Empress spoke of the uncertainty of the fortune of war, but the losses greatly depressed her. She began to feel, like the rest of the country, that something was amiss. Her letters are full of the losses, and she wrote once that nearly all her Siberian rifle regiment had been gassed.

Things got worse toward the autumn as one fortress after another fell. The Empress clung to some crumbs of comfort: the fortresses were old and the loss of life was small.

Still, her letters breathe the anxiety she had for those around her, to whom she always showed a brave face. On August 31, 1915, she wrote to Princess Victoria:

> *They are advancing at great speed. Our misery, the lack of rifles and heavy artillery, like theirs. They bring more and more to our side. Will England and France never help us? We leave the fortresses, nothing can withstand 16inch guns old fortresses after all – and to lose lives uselessly is no good. The further they come the worse for them – the getting out. Must hope for an early, cold winter. We were not prepared for war and they were thoroughly, and then, they are splendid at organizing things, laying lines and so on, but God will help! The misery of the thousands of fugitives, who block up the rear! One does what one can for them, but the quantity is so colossal.*

There were fears for Petrograd at one time and it was suggested that the art treasures of the Hermitage should be taken to Moscow, but this was vetoed by the Emperor who knew what a panic it would cause.

As public opinion became still further disquieted, someone had to be made a scapegoat for the reverses, and the hatred of the moment, therefore, fastened itself upon the Minister of War, General

Sukhomlinov, who, at a memorable sitting at the outbreak of the war, had assured the Cabinet that he could fulfil all demands for munitions. However, he had badly underestimated the amount of supplies that would be needed. A commission of inquiry was appointed by the Emperor, and General Sukhomlinov was dismissed, although the charge of high treason was dismissed by the judgment of the court. General Polivanov was appointed Minister of War in his stead, but this did not solve the immediate problem. The retreat continued.

What was to be done to sustain the morale of the armies?

Chapter 21

Tsarskoe Selo without the Emperor: 1915-1916

The end of the summer of 1915 was marked by many glorious deeds. The officers and men were wonderful in their heroic endurance and resistance to forces superior in numbers, in arms, and in equipment. The losses were terrible. The continual reverses that gave the whole country reason to feel the gravest anxiety pointed to some serious defects in organization.

The Emperor heard much criticism of the management of the war and from the very outset had been displeased to note that orders from Stavka (military headquarters) were often in conflict with orders from the Home Office in the parts of the country closest to the action, causing monumental confusion. The military staff was held most to blame for this and the troops were beginning to be discouraged by the disasters.

Grand Duke Nicholas could not be persuaded to dismiss those who attracted the bitterest criticism and there seemed to be only one way in which to make a complete change and at the same time to inspire the army with new energy, and that was for the Emperor to take the supreme command of the army himself.

His first idea was to retain Grand Duke Nicholas at Stavka so as to avoid any appearance of a slight to him, but this course presented many difficulties and the Grand Duke was appointed Commander-in-Chief on the Caucasian front instead.

The Emperor took over supreme command on September 5, 1915, and in doing so was fulfilling his secret wish since the beginning of the war to be with his armies as Alexander II and Alexander I had been. The Emperor's decision was not wholly approved of by the Government, and at a Council of Ministers meeting held in the

Emperor's presence before the decision was definitively taken, the difficulties of combining the Sovereign's work with that of Commander-in-Chief were pointed out, as was the danger that possible mistakes and failures might be attributed to him personally. The Emperor refused to be deterred by these considerations that he thought were dictated by a desire to safeguard him from shouldering his responsibilities. The war must be won at all costs and he believed that his presence would strengthen the morale of the army, announcing to Rodzianko, "I will perish, but I will save Russia."

Sazonov was among the strongest opponents of this idea. So was the Dowager-Empress, who implored her son not to take over the command, but the Emperor refused to be shaken in his decision as he felt that, if he did not face these added responsibilities, he would be shirking his duty.

The Empress considered that Grand Duke Nicholas was unlucky. Intrigues of every kind were rife in Kiev, where his wife resided, intrigues of which the Grand Duke himself was probably ignorant, but which ill-disposed people attributed indirectly to him. Her Majesty knew that the Emperor's whole soul was at the front and was convinced that his presence would put new spirit into the troops, and although to her personally the separation was a real tragedy, she felt it her duty to support him as it would lead to victory.

So, on September 4, the Emperor left for Stavka and in an Order of the Day, dated September 5, he reaffirmed his former resolution not to conclude peace while a single enemy was left on Russian soil. These words were now even more impressive as nearly all of Poland lay in the hands of the enemy.

The Empress wrote to her sister:

Nicky will take over the command, General Alexeiev will have the chief work to do, as head of Nicky's Staff. He will guide the whole thing here as the other place [Mohilev] is still further off and then he will constantly

215

go and see the troops and know what's going on at last
... It's a heavy cross Nicky takes upon himself, but with
God's help it will bring better luck.

The Emperor's initial idea when taking over command was to limit the time he spent in Mohilev, where Stavka had been set up, to short visits, leaving the actual command to General Alexeiev, his Chief of the Staff. This plan, unfortunately, was not adhered to.

After the decision had been taken, the Empress was calm. She felt sure that the reward would not be delayed and that their luck would turn. She wrote on August 25, 1915, "Times are awfully hard, in every sense of the word, but one lives, hoping in God's infinite mercy." She began working again feverishly after the Emperor had gone and more palaces were turned into hospitals: the Neskoutchnoe at Moscow and the Winter Palace in Petrograd. This latter became a huge hospital of one thousand beds equipped with every modern appliance.

Thousands of refugees poured into the country. The Refugee Committee, which had been formed by Grand Duchess Tatiana, became almost a Department of State. The Committee was directed by Alexei Borrissovich Neidhard, a member of the Imperial Council, while members of the Duma, of the Imperial Council, and of the Union of Towns and Zemstvos belonged to it. Grand Duchess Tatiana took the greatest interest in it and, young though she was, had quantities of papers sent to her every day which she went over with her mother's help, making notes and writing her decisions. The housing, feeding and general welfare of refugees all over Russia were in the hands of the Committee, the budget of which rose rapidly to several million rubles. The money was at first raised by private subscriptions, but the department was eventually financed by the Government. This Committee continued to work after the Revolution of 1917 under the Kerensky Government.

The mass of people of every class and condition fleeing from their homes, some with a few of their goods and chattels, some quite penniless, even reached Petrograd and were put into every available building by the municipality. The Empress immediately went to see all the places where they were housed, even the emergency barracks on the island of Golodai, where hundreds of men, women, and children were all herded together, glad to get even this miserable shelter. The Empress visited every corner, questioning the people about their needs and devising measures to improve their condition.

After the Emperor had taken over command, news from the front became better, and General Alexeiev succeeded in keeping the Germans in check until winter put a stop to serious military operations. This improvement seemed to the Empress to be a good omen and her belief in the wisdom of her husband's decision was strengthened when she heard all the officers in her hospitals praising it.

With the Emperor at Mohilev, twenty-six hours away from the capital, life at the Imperial Palace became, if possible, even quieter. The whole place seemed dead. There was no movement in the great courtyard and we ladies-in-waiting passed through a series of empty halls when we went to the Empress who gave audience daily, but only to those people whom it was imperative to see, including a few who were there on charitable business.

However, her latest bout of activity had exhausted her much more quickly than at the beginning of the war, and a month after the Emperor's departure, Her Majesty, though still visiting the Tsarskoe Selo hospitals as often as she could, spent most of the day and all her evenings on her sofa in a state of utter exhaustion. Nevertheless, no matter what was in her heart, she always had a smile for her children and they always found their mother interested in their activities. Her face would light up whenever the Emperor or one of her children came into the room. After dinner, the Empress and her daughters sat together in the mauve boudoir, the children assembled around her couch. One daughter would play the piano and another would read. Mme. Vyrubova was nearly always there, too. When the Emperor was

217

at Tsarskoe Selo and had a moment's free time, he would read aloud, generally an English novel that relaxed him.

The young Grand Duchesses never seemed to feel the austerity of their lives or to expect the amusements that should have been theirs at their age. The only changes they had from routine were an occasional concert got up at the hospital for the patients or a small party at Mme. Vyrubova's, to which the Empress sometimes accompanied them.

Mme. Vyrubova had a charming little house near the Palace and she knew how to entertain simply and informally, inviting only small parties of a few intimate friends. Her sister, Mme. Alya Pistohlkors (married to the son of the Princess Paley by her first marriage), was generally there, as were Countess Emma Fredericks, Mme. Lily Dehn, Countess Rehbinder (née Moewesz) – looking very like the Empress in appearance, although shorter – as well as some young girls, such as Irina Tolstoy, Daly (Nathalie) Tolstoy, Marguerite Khitrovo, and some officers of the imperial yacht when they were on leave from the front.

The realities of war were known to the Empress because she heard accounts of life at the front every day in the hospitals, and from the reports of officers on leave she realized that the spirit that prevailed at the front was very different from that in the towns. The officers from the army were full of hope, energy and patriotic feeling; those who had been some time in the Petrograd hospitals were dispirited and full of alarming tales.

The hope that the Emperor would be able to keep his visits to Stavka short could not be fulfilled and he did not return to Tsarskoe Selo until October, and then only briefly. When he was there, the Palace sprang to life. Ministers came and went daily, carriages drove to and fro. He was satisfied that all was going well and was full of hope for the future. When the Emperor returned to Stavka, he took the Tsarevich with him. He wanted the troops to know his heir. He also wanted his son to see at close quarters what war meant so that he should be able to understand, in years to come, what the struggle had been and what it had cost Russia.

This was a terrible wrench for the Empress. She had never been parted from her boy for more than a few hours, except for one week on one of her inspection journeys. Every moment she was away from him she was filled with anxiety that something would happen to him, for the sword of Damocles was always hanging over his head, but she made up her mind that she must make this, the greatest of all sacrifices. She would part with her peace of mind and let her treasure go. She was always anxious when her vigilant eye could not guard him, but this was for her son's future and also for the Emperor's sake. The Emperor was often lonely at Mohilev and the boy would cheer him up, but the look of anxiety never left her face from that day.

Her war work had little-by-little shown the Empress many defects in the machinery of Government. She heard that her ambulance trains were often held up owing to the lack of railway lines. There was also a shortage of supplies caused by slowness and disorder, as well as by mismanagement. On December 10, 1915, she spoke in a letter of a "shortage of flour and meat in many places though they exist in quantities, but fugitives and troops take all the trains."

She did not realize how much all this was influencing the political situation of the country as there was no one to give her accurate information on this subject. She never spoke about politics to either her gentlemen or her ladies as the subject was taboo at Court. Rumors of what was being talked about in the capital sometimes reached her, but only through chance remarks from some of the wounded in her hospitals or through nurses and doctors.

Another occasional source of information was Mme. Vyrubova, who got about a great deal in spite of her lameness. Her father, Alexander Sergueievich Tanayev, was not only a prominent government official but also a composer of some repute who had artists, members of society and Ministers of State all meeting at his house. Mme. Vyrubova also frequently went to the house of Princess

Paley, the wife of Grand Duke Paul, who held a kind of salon at the time.

Unfortunately, although she collected many stories from various sources, Mme. Vyrubova was not a very reliable or discriminating informant and found it almost impossible to separate idle gossip and rumor from sound information. Many who knew that she was the Empress' friend flattered her and she was apt to be deceived. Anyone who expressed the slightest criticism of the Government was put down as "bad." Mme. Vyrubova always identified the Government with the person of the Emperor and any censure of the Government was considered by her as disloyalty to the Crown.

The Empress tried to sift out her friend's reports, but they always left an impression, for Her Majesty knew the absolute and wholehearted devotion of her friend Ania to the Imperial Family. She knew, too, that the things Mme. Vyrubova repeated were probably the talk of the town, although, regrettably, she did not know of how small a section of it.

The death of the Empress' devoted lady-in-waiting Princess Sonia Orbeliani in December 1915 was a loss to the Empress in many ways as well as being a great personal blow. Although she had been an invalid for years, Princess Orbeliani had the undaunted spirit of the Georgians, refusing to give in despite knowing that her days were numbered, and retaining to the last an intense interest in life. When she could no longer serve her beloved Empress actively, Princess Orbeliani did all she could to help her socially, putting her in touch with people who would interest her and talking to her frankly, never fearing to give her an honest, and even unfavorable, opinion. She traveled about a great deal in her wheeled chair to houses where the voices of different parties were heard, being the niece of the former Liberal Prime Minister, Prince Sviatopolk-Mirsky.

The Empress was devoted to Sonia and appreciated her honesty and affection. Her Majesty did not easily change her opinions once formed, but in discussing a subject with a person she trusted she could be persuaded in time to see the other point of view, and even to act on it later. Nothing that the Empress did, or did not do, brought about, or could have averted, the catastrophe of 1917, but had she had wiser advice during the critical years, she would have escaped the unjust accusation of influencing the politics of the country.

Sonia Orbeliani died after a short illness and the Empress never left her during her final day. She had promised her friend to close her eyes when she died and she kept her promise. Sonia died in her arms, thanking her Empress and friend with her last smile for all she had been to her. The Empress saw to all details of the funeral, fulfilled her dear friend's last wishes, and wrote to all the relatives herself. She came to the first memorial service (*panihida*) in her nurses' dress. "Don't be astonished to see us [the Empress herself and Olga and Tatiana] dressed as sisters," she wrote me, "but I hate the idea of going into black for her this evening and feel somehow nearer to her like this, like an aunt, more human, less Empress."

Late that same evening, the Empress joined me in the room where the coffin lay. She sat down beside it, looking into the quiet, dead face, and stroked Sonia's hair as if she were asleep. "I wanted to be a little more with Sonia," she said. When she left the room, her face was bathed in tears. She felt the loss of the "true heart," as she called Sonia in a letter to her sister, adding "All miss her sorely."

Misfortunes never come singly. On the day of Princess Orbeliani's funeral, the Emperor arrived unexpectedly from Stavka with the little Tsarevich who was desperately ill. He had broken a blood vessel in his nose and all the doctors' efforts could not stop the hemorrhage which had lasted for forty-eight hours. The poor child had to be supported day and night in a half-sitting posture and could scarcely speak.

The Empress was in agony. Always calm on the surface, she relived the time of her son's extreme suffering in Spala in 1912. Again the last remedy, the prayers of the Healer, was called for. The *Staretz*

221

came, prayed for the child, touched his face, and, almost immediately afterward the bleeding ceased. The doctors tried to explain the medical reasons for this, but the Empress had seen that all their efforts had failed and that Rasputin had succeeded. The Tsarevich recovered and the reputation of the *Staretz* as a man with heaven-sent powers stood higher than ever.

Chapter 22

Visits to Stavka and Elsewhere: 1916

The Empress was but rarely seen in Petrograd in the winter of 1915-1916. Her health was very uncertain and she frequently had to interrupt her hospital work at Tsarskoe Selo. Her cherished plan of going to see the work of the other Grand Duchess Olga, the Emperor's younger sister, near the front and of paying a surprise visit to her ambulance trains had to be abandoned.

The Grand Duchesses Olga and Tatiana replaced their mother as much as they could, visiting Petrograd every week, Grand Duchess Tatiana to preside at sittings of her Refugee Committee and Grand Duchess Olga to receive donations for her soldiers' families at the Winter Palace. Afterward, the young Grand Duchesses would wind up the afternoon by going to the different hospitals in Petrograd which the Empress would have seen for herself had she been able to do so.

The Grand Duchesses also represented their mother at the opening of the British Red Cross Hospital, going there with their grandmother, the Dowager-Empress. The Empress had taken the greatest interest in this hospital and had several conversations with Lady Muriel Paget, Lady Sybil Grey, and Mr. Malcolm, who were responsible for it. It was established in Grand Duchess Ella's former palace, then the property of Grand Duke Dmitri Pavlovich, and was equipped by the British Red Cross and very well run by English doctors and nurses.

The Empress was able to pay a visit to the hospital before the unit left for the front.

Lady Sybil Grey, who went with them, had the ill-luck, after a very short stay, to be hit in the face by a splinter of shell in the trenches near the front line. She was sent back to Petrograd and the wound healed well, but there was considerable anxiety felt for her at one time and the Empress was full of sympathy.

In the spring of 1916, the Empress was able to resume her travels through the country, although on a smaller scale than in the previous year. These journeys always finished now with a short visit to the Emperor at Mohilev, to where the Tsarevich had also returned after a time spent at Tsarskoe Selo recovering from his illness. The sun went out of the Empress' life when she was away from the Emperor, and since the Tsarevich's last illness that winter her fears for him were never at rest.

The little Tsarevich had grown up considerably while being in the Emperor's constant company. He slept in his father's room, for the house at Mohilev was a very small one, and lunched daily with him and his staff, talking merrily to the generals and the members of foreign military missions, forgetting his shyness. He was a great favorite with the officers, and the Empress always begged them not to spoil him, which would have been difficult as he was a delightful boy.

The old Belgian General, Baron de Riquel, and the Japanese military representative, who, in common with all his countrymen, was particularly fond of children, were his special friends. He also made friends at Mohilev with two little boys, the sons of officers' widows in very modest circumstances. The Empress made the acquaintance of their mothers during her visits, and often sent special invitations to the little boys to come and play with her son as she felt that he lacked companions of his own age.

The Empress took her four daughters with her on her travels, and also to Mohilev, where the whole family rejoiced in being together. The Grand Duchesses needed a change from their hospital work. Grand Duchess Olga especially had so much overtired herself in the course of the winter that she had grown nervous and anemic, having to give up actual nursing and limiting herself to supervising the wards, while Grand Duchess Tatiana still worked in the operating theater.

Large supplies of clothes for refugees were always taken on these journeys, which Tatiana distributed.

For about ten days in the spring of 1916 the Emperor and the Empress travelled together in the south of Russia, the Empress inspecting hospitals and the Emperor reviewing troops. It was a terribly wet time and the Empress and her daughters went about in mackintoshes with well tucked up skirts. They went to Vinnitza, a small town near the Rumanian frontier, to see Her Majesty's *sklad* that had been excellently managed all through the war by Mme. de Hartwig, widow of the former Russian Minister to Serbia. This was the central depot for all the Empress' stores and ambulances for the Galician front. From there they went to Bendery, where the Emperor reviewed the Czechoslovak legions, formed from former Austrian prisoners of war, and the beginning of the Czechoslovak army, units of which, while returning to their own country through Siberia, were later the first to help Admiral Kolchak in his fight against the Bolsheviks.

From Bendery, they went to Odessa where the Empress saw the sanatoria for officers that had been set up with mud baths and the first Russian iodine factory. Sebastopol was the next stop. They resisted the temptation to go to Livadia, although the doctors advised the Empress to do so. It was, she said, "too great a treat to indulge in during the war."

As it was, the trip was delightful and did everyone good. The Empress revived, notwithstanding her fatigue, and the Grand Duchesses used to lie like lizards in the sun beside the train at Sebastopol, regardless of their mother's appeals to them to think of their complexions. At Sebastopol, where they had so often stopped in previous years on their way to Livadia, they felt the spirit of wartime. There were scarcely any men about in the streets as it was a naval town and they were all with the fleet. At night all the windows of the imperial train had heavy black curtains drawn across them. Every light was covered and the whole town was plunged into pitch darkness as German cruisers had entered the Black Sea and air-raids were feared. The Empress and her daughters accompanied the Emperor as he visited the forts above the town but they saw the fortifications only from a distance as the Emperor did not attempt to compromise the rule that no women were to be admitted inside the forts.

From Sebastopol they continued on to Eupatoria, where the Empress had established several sanatoria. Eupatoria was lovely, semi-Oriental, and bathed in sunshine, with glowing flowers overhanging the high white walls of gardens and houses whose high railed windows proclaimed them to be the residences of Tartars. Eupatoria had not been visited by any Russian Emperor since the liberal Alexander I, and all the population gave the Imperial Family a warm welcome. The Mahommedans even authorized the *"valide"* (their name for the Empress) and her daughters to attend a solemn thanksgiving service at the mosque, which no woman ever enters.

It was curious to see the rows and rows of prostrate, turbaned men, their shoes all standing before the door. Not a word of the service could be understood, of course, except occasionally the Emperor's name, but their earnest faces, and the Oriental calm and discipline with which they all followed the Mullah in his every movement, made a deep impression.

After visiting the Mahommedan mosque, they visited the Karaim Jews' synagogue. It was a lovely white marble building, covered with sweet-scented glycinia. A fine tenor chanted the Psalms in Hebrew. It was quite a picture of other centuries and other worlds.

Those were the lighter sides of the visit – the official side including a service at the cathedral, and visits to numerous hospitals – and the day was brought to an end by a visit to Mme. Vyrubova who was undergoing treatment and staying in a seaside villa. Here all the family basked in the sun and forgot their cares for a few hours. Months afterward, this one day in the quiet little town with its marvelous sun was remembered and cherished. They had a few hours' relaxation and quiet there, and were very grateful for it.

In the summer of 1916 the Empress traveled several times to Mohilev. The whole party lived in the imperial train drawn up in the pine woods near the station. In the morning, while the Empress was resting, her daughters visited the cottages in the neighborhood, played with the children of the peasants, and gave them sweets and presents. All went to luncheon with the Emperor in the house which, to his amusement, was pompously called "the Palace" by the people at Stavka. It had formerly been the Governor's residence, and bore traces of the progressive bad taste of all the governors who had lived in it. Such hideous fabrics and such terrible imitation oak-grained wallpapers could rarely have been seen together, but the Emperor had other things to think of and no changes were made.

All the members of foreign missions were invited to these luncheons, as well as the numerous generals attached to Stavka and any who came in from the front. The Empress told me that she always felt desperately shy at Stavka. She had grown unaccustomed to making a big circle and felt that she was out of her element in such purely masculine surroundings. When she stood in the corner of the room with her daughters, having given her hand to all to be kissed, the bright red spots on her cheeks were sure signs of her nervousness. While the Emperor was engrossed in conversation with some general, she would timidly send one of her daughters to call someone to her, although she never had the opportunity of talking to some of those whom she would have appreciated most. Her neighbors at luncheon were generally the chiefs of the British and French military missions, at first Sir John Hanbury-Williams and the Marquis de La Guiche, then General Waters and General Janin.

She particularly liked Sir John Hanbury-Williams and talked quite simply to him. He quotes in his book ("The Emperor Nicholas II as I knew him") a remark she made to him at one of these luncheons: "War is the passing out of darkness into the light of victory, but

227

victory we must have." This same feeling about victory can be seen in a letter to Princess Victoria on December 10, 1915: "Oh, how one longs for 1916 to bring us Allies glorious victories and peace!"

After luncheon, the imperial party would go out by motor, or down the Dnieper on a small steam launch, to an appointed spot where the car or launch would be left, and the Emperor and his daughters, accompanied by the most intrepid walkers of the Court suite, would go off on a long expedition through the country. It was amusing to see some of the gentlemen lagging behind to avoid the inviting eye of the Sovereign, for to the stout these walks were more of a pain than a pleasure.

The Emperor walked through fields and woods and villages, once or twice even through private gardens when he missed his way. The surprise of one family of small landowners can be imagined when the whole imperial party of some ten ladies and gentlemen walked through their garden, and appeared unexpectedly in front of the balcony where they were sitting around a steaming samovar enjoying their afternoon tea. The Emperor politely apologized for the intrusion, but was met with rather black looks. Then someone said, "It is the Emperor," and all the flowers in the garden would have been pressed on the Grand Duchesses if the hospitable owners could have had their way.

Another time the young Grand Duchesses and I nearly fell into a pond from a raft onto which we had climbed to pick some water lilies for the Empress, and had to be rescued by the Emperor, although he said he had never before provided Her Majesty with flowers under such difficult conditions.

The Empress stayed near the cars or by the river with Mme. Vyrubova during these expeditions, for she could not take long walks now. She liked to talk to passing villagers and the conversation generally resulted in some private charity to the people who, at first, did not know who she was.

After the walk came tea, and then the Emperor had to return to his work. Sometimes special guests were invited – officers returning from the front, doctors, etc. – and the Court suite, of course, was present. After tea, the ladies returned to the train, where the Emperor joined his family for dinner, returning immediately afterward to his work. About eleven o'clock, tea was served again, in the Russian fashion, when the Emperor would reappear to read the daily papers and to drink the same number of glasses of tea each evening, while his daughters and Grand Duke Dmitri, who sometimes spent the evening with Their Majesties, kept up a lively conversation together.

The Grand Duke teased both mother and daughters, and the Empress was often laughing and talking as gaily as the girls, infected by the buoyant spirits of the young people. Only those members of the Court suite who were living on the train, and the two gentlemen who had come with the Emperor, were present at their last meal, and the conversation then was generally quite informal and the Emperor commented on the news he had read.

It was said that the whole of Stavka disliked the arrival of the Empress at Mohilev as they had an idea that she influenced the Emperor much more than was really the case, and every appointment or every change that occurred after she had been there was laid at her door. This was not so.

I myself happen to have witnessed an incident that proves that the dismissal of Sazonov, which has always been attributed to the Empress' influence and most bitterly commented upon, was not brought about by Her Majesty. I was with the Empress in her coupé in the train at Stavka when a note from the Emperor was brought in. The Empress read it with signs of the greatest surprise, and, on the spur of the moment, told me its contents. The Emperor wrote that he had decided to dismiss Sazonov. This was news to the Empress who seemed dubious and expressed the opinion that she feared the moment was inopportune.

The last journey that the Empress took was in December 1916, when she went to Novgorod, a town she had longed to visit on account of its numerous beautiful old churches. Now she had no time to see these, as her visit was mainly to the war hospitals. The Governor escorted her around them, and the nobility gave a large tea party in her honor, but it was clear to those who were with her that there was no warmth in the welcome, although the Empress did not realize this.

The Empress managed to see some of the old church treasures and the cathedral, and she went also with her daughters and the Prince Ioan Constantinovich to see a *Staritza* who was over a hundred years old and much reverenced in the town.

The old woman greeted her with the words, "Here is the martyr, Empress Alexandra." Her Majesty seemed not to hear. She received the *Staritza's* blessing and went away, cheered and comforted, but those who had been with her came back depressed and apprehensive, for they felt the reception was an omen.

Chapter 23

Before the Storm

During 1916, the political atmosphere in the capital and in all the big towns became more and more threatening. The reverses of 1915 had unsettled the public mind and given rise to a natural anxiety. The Russian temperament always fluctuates from extreme optimism to utter pessimism, and now the blackest view of the future was generally taken. The responsibility for all disasters was laid on the Government, without any allowances being made for the inordinate difficulties of the situation.

There was bitter criticism behind the lines of what was done at the front and the revolutionary organizations, which had been lying low, started to stoke the flames in pursuance of their own ends. They particularly directed their efforts toward encouraging attacks on the Sovereigns. The revolutionary movement of 1905 had been thwarted mainly by the people's innate fidelity to the throne, and there was nothing in the personal conduct of the Emperor that could shake his prestige, so the undercurrents began to be directed against the Empress in the hope of weakening his position through her.

Besides exploiting exaggerated tales of Rasputin's influence, much was made of the Empress' German origins. Tales of her pro-German sympathies were invented and assiduously spread. Stories were circulated of her desire for a separate peace, rumors that could gain credence only in the public's total ignorance of the Empress' character. This gossip would never have been listened to for a moment had not the whole country's nerves been strained to such a pitch that nothing seemed too wild to be thought possible. I myself was asked in all seriousness whether the Grand Duke of Hesse was not hidden in the cellars of the Palace! After the Revolution, the whole Palace was searched for mythical wireless stations that were supposed to have been used for secret communications with the enemy.

Needless to say, all these wild allegations were without the slightest foundation, and I mention them only to show the state of "war nerves" that had been reached at the time. The Empress' sympathy with the Allies and her fidelity to the cause for which Russia was fighting are known to everyone now. Sir George Buchanan, Sir John Hanbury-Williams, and M. Paléologue, all of whom knew her personally, have explained in their books that even at the time the stories were not believed by sensible people. Even Rodzianko, the President of the Duma, and one of the Empress' most virulent enemies, says that "the wicked idea of treason on the part of the Empress must be rejected once and for all. This charge was absolutely repudiated by the commission under Muraviev, who was appointed by the Provisional Government for the purpose of elucidating this matter in the light of documentary evidence." I may as well say here that the authenticity of some of the Empress' published letters is in my opinion open to doubt.

An episode out of which a defamatory tale against the Empress was constructed was the arrival in Petrograd in the late autumn of 1915 of a former friend of Grand Duchess Ella, whom the Empress had known since her girlhood – Mlle. Marie Alexandrovna Vassiltchikov. This lady had settled in Austria long before the war and returned to Petrograd, bringing with her letters from her friends in Germany to different prominent people, among them one to the Emperor and another to Sazonov. The Emperor immediately sent his letter to Sazonov, with the remark that it needed no answer, and neither the Emperor nor the Empress ever saw Mlle. Vassiltchikov. The Empress thought that she was trying to create a link between the countries and considered her action wrong as she thought that a separate peace would be dishonorable on Russia's part. She said so strongly and was firm in refusing to have anything to do with Mlle.

Vassiltchikov, who was sent to her estate in the provinces and ordered to reside there until the end of the war.

The Empress was very English in her feelings. Her upbringing and her long visits to Queen Victoria had all fostered her love for her mother's country. English was the language which came easiest to her; the Allies' cause was hers; all her recorded conversations and published correspondence show this clearly and she rejoiced at the Allies' successes nearly as much as at the Russian ones.

Her letters to her sister Princess Victoria show that she followed with sympathy the movements of the British Fleet and British naval actions, both in the Dardanelles and in the Baltic. The sinking of the Lusitania and of the Portugal by the Germans moved her to the greatest indignation. The Breslau's bombardment of defenseless spas in the Crimea excited her nearly to fury. She was always longing, praying, and hoping for victory over Russia's enemies.

On August 15, 1916, she wrote to Princess Victoria, "How one longs for this terrible war to end – two years strain. Such awful losses all over the world. But I do not think it can be yet for a long while."

It must be said, to the shame of the upper classes of Petrograd society, that every idle piece of gossiping was believed, or at least repeated and spread all over the country until the stories reached the masses, who accepted them as facts. When the stories drifted back to the Empress, they distressed her terribly. How could it be said that she was untrue to the country she loved fanatically, the land of her husband and son? To her, Russia was God's chosen land, Holy Russia.

Happily for her, she was spared the bitterness of ever believing that the peasants had been poisoned by the revolutionary spirit. The Empress has often been accused of surrounding herself with a German cabal, so it may be worthwhile to note those who were with her all through the war. Her ladies were Mme. Narishkin (née Princess Kurakin), Mistress of the Robes, and four maids-of-honor: Princess Orbeliani (who died December 15, 1915), O. E. Butzow (until the summer of 1915), Countess A. W. Hendrikov and myself. Her gentleman was Count Apraxin, who was often away looking after her war charities and lived in Petrograd. She had practically no man in the house between 1915 and 1917. The Grand Maréchal, Count Paul Benckendorff, came to assist at her receptions in Apraxin's absence. The Minister of the Court, Count Fredericks, and Count Benckendorff were among the noblest and most respected figures in society. All their sympathies were with the Allies, as Sir John Hanbury-Williams and Sir George Buchanan have attested in their books. The Empress' most intimate friends at the time, Mme. Vyrubova and Mme. Dehn, were of purely Russian origin. These formed the whole of the Empress' entourage.

The Empress' committee for Russian prisoners of war was also used as a means of distorting the truth. From the very outbreak of the war, Her Majesty had been distressed at the plight of the Russian prisoners in Germany and Austria, and had set up a committee to help them under the presidency of Prince Nicholas Galitzin, the last Prime Minister, whom she received constantly in connection with this work. She was much disappointed at not being well enough to meet the first batch of exchanged prisoners from Germany and to hear their stories herself, and went to see them later at Princess Helena Petrovna's hospital.

She wrote to Princess Victoria on August 23, 1915, that the returned Russian prisoners were sad to look at. "Clothes in an awful state, faces of those that had no arms covered with crusts of dirt, thin and famished looking, but intensely happy [to be back]. Very kindly treated in Sweden. The Swedish correspondent found those we sent to Germany better dressed and looking well fed. Sad things they told, if one only believes the half of what they say."

The Empress wrote this from the Emperor's account to her. In the same letter she spoke of her horror at the treatment that was meted out to Russian prisoners. At the suggestion of the Swedish Red Cross, Russian nurses were sent to inspect the German and Austrian camps, while Austrian and German nurses came to Russia. Both parties were accompanied by neutral delegates. The Emperor of Austria and the German Empress having received the Russian nurses on their journey through Vienna and Berlin, the Empress, in the absence of the Dowager-Empress, who was the President of the Red Cross Society, received the German and Austrian nurses in an official audience. The Empress received the Russian nurses before they started, and saw them also on their return, to hear what had been achieved by them.

This exchange of visits bettered the conditions of the prisoners in both countries. The Russians in the German camps were suffering greatly from hunger in 1916, and to the Empress' distress, her committee had to stop sending them food in January 1916, as the Germans "eat it all up." German prisoners of war were not in the Empress' concern; she had nothing to do with them.

Princess Irene wrote to her sister officially through the Swedish Red Cross to point out the unwholesome conditions in which the German prisoners were working on the Murman railway. The Emperor had the matter inquired into and the Empress sent an official answer to Princess Irene.

She wrote to Princess Victoria on December 2, 1916:

What one says about the Murman railway is untrue. We have just seen people we sent to see all.

The German prisoners won't eat cabbage, therefore fall ill more than ours of Zinga [i.e. scurvy].

They get paid 60 rubles a month for their work on the line, as they do it well. Out of that they eat for 40 rubles – have beds, huts and barracks.

In summer they sleep out of doors.

At the beginning, of course, things were not famous as so awfully far away.

She believed what she was told and had done all that ordinary humanity dictated by having the matter investigated. This was also done in the few isolated cases when the Swedish Red Cross appealed to her personally, although it generally wrote direct to the Russian Red Cross Society.

Already by the autumn of 1915 the relations between the Duma and the Government had become strained, the former claiming that the latter was mismanaging the affairs of the country. Some of the ministers shared the view that radical changes in the Cabinet were necessary. They considered that the Prime Minister, Goremykin, was out of date in his views, and presented a memorandum to that effect to the Emperor.

The Emperor would not agree to Goremykin's dismissal, but, at the latter's instance, he gradually replaced those members of the Cabinet who were not in political agreement with the Prime Minister. This was the beginning of a series of political changes in the Ministry, which was called by some wit in the Duma "the ministerial leap-frog."

The Emperor was still seldom at Tsarskoe Selo. During one of his brief visits, on February 23, 1916, he went to the Duma with his brother, Grand Duke Michael, to be present with the representatives of the people at the *Te Deum* sung in thanksgiving for the taking of Erzeroum. The Emperor was warmly received, loyal speeches were made, and the visit was heralded as the healing of the misunderstandings between the ministers and the Duma. There seemed to be a promise of unity on the "Inner Front."

This did not last, however. The Duma disapproved of the choice of Sturmer as Prime Minister, and the appointment of the Vice-President of the Duma, Protopopov, as Minister of the Interior. Protopopov was greatly criticized. Later on, the Duma clamored for a Ministry of "National Confidence," similar to what existed in England. That

236

would have meant a radical change in the whole system of government, which the Emperor hesitated to sanction while he was only intermittently in complete touch with his Cabinet.

Things seemed to have reached a deadlock. The French delegate, M. Thomas, said to Rodzianko, the President of the Duma, *"Ce qui manque, c'est l'autocratie du gouvernement."* (There needs to be autocratic government). This was aptly said. There was no sign of the strong man whom the Empress had always hoped would appear to help the Emperor.

The Empress was anxiously following the course of events. She felt intuitively that things were going wrong and feared that governmental difficulties might affect even the war itself, and that her husband's hard work would all have been in vain. What would become of Holy Russia should there be a recurrence of the events of 1905?

She knew that the Emperor was anxious: He was worn out with his double work and was tied to Stavka when he felt he ought to be in touch with his Government. He was unable to see many people at Stavka except the military around him, and he had no time to look about for new elements to be brought to the fore in this time of national danger.

The Empress felt that, whatever it cost her, she must help him in this and bring him into contact with fresh people to choose from. She had always been in awe of the ministers and had never discussed any matters of importance with them, however in 1915 she began to know some of them better. The Prime Minister, for instance, whom called "Good old Goremykin," and whom she trusted, and some of the other ministers sat on her charity committees, and she had to receive them often in connection with her work.

The ministers took advantage of their audiences with the Empress during the Emperor's long absences to express their opinions to her, in the hope that she would pass them on to the Emperor. In her desire to find people, and realizing all the intrigues that were going on, she communicated to the Emperor all the names of people mentioned by the ministers and those who were well spoken of in connection with her charities.

In a conversation with me, she once said that one of the great trials of their position was that they constantly saw people intriguing against one another, and that it was very difficult to know who was really sincere in his advice. People whom they knew to be loyal to themselves would also, after some time, suddenly become touched with the spirit of intrigue and speak to the Emperor against others who were believed to be the Sovereign's friends.

Therefore the Empress groped blindly about, unable to verify the information she got, for she did not know the people herself and had met them only cursorily. Her one criterion was whether people were strictly faithful to the Emperor. Were they loyal?

She believed that she was beginning at last to hear public opinion and not only the opinion of the Court. Although she did not realize it, she was often mistaken in this, and was misled by those in whom she put her trust, and, of course, she never really 'discovered' anybody. All the names she mentioned to the Emperor were those of prominent officials who had some important post or other. They were often brought to the Emperor's notice by others at the same time as by her, for the choice among his conservative statesmen was small.

The Emperor preferred to appoint a man whom he heard favorably spoken of in several quarters and who was also suggested by the Empress, in preference to someone else about whom he knew less, but this does not mean that he was solely guided by the Empress' opinion. When he disagreed, he did not like to refuse her directly, but rather went his own way in silence.

In happier times, the Empress thoroughly disliked even mentioning anything reminiscent of the Emperor's work to him. In 1905, when Count Fredericks had, on one occasion, asked her to speak of some matter to the Emperor, she was with difficulty persuaded to do so, and when he asked her to repeat the attempt, she burst into tears. She was so ignorant of affairs that she was diffident, and she knew few men of note. She was, as a true woman, always guided by the impression of the moment, and she had now to rely on the few people she trusted. She thought Goremykin a good judge of men, and Protopopov had instilled into her a belief that he fully understood the mentality of the provinces, and was an active and loyal man who would manage to put things right if he were given time and not interfered with. In her own household there was nobody whose advice would have been of any value.

When the Empress once thought well of a person – in politics as in friendship – he had to reveal himself virtually to be a criminal before she would give him up. She was extremely conservative in her political opinions. Her idea was that the current government policy was the right one and that the peasants (the salt of Russia in her eyes) would not approve of a change, and this was strengthened by hundreds of letters which she received purporting to be written by the rural population, in which approval of the Government and loyalty to the Sovereign were expressed. Even if the Empress had been told that the letters were fraudulent, she would, in her inherent honesty, have disbelieved the story. She also received telegrams to the same effect from an ultra-Conservative "Union of the Russian People." All this convinced her that the salvation of Russia lay in autocracy.

On October 9, 1916, the Holy Synod came as a body to Tsarskoe Selo to present the Empress with a *Gramota* (letter of commendation) as well as with a beautiful antique icon. In the *Gramota* she was greatly praised for her work. The Empress was deeply touched by this. The *Gramota* was very rarely given – it was something like the Papal gift of the Rose – and she was especially pleased at this public approval shown to her by the highest Church authority, as she knew what criticism her faith in Gregory Rasputin had excited. The commendation of her work by the Church was believed by her to mean that her efforts to be a help to the Emperor were also rightly understood by well-meaning people who gave her their support.

She was often mistaken in her views; events have tragically proved this. She had no party behind her and no regular advisers. She acted largely on impulse. She saw Russia from one angle only and that from a romantic one. Her belief in Russia's great future and her natural desire to preserve her son's inheritance were her only motives. She was no born politician but a religious woman, highly strung, who struggled through a maze of difficulties and opposition, the full extent of which she did not realize, to help her husband. It was the Emperor's fate to face a task so titanic that it would have demanded a reincarnation of Napoleon and Peter the Great thrown into one to carry it through successfully.

Chapter 24

Warning Voices: 1916-1917

There were no entertainments at Tsarskoe Selo during the war, only a few private cinema exhibitions of special military films, and on these occasions the members of the Household, and sometimes a few guests, were invited. Once Sir George Buchanan was asked to see an English war film; another time M. Paléologue was invited to see a French one. No ladies were asked, except the members of the Household, as the Empress felt too tired to entertain them and the men she could leave to the Emperor.

In the Emperor's absence, she scarcely ever invited anyone to lunch or dine with her. The Empress used meal-times to rest and write letters. The young Grand Duchesses' table was close to her couch. To her, meals were an unimportant matter. She ate very sparingly and had been practically a vegetarian for years. She, of course, fasted all through Lent, as prescribed by the Orthodox Church.

Only once did the Empress give an official luncheon in the Emperor's absence. It was on the occasion of the arrival of the Japanese Prince Kanin in September 1916. She was very nervous, but as the Prince came specially to Tsarskoe Selo to see her, after having been to Mohilev and to Kiev to see the Dowager-Empress, she felt it to be her duty, and was as proud as a girl when her lunch proved to be a success.

The Emperor was almost uninterruptedly at Mohilev during the summer and early autumn of 1916, coming back for short spells in October and November. During his second stay, a slight stir was caused at Court by the visit of the Crown Prince Carol of Rumania on his second visit to Russia. This was the last time a State dinner was given. It was marked by the first official appearance of Grand

Duchess Marie, the Emperor's third daughter. She looked extremely pretty in her pale blue dress, wearing the diamonds that her parents gave to each of their daughters on her sixteenth birthday. Poor child, she felt that the world was coming to an end and that she was disgraced in its eyes forever when she slipped in her new high-heeled shoes and fell down as she was entering the dining-hall on the arm of a tall Grand Duke.

On hearing the noise, the Emperor remarked jokingly, "Of course, fat Marie."

In November 1916 the state of tension in all circles had increased so greatly that it was evident that a serious crisis was imminent. Only the Emperor and Empress did not realize the full gravity of the situation. They believed that alarming reports were spread in order to force reforms on the Emperor which he considered inopportune in time of war. He had listened to the voice of public opinion and had dismissed the unpopular Prime Minister Sturmer. It was said that the Dowager-Empress had urged this when the Emperor had seen her at Kiev in the November. However, Protopopov still remained as Head of the Ministry of the Interior and had succeeded in gaining Their Majesties' confidence, reassuring them that he had the situation in hand and convincing the Empress of his absolute devotion to the Crown. He had been in voluntary service in the Provinces for many years before being in the Duma, which had elected him to the post of Vice-President. This, coupled with his well-known conservative views, made the Emperor trust his knowledge of the country and think that the criticism of him was the result of a cabal trying at all costs to enforce changes.

Protopopov had known Rasputin for a long time and it was said that his whole policy was influenced by the *Staretz*. There were wild stories after Rasputin's death that the Empress had séances with Protopopov to summon his ghost. This was pure invention as the Empress had never practiced spiritualism. Indeed, she often said to me that she considered it wrong to call up "the spirits of the dead, even if this were possible."

Gradually the hostility toward the Empress, based on the political role she was supposed to be playing and on the totally unfounded report of her pro-German tendencies, crept from the corridors of the Duma to the floor of the assembly itself. The deputy Purishkevitch made a speech against the "Dark Powers" which, although ostensibly directed against Rasputin, was really a thinly-veiled attack upon the Empress. Millukov followed, quoting a German paper that said that the Empress influenced Russia's politics. Millukov was a bitter enemy of the Emperor and the Empress, and spoke strongly, referring to German spies and making insinuations against Court officials.

People who heard the debate realized that animosity was spreading from the Empress to drench the whole imperial regime. The instigators of the Revolution of March 1917 were indefatigable in encouraging opposition to the Government. The Bolsheviks for their part were independently pursuing their deadly propaganda against the State. The upper classes, particularly those of Petrograd, had always criticized the Empress. They thought she had ignored them after 1905, during the years which had left her as a semi-invalid. They had wanted to be amused and the Empress had not entertained them as she considered the times were too serious. Her charities and her devotion to her children were ridiculed. Her shyness in her rare public appearances was resented as aloofness. The wildest tales were spread. The name of Rasputin was in every mouth. Sadly, every story was immediately believed by the middle and lower classes who did not know the utter impossibility of the gossip they repeated.

The Imperial Family did not support the Empress as there was a good deal of personal animosity against her there too. She was rigid in her ideas and had more than once expressed her disapproval of youthful follies and other behavior that she had quite justly considered wrong.

243

Sturmer had been succeeded as Prime Minister by Trepov, whose Government met with little support because the more reasonable elements stood aside. Trepov was soon succeeded by Prince Nicholas Galitzin, a senator and formerly a provincial governor. Neither of these was the strong man that the situation demanded. The ship of state was drifting towards disaster. In his memoirs, Rodzianko speaks of a tentative offer made to him to accept the premiership. He says that one of his conditions was that the Empress should be sent to Livadia for the remainder of the war, which was clearly an impossible suggestion for the Emperor even to discuss.

Warning voices began at last to reach the Emperor. Unfortunately, most of the people who tried to speak to him of the danger of the situation coupled their warnings with attacks on the Empress, and the Emperor knew better than anyone the injustice of the charges against her. Both as Sovereign and as her husband he had to refuse to discuss the subject any further. Other people seemed to the Emperor to be speaking from personal motives and he was not convinced that their advice was disinterested.

The tone of some of the letters annoyed him. A revolutionary blast was in the air. A letter of this kind was written to the Empress by a well-known lady in society. By accident or design, the writer managed to hurt the Empress deeply. The letter was meant as an eye-opener but was full of bitterness. It was written, evidently in haste, on small sheets of paper torn from a note pad, although perhaps the writer did not realize how wounding she was alike in tone and in manner. The Emperor was prepared to ignore letters to himself, but this one, addressing the Empress, exhausted his patience and he was advised to make an example of the writer to prevent anything similar happening in the future.

The lady in question was asked by Count Fredericks to retire to her country seat for a time. It was perhaps an injudicious measure, as it made a martyr of the lady and people flocked to her house in sympathy. A few of the older leaders of society expressed their disapproval of her action but the whole incident only created bitter feeling on all sides.

Several members of the Imperial Family also warned the Sovereigns of the increasing disaffection in the country, among them Grand Duke Nicholas Mikhailovich, a well-known historian and a cousin of the Emperor who was murdered by the Bolsheviks in Petrograd in 1919. The Emperor had received earlier letters from the Grand Duke, drawing attention to the dangers of intrigue. He knew his cousin's liberal tendencies and that he openly criticized the Government, the Empress and himself, and he had little faith in his advice, astute though he knew him to be. He had disregarded the Grand Duke's earlier letters and he disregarded this latest one too, and when the Grand Duke spoke vehemently against the Empress in the clubs, he was asked to retire to his country estates.

At about the same time, Grand Duchess Victoria Feodorovna spoke to the Empress of the unpopularity of the Government. The Grand Duchess was restrained in her language and the Empress did not believe that her cousin's apprehensions were well founded. She always thought that she and the Emperor understood any situation better than anyone and she had the assurance, backed up by the authority of the Minister of the Interior, that it was only the desire to frighten the Emperor into granting hasty reforms that caused the spread of these rumors, and in her mind the letters she received from the provinces proved Protopopov right.

Finally, Grand Duchess Ella arrived from Moscow. Even this saintly woman was now reviled and slandered by the seditious elements. She was frightened at the hostility displayed towards her sister and implored her to send Rasputin to his home in Siberia, pointing out that his presence in Petrograd lent credibility to the report that he was influencing the Cabinet, the Empress, and even the politics of the country. The Empress was obdurate. She would not believe in the approaching disaster. She kept her blind faith in the millions of Russia's peasant population. They would understand her faith in the

245

Staretz, whose bodily presence seemed to her necessary to save the Tsarevich. To send him away when the child was continually liable to accidents or illness was impossible. She considered her son's life to be at stake and her sister spoke to her in vain.

The British Ambassador, Sir George Buchanan, was among those who at the last hour tried to open the Emperor's eyes and persuade him to avert disaster by granting constitutional reforms. Unfortunately, the British Ambassador had lost much of the Emperor's confidence during the last year as he had been told that Sir George was in touch with Millukov, Gutchkov, and others of the most advanced liberal group, personal enemies of the Emperor, whom Sir George, as he says in his memoirs, considered simply as members of the 'Opposition' in the British Parliamentary sense. They became those in power after the Revolution of 1917. For this reason the Emperor no longer considered Sir George's opinions impartial, and the friendliness with which both the Emperor and the Empress had always met the British Ambassador, whom they had known as the British Minister in Darmstadt, had been replaced by more official relations.

On January 12, 1917, Sir George sought an audience with the Emperor, whom he says he had personally always liked, to offer him advice on the government of the country. He admits himself that he was acting against all diplomatic precedent and that he felt like a man trying to save a friend he sees falling over a precipice. All the arguments Sir George used had no doubt been heard by the Emperor many times. They might, however, have carried more weight than those of opposing ministers if the Emperor had not believed that Sir George got much of his information from the Opposition in the Duma. The British Ambassador also made the grave mistake of speaking about the supposed political influence of the Empress. These allusions to the Empress wrecked all chances of his advice being accepted and the Emperor dismissed the Ambassador coldly.

I heard from most reliable sources that, if it had not been for the inadvisability of making changes in the Allied representation during the war, the Emperor would have written personally to His Majesty King George to demand Sir George Buchanan's recall. After this interview, the Emperor saw the British Ambassador on official occasions only and all their subsequent conversations were purely formal.

Chapter 25

Rasputin's Murder and the Last Days of Sovereignty: December 1916 to March 1917

The first to suffer in the coming cataclysm was Rasputin. Hatred for the man who was supposed to be responsible for all the Government's mistakes became a real obsession, even with generally level-headed people.

Rumors spread, not without foundation, that he was visited by all kinds of influential people – ministers, like Protopopov, and high officials – and that he used to send short, illiterate notes demanding their help. These rumors firmly established the belief in his hidden power, which was further increased by the way in which Rasputin bragged on all occasions about himself and his influence.

The feeling against him became so intense that a plot was formed to murder him, in which Purishkevitch – a member of the Duma – Prince Felix Yussupov, Grand Duke Dmitri and some others were involved.

It was difficult to lure the *Staretz* into a trap, as, by order of Protopopov, he was constantly guarded by detectives. Prince Felix Yussupov, a personal acquaintance of Rasputin, undertook the task and invited him to an alleged party at his house on the evening of December 29, 1916.

The story of the murder has been so often told that there is no need to repeat it. It is enough to say that Rasputin was first offered poisoned wine – the amateur murderers not knowing that for the poison they chose, alcohol is an antidote – so that their victim survived what appeared to be a deadly dose. Prince Yussupov and Purishkevich then took the *Staretz* into an adjoining room and, as he was admiring an ancient crucifix, shot him several times in the back.

Rasputin's strong frame resisted even this, and when Prince Yussupov returned to remove his body, he got up and staggered across the room.

More shots were fired, this time with effect and the body was taken in a car and thrown into a hole made in the frozen Neva. The strength of the current drove the body down under the ice and it was washed ashore some days later.

The *Staretz* does not seem to have been dead even when he was thrown into the water, for the cords bound around his body were loosened and his rigid hand was folded as if making the sign of the cross.

When the police came to Prince Yussupov's house to ask about the gun shots in the dead of night, they were told that a dog had been shot. The authors of the murder lay low at the time and some even denied any knowledge of it.

In spite of the efforts of the Censor, however, the story of the *Staretz's* disappearance got almost immediately into the Press and caused a tremendous sensation. Although patriotic feeling was supposed to have been the motive of the murder, it was the first indirect blow at the Emperor's authority, the first spark of insurrection. In short, it was the application of lynch law, the taking of law and judgment forcibly into private hands.

No inquest was ordered, on account of the social standing of personalities involved. An imperial order forbade any legal procedure and the murderers of the *Staretz* went unpunished. Both Prince Yussupov and Grand Duke Dmitri were, however, exiled by the Emperor, Prince Yussupov to one of his properties, Grand Duke Dmitri to the Caucasian front. The whole Imperial Family signed a petition to the Emperor, asking leave for the Grand Duke to stay in Petrograd on account of his health, but the Emperor refused, making a marginal note on the petition that "no one had the right to commit murder."

After the first horror-stricken moment of the news of Rasputin's disappearance, the Empress showed her usual spirit. She was holding a reception of ladies, and between the audiences Mme. Vyrubova managed to tell her what had happened. I knew nothing, and went to Her Majesty to tell her that there was still a lady to be received. I heard the door close on Mme. Vyrubova and found the Empress outwardly perfectly calm. I told her that Mme. Vera Narishkin (née Witte) was waiting, and Her Majesty told me to bring her in. Mine. Narishkin had come to talk to the Empress about a workshop for disabled soldiers and she notes in her reminiscences the deep interest that the Empress took in her work and the detailed knowledge that she displayed of the subject.

The body of the *Staretz* was recovered and buried in a piece of ground at Tsarskoe Selo on which Mme. Vyrubova meant to build a chapel for a home for disabled soldiers. The Emperor, Empress and their daughters, Mme. Vyrubova and Father Alexander, their confessor, went early in the morning to the funeral. Then the Empress nerved herself to attend to furnishing the usual numerous Christmas trees for the servants, the escort, and the hospitals, and when Protopopov came to report an alleged plot to murder Her Majesty, she was perfectly cool and calm.

She asked me if I were afraid to drive with her, and this, of course, I energetically denied, but I noticed after this that she seldom took either Countess Hendrikov or myself with her on outings. Her greatest fears were for Mme. Vyrubova, who was almost as hated by the public as was Rasputin himself, and the Empress made her move into the Palace for her greater safety. However, the underlying reason for the unpopularity of Mme. Vyrubova had now ceased to exist, for she could no longer form the link between the Empress and Rasputin, which had been one of the chief allegations made against her.

Letters now began to pour in threatening the Empress herself, and she felt sad and tired, and in her letters to her intimates she signed herself as "an old woman."

Her anxiety for Mme. Vyrubova is shown in a letter to Countess Anastasia (Nastinka) Hendrikov in which she says, "Besides

250

everything, try for a moment to realize what it is to know a friend in daily, hourly danger of also being foully murdered. But God is all mercy …"

Rasputin's death had been a shattering blow to the Empress as she had pinned all her faith on him as the savior of her child. With Rasputin at hand, she had been calmer about the fate of her boy, whose days she now felt were numbered. Then, too, the *Staretz* had said, "When I go, you shall go also," predicting the fall of the Empire.

What would happen now?

Shortly before the New Year, the Emperor left again for Stavka. The Empress was too dispirited and unwell to attend even the customary New Year *Te Deum*, sung at midnight on December 31 in the private chapel of the Alexander Palace.

The food and fuel shortage was becoming more critical by the month in Petrograd. The measures taken by Protopopov were insufficient and long queues of people stood every day for hours in front of the bakers' shops. The Empress was still confident about the political situation, thinking it was only a passing crisis, and that in a couple of weeks, when food distribution was back in working order, all would be well.

At the end of November 1916, Prince Vladimir Mikhailovich Volkhonsky, the late Vice-President of the Duma, told me that the mismanagement of food distribution was such that by the middle of February the population of Petrograd would be without flour, and that we should have famine riots in the capital which, in the alarming state of the country, might imperil the safety of the throne.

Prince Volkhonsky wanted to see the Empress and warn her of the danger and I gave Her Majesty his message. The Empress liked Prince Volkhonsky personally. He had been a playfellow of the Emperor in childhood and had worked with Grand Duchess Olga on one of her charity committees. The Prince was, however, at that time Under-Secretary to the Ministry of the Interior under Protopopov, and the Empress thought it would be disloyal and undermining on her part to listen to the complaints of a second-in-command "behind the chief's back," so Volkhonsky was never received.

The Emperor had contemplated forming a Ministry of National Confidence in January 1917, but in consequence of the great state of ferment the country was in, the plan had, been postponed.

The year began in an atmosphere of anxiety and gloom. The Emperor returned to Tsarskoe Selo shortly after the New Year and remained in the Palace until March 8, anxious and worried. Ministers came and went. All the audiences that had been postponed, and all the business that had been held over, were now dealt with.

Physically, the Emperor was much changed. He looked worn and pale, and had grown extremely thin. His kind eyes had a constant look of worry and sadness, and there were deep lines on his forehead and a suspicious bagginess under his eyes, suggestive of potential heart complications.

His presence was a great comfort to the Empress. Mme. Vyrubova and Mme. Lily Dehn were spending even more time with her now. Mme. Vyrubova was living in the Alexander Palace and gave three small musical parties in her rooms for the young Grand Duchesses, to which the Emperor and Empress came. She invited her usual circle: Mme. Dehn, Countess Emma Fredericks with her sister Mme. Voyeikov, a few girls, and some officers of The Standart who were on leave; also Prince Dolgorukov, Duke Alexander Leuchtenberg and myself. A Rumanian band played, yet although the Grand Duchesses enjoyed any change to the monotony of their lives, there was no gaiety in these entertainments. Everyone was weighed down by the gloom of coming events and all the songs seemed to strike the saddest of notes. I distinctly remember the anxious look on the Emperor's face and the deadly sadness in the Empress' eyes.

Events were now so threatening in the capital that the Emperor decided to stay at Tsarskoe Selo and give all his attention to home affairs. He felt that the disaffection in the rear was seriously beginning

252

to endanger the prospects at the front. To win the war was his sole preoccupation day and night, for he knew that Russia's future as a Great Power depended on victory.

The Emperor's loyalty to his Allies has never been questioned, and he put faith in the great advance that had been planned for the spring both in Russia and in France. All through this winter the Russian armies were preparing, and were being reorganized and reformed. It was in connection with this reorganization that the Emperor was persuaded, against his will, to return to Stavka on March 8. It was only after an urgent telegram from General Alekseyev that he decided to go, and he went with the intention of staying only eight days.

I happened to be with the Empress on business when the Emperor came in with General Alekseyev's telegram in his hand. He told me to stay, saying to the Empress, "General Alekseyev insists on my coming. I cannot really imagine what can have happened to make my presence at Stavka so urgently necessary now. I shall have to go and see myself. I am determined to stay only a week at the utmost, for I must be here."

Was it a plot? God knows! The Revolution broke out during those eight days. Had the Emperor been at Tsarskoe Selo, and had Rodzianko been in direct communication with him, the Emperor would have had the whole machinery of government in his hands. The Revolution, which was at first only a local rising in Petrograd, might have been stamped out and all the subsequent tragedies averted.

After the Emperor's departure, the Tsarevich and Grand Duchess Olga fell ill with measles, caught from one of the Tsarevich's friends who had been spending the weekend at the Palace. The Empress held diplomatic receptions on March 9 and March 10, warning all those who might have been afraid of infection. It was the first time for many years that she had received the Diplomatic Corps. Her health had for a long time prevented her from accompanying the Emperor to the New Year receptions and often foreign ministers came and went without ever seeing the Empress. This year she felt stronger, as she had not tired herself so much in travelling, and she received together all the Ministers and Secretaries of Foreign Missions whom she had not yet seen.

In Petrograd many of the workmen were already on strike. There had been minor riots in consequence of the "lines" and the atmosphere was thunderous. The Danish Minister, M. de Scavenius, said to me on March 10 that the situation in the town was very grave. I was alarmed, for in the Palace we had lulled ourselves into believing that no serious uprising would take place during the war and the Emperor's gentlemen had confirmed this opinion.

The Diplomatic Reception went off with its usual pomp – Masters of Ceremonies, runners in feathered hats, servants in gold-laced liveries, preceding the Diplomatic Corps. The Empress was very gracious to all and they went away captivated by her charm.

This was the last function – for five days later the Empire of Russia was no more.

Chapter 26

Revolution: March 1917

In Petrograd, the strikes spread gradually from one factory to another, the non-political workmen joining the seditious elements as the scarcity of food became more serious. Dissatisfaction with the Government was turning into hostility toward the monarchy and was expressed openly and extended to everyone and everything connected with the Court. I myself saw an inscription that said "Down with the Tsar!" written on the frozen wall of the Headquarters of the Staff close to the Winter Palace. It was removed but appeared again the next morning. On March 4, as my carriage was stopped in the street, a passerby deliberately spat through the open window. The hostility was out in the open now.

At Tsarskoe Selo, the gravity of the situation was still barely realized even by members of the Household, and not at all by the Empress. So unexpected was the turn of events that as late as March 11, Countess Hendrikov, one of the ladies-in-waiting, left on a visit to a sick sister in the Caucasus – a four days' journey. On the day of her arrival at her destination she heard of the revolution in Petrograd and rushed back, arriving at Tsarskoe Selo on March 22 and remaining with the Empress from that moment on.

The Imperial Household believed that these strikes were like previous ones, merely an outpouring of dissatisfaction caused by the food shortage, and that the fresh supplies ordered by the Government would prevent the movement from spreading. Protopopov had succeeded in persuading the Empress of this, and also that all the necessary measures had been taken by the police to prevent any serious uprising.

It was at this moment that Alexei and Olga fell ill with measles. Tatiana and Mme. Vyrubova soon followed. As her rooms were at the far end of the Palace, the Empress spent her days running from the sickrooms of her children to that of her friend.

On March 11, although there were street riots in Petrograd, the Empress received Professor Madsen of the Copenhagen Serum Institute, who had come to discuss the possibility of producing more anti-tetanus serum in Russia. On Monday, March 12, I telephoned Mme. Sazonov in Petrograd at nine o'clock a.m., at the Empress' request, asking her to lunch that day. Mme. Sazonov said that it would be impossible for her to reach the station. There was fighting in the streets and the Preobrajensky Regiment, whose barracks were opposite her house on the Kirotchnaia, had mutinied and were using machine guns. Senator Neidhardt, her brother, in whose house she was staying, continued the conversation with me, and when he discovered that we knew nothing in the Palace, gave me an account of the happenings of the night before and of the mutiny of the Paul, Preobrajensky and Volhynsky regiments, asking me to report it to the Empress.

I went at once to Her Majesty's room. She was still in bed, but her maid, Madeleine Zanotti, told her I wanted to see her urgently, and I was called in. I told her everything Neidhardt had said. She listened with perfect self-possession, only remarking that, if the troops had mutinied, "it was all up," and asking me to send for Colonel Grooten, Acting-Commander of the Palace in General Voyeikov's absence.

Grooten told her that, although several regiments had mutinied in Petrograd, the garrison at Tsarskoe Selo was still perfectly loyal, that the events of the past night had been reported to General Headquarters, and that General Ivanov was coming, by the Emperor's orders, with trustworthy troops to put down the rioting in the capital.

Count Benckendorff had telephoned to General Voyeikov at General Headquarters on the previous day, asking for the Emperor's instructions should the riots become worse. General Voyeikov had

256

replied that "according to his information, things had been greatly exaggerated." The Emperor was sending General Ivanov with the St. George Battalion to quell the rebellion and did not want the Empress to be troubled by any idea of leaving Tsarskoe Selo unless the danger became imminent, as the Emperor was himself returning.

General Voyeikov was optimistic all through and succeeded, apparently, in imparting his optimism to the Emperor. Their Majesties had so often heard reports of dangerous conspiracies, and so many alleged plots were supposed to have been discovered by the police, that they were almost fatalistic about it. They were always inclined to think, too, that reports were exaggerated by those who wanted to keep them at Tsarskoe Selo, out of harm's way. The Emperor in particular always disliked alarmist reports.

General Ressine, Commander of the Svodnyi Regiment which mounted guard inside the Palace, who was under General Voyeikov's orders, told me in January 1917 that he was very anxious about the morale of the men of the Palace Guard, as there had been much revolutionary propaganda. The Department of Police had also given him serious warnings. Ressine had passed all this on to Voyeikov, but, to his despair, his chief had brushed it all aside. So, it was only natural that the Emperor should disregard the hints of private individuals when the Minister of the Interior and General Voyeikov, who were responsible for his personal safety, both assured him that there was no real danger.

The Empress telegraphed to the Emperor on March 11 and was uneasy when she got no answer from him. From this moment, indeed, no communication was allowed to pass between them. She had also written to the Emperor, begging him to make political concessions, the letter being sent by the wife of an officer who volunteered to take it by hand. It reached the Emperor too late. He was never able to act on it, or to answer her.

March 12 passed quietly at Tsarskoe Selo. The Empress begged her ladies to go on working at the *sklad* so as to discourage any idea of panic. She herself spent the whole day with her sick children, who were getting worse. She wrote to me on the evening of March 11 that their temperatures were high:

> *Olga 39-9 [103F.], Tatiana 39-3 [102F.], Alexei 40 [104F.], Ania [Mme. Vyrubova] 40-3 [104F]. It's normal when high, the rash coming out very strong. Thank God, none have so far complications. Yes, indeed, a heavy time. [The Empress often unconsciously translated from Russian when writing in English.] But faith keeps up. Kiss-sleep well! A.*

The complications soon appeared, however, for Tatiana developed abscesses in her ears and Olga developed pericarditis. Grand Duchess Anastasia soon joined her sisters in the sick room, although the Grand Duchess Marie remained well for a few days longer. She was constantly with her mother, acting as her "legs," as she said, trying to persuade her to rest, and running messages because the electric current for the lift had been cut off on March 13. These days, in which she was her mother's sole support, turned her from a child into a woman.

On March 12, unknown to the Empress, the question of her leaving Tsarskoe Selo was discussed by Count Benckendorff and Colonel Grooten. They came to no decision as they knew that the Empress did not want to go, and no orders to that effect had been received from the Emperor, who was believed to be on his way back.

On the same evening, the President of the Duma, Rodzianko, telephoned to Count Benckendorff, ostensibly to inquire about the Tsarevich, rumors of whose death had been circulating in Petrograd, but really to advise the Empress to take her children away as the situation was so serious that it demanded extreme measures.

The Empress had said to me that to go "would look like flight," and she was also afraid of the risk to the children in moving them while they were still so ill. On the morning of March 13, however, she told me that I should "quietly pack my bag to be able to start with them at any moment, should this prove necessary."

That morning, the gentlemen raised the question of the Empress' departure, but it was too late. When they asked the commander of the railway battalion if the imperial train could be immediately brought from Petrograd to Tsarskoe Selo for the Empress' departure, stating at the same time that four hours would be needed for the Court's preparations before they could start, he said that even if he could get the train from the capital – which was doubtful – he feared that in four hours' time events might have developed to the point that the train would be halted further up the line. Had the Empress and her children started out on March 12, or even early on March 13, in an ordinary train, they would certainly have been able to reach the Emperor at Mohilev or at least on the way.

The Empress was still without news from the Emperor and she could scarcely master her anxiety. The Emperor usually answered a telegram from her within a couple of hours, and she read into his silence that the situation had become critical outside Petrograd too.

Mme. Dehn now volunteered to help the Empress in nursing the children, and her sympathy and calmness made her a real support. Of all the Empress' ladies, only I and the *lectrice*, Mlle. Schneider, remained in the Palace. Mme. Narishkin was in Petrograd and was not able to come until March 20, and Countess Hendrikov had left for the Caucasuses. General Ressine, General Dobrovolsky and Colonel Grooten were there all the time, as were Drs. Botkin and Derevenko, and M. Gilliard. Count Apraxin came at Count Benckendorff's request on the morning of March 13, and Count and Countess Benckendorff came over from the Lyceum building on the evening of March 13 and took over Countess Hendrikov's rooms.

The Empress saw the gentlemen and me several times a day in a quarantine room, so as to avoid spreading the infection further, and according to her habit she wrote me short notes in between. She was

259

always a great letter-writer and preferred writing notes to the trouble of coming to the telephone. Her friends and the members of her household used to get many such little notes containing her orders or comments on any events that had impressed her.

Count Apraxin arrived from Petrograd with a most alarming tale. Nearly all the regiments in the capital had joined the revolutionaries. The Government had entrenched itself in the Admiralty under the protection of the few remaining loyal troops and was having continuous sittings, which led to no result as executive power had slipped out of their hands. The Duma had ignored the imperial decree for its prorogation, which had been issued before events had reached their present crisis, and had assumed the direction of affairs.

On the evening of March 13, the Tsarskoe Selo garrison, which had until then refused to join the rebels, left their barracks, and marched out, firing their rifles into the air and at houses as passed them. They went first to the local prison and threw open the doors, to the delight of its inmates. These were mostly thieves, as only less serious offenders were kept in a prison near to the imperial residence. From here they looted the neighboring wine shops. Thoroughly aroused, and mostly drunk, several thousands of them started for the Alexander Palace, intending to seize the Empress and the heir, and take them to the Revolutionary Headquarters in Petrograd. Their wild firing gave the alarm to the Palace Guards consisting of two battalions of the Svodnyi Regiment, one battalion of the Naval Guards (1,200 strong), two squadrons of Cossacks of the Escort, one company of the 1st Railway Regiment, and one Heavy Field Battery from Pavlovsk, under the command of Count Rehbinder.

It fell to me again to bring the news of the mutiny of the troops to the Empress. She was in the sickrooms and was just crossing the corridor when I came upstairs. She was quite alive to the danger but most painfully surprised at hearing that the Tsarskoe Selo garrison, on whose loyalty we had all counted, had mutinied.

She went at once to the children to tell them that maneuvers were going on so that they should not be frightened by any sound of firing. She then asked me to call the gentlemen and came down to discuss the situation with Count Apraxin and General Ressine.

The Empress could not bear the idea of people fighting on her account and begged that the troops defending the Palace should not in any way provoke their assailants, so not a single shot was fired by the Palace Guards. She then threw a black fur cloak over her white nurses' dress and, accompanied by Grand Duchess Marie and by Count Benckendorff, went out herself to speak to the soldiers of the Guards.

She went into the courtyard and all through the Palace basement, where the men came in turns to warm themselves, telling the soldiers how fully she trusted in their loyalty to the Emperor, and how well she knew that, if need arose, they would defend the heir, but that she hoped that no blood need be shed.

The scene was unforgettable: It was dark except for a faint light thrown up from the snow and reflected on the polished barrels of the rifles. The troops were lined up in battle order in the courtyard, the first line kneeling in the snow, the others standing behind, their rifles in readiness for a sudden attack. The figures of the Empress and her daughter passed like dark shadows from line to line, the white Palace looming a ghostly mass in the background. Firing from nearby could be heard amid wild gusts of wind. The mutinous troops had reached the so-called "Chinese village" near the Big Palace, but the Cossack patrols reported that they would not venture farther as they had heard that immense forces were massed in the Palace courtyard and that machine guns were stationed on the roof. Neither of these rumors was true but they served our purpose, for the mutineers decided that they would not attack the Palace until the morning.

Inside the Palace, the night was passed in great anxiety. Firing was heard at intervals and the Cossacks reported that an armored train manned by rebel troops from Petrograd was moving up and down the line between the capital and the imperial station at Tsarskoe Selo. It was rumored that the rebels were anxious to get possession of the Empress and her children to hold them as hostages in case things went against them, while further rumors said that they had sworn to murder the Empress.

The Benckendorffs, Count Apraxin and I spent the whole of that night in the Empress' rooms so as to be near her in case of a sudden attack. Our small company had been increased by the addition of one of the Emperor's aides-de-camp, Count Adam Zamoyski, who, hearing of the danger to the Empress and her children, had come with the greatest difficulty from the capital, part of the way on foot. He stayed at the Palace until he was recalled by orders of General Headquarters. I must place his conduct on record, for he came at once to the Empress in her hour of need although he was one of the A.D.C.s whom she had known least.

A little later Colonel Linevitch, another A.D.C., also arrived. During the evening the Empress was wheeled in her bath chair over to Mme. Vyrubova's room. Mme. Vyrubova was terrified by the sound of firing and felt that something was being kept from her, which was indeed the case as it was considered that the agitation of knowing the truth would increase her already high fever.

I went with the Empress across the vast dark halls – the electric light and water supply had been cut off by the revolutionaries – and our feet echoed uncannily in the empty rooms. We did not meet a soul: All the servants who were usually about the house had fled; only the Empress' personal staff remained at their posts.

Even now the Empress was thinking of others. She tried to calm old Countess Benckendorff, and in the evening, when the Countess and I were preparing to camp on sofas in the green sitting room, Her Majesty suddenly walked in with pillows and blankets from her own bedroom. She went to her room herself, but did not sleep, only resting for a few hours while Grand Duchess Marie, who was quite worn out, slept on the bed beside her, and three or four times during the night she came in to us, looking like a ghost in her nurses' dress, her face pale, her features sharpened by anxiety, to share what news we might have of events outside or of the Emperor's movements. On one of these occasions she brought some biscuits and fruit for the Countess. She always had some in her bedroom to eat during sleepless hours. I saw then how oblivious she was to outward things, for she had not noticed that she was in stockinged feet, having taken off her shoes to lie down.

At one moment during that night we heard a sudden rush of heavy feet along the balcony outside the Empress' rooms and the same thought struck the Countess and myself, that the insurgents had broken through the lines of defense and had come to lay hands on the Empress. I went to the balcony door, asking Countess Benckendorff to take the Empress upstairs to the children while I parleyed with the men. To my immense relief, I found, on opening the door, that the men who were hammering so violently were only some of the sailors who did not understand the geography of the Palace and had come to the wrong entrance on their way to warm themselves in the basement as it was twenty-two degrees Celsius below zero outside. The gentlemen of the Court spent the night walking about the corridors and descending at intervals to the guardroom.

It was known that the Emperor had left Mohilev and at six in the morning the Empress came in again to ask for news of him. Nothing had been heard and we were all seriously alarmed. The Empress grew whiter than ever when Countess Benckendorff volunteered the unfortunate remark, "Et cést le premier mars aujourd'hui," (And it's the first of March today – the anniversary of the assassination of Alexander II).

The Empress pulled herself together and said, "Il y a des difficultés en chemin, probablement, le train ne tardera pas à venir," (There have probably been some delays along the way. The train will be here soon). It was not until eight in the morning on March 14 that Grooten heard that the Emperor's train had been held up at Malaia Vischera and was coming to Tsarskoe Selo via Gatchina.

It was lucky that the insurgents did not continue their attempt to storm the Palace. Had they done so, they would have taken it easily, for they would have found the troops guarding it completely unprepared to resist their assault. Until patrols were set up, no one knew exactly where the revolutionaries were, nor what they were doing. No plan of defense had been set up and great anxiety was caused by a rumor that the revolutionaries had mounted two siege guns in the Sophia in Tsarskoe Selo, and intended using them against the Palace in order to destroy it completely. Fortunately they had no ammunition, although this was not known at the time.

The whole of March 14 passed without news of the Emperor. Outside the Palace, the firing ceased and the revolutionaries decided to join their comrades in Petrograd to await further developments.

On March 13, the Empress sent for Grand Duke Paul, the Emperor's uncle. I was told by Grand Duchess Marie, who was in the next room, that their interview was a very stormy one and that the Empress severely criticized the fact that all the troops in the Petrograd military district were reservists from the adjoining factories. After this one heated conversation, however, Grand Duke Paul – who was murdered by the Bolsheviks on January 29, 1919 – was kindness itself to the Empress, and he and his wife, Princess Paley, wrote several times to Their Majesties during their imprisonment.

During these first days, the only way in which the occupants of the Palace could get news about what was happening in the town was during short conversations on the private telephone that connected the Winter Palace in Petrograd with the Alexander Palace at Tsarskoe Selo, and the people in the Winter Palace only knew what was going on in its immediate neighborhood.

One or two servants came on foot from the capital, as there was no longer any train service, and some of these described the murders of officers and police, which they or their relations had seen or heard of. Others said that the Duma was taking the situation in hand and that things were improving. There was complete confusion, and since no newspapers appeared, there was no way of getting reliable information.

A kind of agreement had been reached at Tsarskoe Selo between the soldiers inside and outside of the Palace that they would await developments, for it was reported that two delegates from the Duma had gone to meet the Emperor. In the meantime the Palace guard, who wore white bands on their arms as a distinguishing mark, saw that no one left the Palace.

On March 14, Grand Duke Paul sent the Empress the draft of a manifesto granting a constitution which he wanted Her Majesty to sign, some of the Grand Dukes having already signed it. However, the Empress refused to do so, telling me that, although she considered it necessary for concessions to be made, for her to sign such a paper would look "as if I did just the things that I am accused of doing that I do not do. I am not the Regent and I have no right to take any initiative in the Emperor's absence. Besides, such a paper would be quite without legality and worth nothing at all."

Later on that same night, General Ivanov arrived from General Headquarters and asked to see the Empress at 2am. He had been sent in command of the troops that were to put down the rioting in the capital and had left them at Vyritza, some twenty versts away. He wanted the Empress to give him authority to use the troops guarding the Palace to protect his rear while he himself marched on Petrograd with the St. George battalion.

The Empress replied very reasonably that he had full powers and instructions from the Emperor and that he must act as he thought best, as she could not interfere in military matters.

General Ivanov, as a matter of fact, did nothing at all. He stayed with the St. George's battalion at Vyritza and did not even disembark his men from the train, and after the Emperor's abdication, he returned

265

by orders of General Headquarters to Mohilev. The fact that he had seen the Empress was used as another point against her and she was accused of having plotted with him to bring about a counter-revolution.

In the meantime, the number of troops at the Alexander Palace dwindled. Early on March 15, the Equipage de la Garde was recalled to Petrograd, by order of their commander, Grand Duke Cyril Vladimirovich, or so it was said. It was a poignant moment for the Empress when she saw the colors that had always been kept at the Palace taken away. Count Benckendorff insisted that this should not be done secretly and the colors left with the usual ceremonial and with the guard drawn up in the courtyard and the band playing. The Empress had always loved the Navy, and the officers and men of their beloved Standart had been greatly spoilt by the Imperial Family, and now the Naval colors were the first to leave the Palace.

The Empress heard the sound of drums and looked out of the window at the exact moment they passed below, watching the scene with tears that no danger to her personally had been able to make her shed. The loss of the colors seemed symbolic of all the other things that were slipping away.

Chapter 27

The Emperor's Abdication – March 15, 1917 – and the Arrest of the Empress

On March 16, some of the imperial servants who had been in Petrograd returned on foot and we learned from them that leaflets announcing the Emperor's abdication at Pskov were being distributed to people in the capital.

At first no one in the Palace could believe this terrible news. It seemed incredible, and how could the Emperor be at Pskov, when the last that had been heard of him was that he was on his way from General Headquarters to Tsarskoe Selo? Then, late in the afternoon, Grand Duke Paul came as the bearer of bad tidings to the Empress. Count Benckendorff had already warned her of the rumors reported by the servants, but she had refused to believe them. The Grand Duke, however, had come to confirm the news, which at first she found almost impossible to grasp. Count Benckendorff told me that the Grand Duke was terribly upset and very apprehensive as to the future. The uncertainty of the whole situation seemed bound to lead to disaster.

After dinner I went with Count Benckendorff and Count Apraxin to the Empress, wishing to assure her of our personal loyalty. The Empress received us in her daughters' schoolroom. She was deadly pale and supported herself with one hand on the class room table. I could not think of any words in which to say to her what I felt, and when the Empress kissed me, I could only cling to her and murmur some broken words of affection. Count Benckendorff held her hand, tears running down his usually immobile face.

The Empress spoke to us in French, as neither Count Benckendorff nor Count Apraxin could speak English, translating, as she often did, unconsciously from English. "Cest pour le mieux. C'est la volonté de Dieu. Dieu donne que cela sauve la Russie. C'est la seule chose qui signifie." (It is all for the best. It is God's wish and may God ordain it that it Russia be saved. That is the only thing that matters.) Before we shut the door we could see her sinking into her chair by the table, sobbing bitterly and covering her face with her hands.

Later that same night, the servants brought us Grand Duke Michael's manifesto, in which he refused to take up the reins of government before a Constitutional Assembly had decided what the future form of that Government should be. This was the starting-point of chaos and in one moment all the structure of the Empire was broken down as it left nothing to which the nation could cling. What had begun as a military revolt, supported, it is true, by the general discontent caused by the mismanagement of a weak Ministry, led to complete disaster. The strong monarchist element that still existed both in the country and at the front had now no rallying point, while the revolutionaries profited from the general confusion to take the power into their own hands.

In one of her notes to me at this time, the Empress wrote, "It is a merciful Providence that fits the back to the burden."

At the moment when her fears for the Emperor were at their most acute, her children's health began to give her the gravest anxiety. Tatiana was suffering terribly from her ears, and had, temporarily, become quite deaf. Anastasia also had abscesses and her ear drums had to be pierced. Brave little Marie had fallen ill too. During that agonizing day she told me that she felt that she was "in for it." I implored her to go to bed, as she seemed to be very feverish, but she would not think of doing so "till Papa is back," and she insisted I keep her illness secret from the Empress. I agreed to say nothing on her express promise that she would not go out of doors.

As it turned out, Marie could not wait for the Emperor's arrival before giving way to her illness. She had caught a chill while the rash was emerging and developed double pneumonia, to lie at death's door, her temperature always 104 Fahrenheit. In her fevered dreams she was haunted by imaginary soldiers all coming to kill her mother!

Rumors reached us that the Emperor had left Pskov, where the abdication had taken place, presumably for Mohilev, but everything we heard was vague and I had never seen the Empress in such distress. She did not put her fears into actual words, but she was tormented by the dread that the Emperor had been murdered. She could not believe that, after his abdication, he would still be prevented from giving her news of himself or from inquiring after his children. She hid everything from the children themselves, who were too ill to keep abreast of what was happening in any case, and as their rooms were darkened, they could not see her tell-tale haggard face.

At our daily interviews I could feel the force of her suppressed anxiety. "There is nothing I would not do! Let them kill me, put me in a convent – only that the Emperor should be safe and should be with his children again," she wrote to me. Her chief sorrow was for the loneliness she knew he must be feeling at such a moment. These were her moments of weakness. "God will help. He will not leave us," she said.

Her faith came to her rescue. Gradually out of that terrible mental suffering she gained a serenity in which she could bear anything, and could be a support to all those round her.

There was one night when Marie was so ill that Dr. Botkin wanted me to warn the Empress that he feared she would not live. I refused to speak to her about it, saying that Her Majesty knew enough of illness to realize her daughter's danger, and I would not cause her additional suffering by putting it into words. I was right in this, for that night the crisis abated and the Grand Duchess's strong constitution pulled her through.

In one way, the children's illness was a help to their mother, for it absorbed her thoughts and kept her constantly busy. On the other hand, had they not been ill, the whole Imperial Family would probably have left the country at the very outbreak of the Revolution.

It was not until March 17 that the Empress got a telegram from the Emperor announcing his arrival at Mohilev. Here he was to hand over the military command to General Alekseyev and to see the Dowager-Empress. Much though the Empress must have longed to be in her mother-in-law's place, she still said gratefully that she thanked God "that he had his mother with him."

Later on the same day, the Emperor was allowed to telephone his wife. Volkov, the Empress' old page, told me that she ran down the stairs like a girl when she heard that the Emperor was on the line. Their conversation was short, listeners at both ends preventing any intimate conversation. They only spoke of the children's health, the Emperor opening the conversation by saying "You know?" and the Empress replying, "Yes." The Emperor was also able to announce his early return to Tsarskoe Selo, which relieved the Empress' mind greatly, but from this time a premonition of dire calamity began to grow upon her.

Little by little news sifted through from Petrograd, as it was still possible to keep up telephonic communication on the private line to the Winter Palace, although the ordinary telephone had been cut off. In this way we heard of the murders of police and of officers by their men in the barracks, and of the burning of law courts and of police stations by the escaped and liberated prisoners who took care to destroy all police records in which their own past misdeeds were recorded. Many private houses had been set on fire, among them that of old Count Fredericks, whose eighty-year-old wife was only carried to safety just in time.

There was constant fear that the maddened and drunken hordes of soldiers would come to Tsarskoe Selo and vent their fury on the Empress and her children and there was no sleep for anyone in the Palace during those first nights, and no one thought of meals.

There were constant alarms when motorized trucks full of armed soldiers stopped in front of the locked gates of the Palace and for three days the courtyard looked like a camp. The men, fully armed, warmed themselves at open fires, and field kitchens, where the regimental cooks were preparing the men's meals, smoked. It became more and more difficult to cater for them as the provisions in the Palace, as well as those in the Cossack barracks, were becoming exhausted. The water supply had been cut off and water could be obtained only by breaking the ice on the pond.

The situation could not last, and with the abdication of the Emperor the state of siege was brought to an end. When this news was known, it caused the deepest dejection among the faithful members of the Palace Guards. There was nothing they could do now, they felt, but to show their allegiance to the Provisional Government that had been formed by the Duma from among its members. During that night, one detachment of soldiers after another left for the capital. In the morning, when the reliefs came round, they found their predecessors gone and they, too, melted away.

Count Benckendorff realized the danger to the Empress if she were left wholly unprotected and persuaded Her Majesty to ask the Provisional Government to take some measures to safeguard the Imperial Family. The Emperor's A.D.C., Linevitch, who was now also at the Palace, went with a white flag to Petrograd on this mission, but although he had been promised that he would be able to reach the Duma, he was arrested on arrival and unable to deliver his message.

At Petrograd, nearly all the members of the Cabinet had been arrested and at Tsarskoe Selo the same fate befell the higher Palace officials. Finally Count Benckendorff managed to get into communication by telephone with Rodzianko, and on the March 18 the latter sent the newly appointed Minister of War Gutchkov and General Kornilov to Tsarskoe Selo to see how matters stood.

Gutchkov came late at night, accompanied by a large retinue of suspicious looking men who went everywhere, abusing the servants for working for the oppressors and reviling the Court suite, whom they described as "bloodsuckers."

The Empress telephoned Grand Duke Paul to ask him to be present at her first interview with the representatives of the new Government. The Grand Duke duly arrived, and toward midnight the Empress and he received Gutchkov and Kornilov. They asked the Empress if she had everything she wanted. She said she had all she needed for herself and for her children, but asked that her hospitals at Tsarskoe Selo should be kept up and their needs attended to. After this visit Gutchkov made arrangements for a guard at the Palace, and at Count Benckendorff's request appointed an officer to be an intermediary between the Government and the Palace. From this time, little by little, the soldiers seemed gradually to cease being guards and protectors and to become jailers.

Before the town telephone was cut off, some people sent messages of sympathy to the Empress and inquired after the children. There were not many of these inquiries, but the Empress' gratitude for them was extreme. Too many people to whom she had been kind in the time of her prosperity were neither seen nor heard of. Many more did not answer the letters that the Grand Duchesses wrote to them, fearing to be compromised by association with the Court. Even one of the children's doctors felt it necessary to sever his connections with the Empress, and sent a message to say that he no longer considered himself a Court doctor. Conversely, another doctor, a man who had never attended the Grand Duchesses before, came to Tsarskoe Selo during the worst days and offered his services, and the Emperor's dentist, Dr. S. S. Kostritsky, came all the way from the Crimea to Tobolsk, at great personal risk, to attend his old patient.

On March 20, when the trains were running again, Captain D. V. Dehn, also an A.D.C., came from Petrograd to place himself at the Empress' disposal, offering to come with his wife (née Scheremetiev, a distant relation of the Emperor's) to live in the Palace. The Empress gratefully accepted this offer, but as Captain Dehn was leaving the Palace, he was arrested and prevented from returning.

Princess Obolensky, the Empress' former lady-in-waiting, arrived about this time with the same offer, but was not allowed to stay in the Palace. Madame Voyeikov and Countess Sophie Fersen also came to express their sympathy. These evidences of friendship comforted the Empress, but how few they were compared with the many that were silent.

The officers of the regiments that had formed the Palace Guard were faithful to the last. When they were ordered away, they all came to take leave of the Empress, and some of the Cossacks wept bitterly.

An incident that struck us as being particularly characteristic of the tragedy of the moment occurred immediately after news of the abdication was received. Looking out of the window, I saw dimly through the falling snow a small, bedraggled group of horsemen parleying in front of the great closed gates. Horses and riders looked exhausted: The animals were hanging their heads from sheer weariness, while the men still tried to retain a military bearing. After the conversation had lasted some time, I saw them moving slowly away. This was a reserve squadron of the Chevalier guard regiment, which was stationed at the Muraviev barracks, near Novgorod, some 150 versts from Tsarskoe Selo. On hearing what was happening in Petrograd, the young officer in command had set off with his men for Tsarskoe Selo. They rode for two days through the bitter cold and over roads deep in snow, hardly ever stopping, so the men and horses were on their last legs by the time they reached the Palace, where they were told that they had come too late: There was no longer an Emperor and there was no monarchy to defend. They rode away, the picture of utter dejection, and the Empress was unable even to send them a message of thanks, although their loyalty was one of the things that she never forgot.

It was especially hard for the Empress, with her inherent belief in the goodness of human nature, to bear the bitter disappointment that she felt in the change of attitude of those she had thought of as friends, but she still held to the conviction that it was not the whole country that had turned against the Imperial Family and that there remained many people loyal to the Emperor who could not show what they felt.

Of the members of the Imperial Family at Petrograd only a few showed any sympathy for the Empress. Grand Duchess Xenia wrote her sister-in-law a letter full of affection and Grand Duke Paul was chivalrous and kind, and he and his wife, Princess Paley, offered the Empress the use of their house in Boulogne in case she should ever need it. The Empress was grateful for the offer, but it gave her a shock to realize that, in addition to everything else, it might be necessary for them to leave Russia. The aged Queen Olga of Greece and her niece, Princess Ioan of Russia, continued to come to the Palace for as long as they were allowed, and whenever possible they wrote and sent flowers to the Empress. Grand Duchess Ella was in Moscow and not allowed to leave the precincts of her convent or even to communicate with her sister.

On March 21, the day before the Emperor's return, General Kornilov came to place the Empress officially under arrest by order of the Provisional Government. The Empress received him in her green drawing room, dressed as usual in her nurses' white overall. When he read her the order of arrest, she said she was glad that the task had fallen to him, as he himself knew what it was like to be a prisoner, as General Kornilov had been a prisoner of war in Austria, and she was sure he would know what she felt. She repeated to him the request she had made to Gutchkov about her hospitals and ambulance trains, and asked that the servants in attendance on the invalids might be allowed to stay, saying that now she was only a mother looking after her sick children. Count Benckendorff, who was present, said that her dignity was wonderful during this interview.

Kornilov told Count Benckendorff that all those who wanted to stay with the Empress would also be placed under arrest and would have to follow the same regulations; those who preferred to remain at liberty must leave within twenty-four hours. The Benckendorffs, Mme. Narishkin, Mlle. Schneider, M. Gilliard, and myself said we would certainly remain, as did Countess Hendrikov, who arrived from the Crimea the next day. General Ressine left, as his regiment had failed to elect him as their commander. Count Apraxin asked for permission to stay for a couple of days and then left too, considering that he could be of more use to the Empress if he were looking after her affairs in the capital.

The Empress awaited the arrival of the Emperor with great impatience as he was expected the next day following her arrest, and the first realization of her changed circumstances was when she asked to have the usual *Te Deum* sung in the Palace Church for his safe arrival, and her request was refused.

The Alexander Palace was now completely cut off from the outer world, as I was told by the girl at the telephone exchange when I tried to send a message of thanks from the Empress to a lady who had inquired after the children. All the entrances to the Palace, except one, were securely locked and sealed, the keys being placed in charge of the newly appointed Commander of the Palace, a former Lancer, Colonel Paul Kotzebue, who was in a very difficult position. He was being spied upon by the soldiers, who were becoming very undisciplined since they had acquired their "rights," and at the same time he could not forget that he was one of the officers of the Empress' regiment. He was courteous to the Imperial Family and did his best to smooth matters over, but the soldiers were really the masters and he had to be guided by their moods.

The Empress now had the difficult task of explaining to the children what had happened, so as to spare the Emperor when he arrived. She asked M. Gilliard to tell the little Tsarevich, while she herself told her daughters. The children were as brave as their mother, and not for a moment did they think of anything except how to help their parents. Although they were still weak from illness, they all mastered their emotions while she was with them. Tatiana was still so deaf that she could not follow her mother's rapid words, her voice rendered husky with emotion, and her sisters had to write down the details before she could understand. No one knows what they said to one another when they were alone, but when the Empress came back to them, the four girls did their best to cheer her up by speaking with joy of the Emperor's return the next day.

Chapter 28

Prisoners at Tsarskoe Selo: March-August 1917

On a gray, cold morning, the Emperor, accompanied by Prince Vassili Alexandrovich Dolgorukov, drove from the station to the Alexander Palace at Tsarskoe Selo. His car was stopped at the gates. "Who goes there?" came the challenge, the reply from one of the soldiers being, "It is Nicholas Romanov." A long parley followed before the gates were opened and the car was allowed to drive up to the private entrance, the soldiers wanting to show by this reception the way in which they intended to treat their former Sovereign in the future.

The Emperor got out and crossed the hall, where he was met by Count Benckendorff and Count Apraxin. He saluted, mechanically the score of curious men and officers who were collected there. Very few of them deigned to acknowledge the salute. The men were already beginning to lose their military bearing and seemed to think that they could best show their liberal feelings by neglecting their outward appearance.

The Emperor went at once to the children's rooms, where the Empress was waiting for him. No one was present at their meeting. As the Empress said to me afterward, the joy of finding each other alive was the only consolation they had. We, meanwhile, were hearing the story of the abdication from Prince Dolgorukov.

When the news from Petrograd had first become alarming, it was decided that the Emperor should return to the capital as he had heard from Rodzianko, the President of the Duma, that this was the last chance for him to gain concessions from the Government. However, with the usual slowness of Court mechanisms, the Emperor's departure was delayed by long preparations until the night of March 13-14, by when much valuable time was lost.

The Emperor did not want his movements to interfere with the planned movements of munition trains bound for the front, so that, instead of following General Ivanov's military trains, the imperial train had taken the Bologoe-Vischera route and was not even preceded by the usual pilot engine. At Vischera, crowds of railway workmen with dark and hostile faces hung about the station and the engineers announced that the line farther on was in revolutionary hands. The imperial train had then to turn back and try to reach Tsarskoe Selo via Pskov-Gatchina.

At Pskov, the Emperor was held up by General Russki, who told him of the imminent arrival of delegates from the Duma. When the Emperor gave him a telegram to send to Rodzianko, granting wide concessions, General Russki delayed sending it, and when the members of the Duma – Gutchov and Shulgin – assured the Emperor that the only salvation for the country lay in his abdication in favor of his heir, General Russki vehemently supported them.

The Emperor, who was not allowed to communicate with his Cabinet, asked all the chiefs of the Army Corps for their opinions. All, even Grand Duke Nicholas Nicholaevich, telegraphed him advising his abdication.

At first, the Emperor wished to abdicate in favor of the Tsarevich Alexei, as had been suggested, but after a conversation with Doctor Fedorov about the Tsarevich's health, he decided to abdicate in favor of his brother, Grand Duke Michael, the Doctor having swept away any remaining illusions the Emperor might have been harboring about his son's future health. The Doctor told him that the Tsarevich's illness was incurable, and that, although he might live for many years, he would always be subject to attacks and would have to take the greatest precautions, so it was clear to the Emperor that his son would not be the strong, vigorous sovereign who could lead Russia out of her troubles. Dr. Fedorov also said that it was most improbable that the new regime would allow the Tsarevich to remain in his parents' care, so who would be the Regent and how would he train the boy?

Therefore, to save Russia – to his mind the only thing that mattered – the Emperor decided to pass on his rights to Grand Duke Michael, a man in the prime of life, whose whole early training had been planned with a view to his possible succession.

The Act of Abdication was changed by the Emperor himself to reflect his decision and he sent a telegram to "the Emperor Michael Alexandrovich," assuring him of his brotherly love and loyalty.

This telegram and the beautiful Order of the Day in which he took leave of his army, concluding with the words, written in his own hand, "God help Russia," were suppressed as they might have aroused some inconvenient feelings of loyalty.

As it was, everyone was stunned by the Emperor's decision, and the members of the Duma did not know how to adjust themselves to the prospect of a new Emperor in the person of Grand Duke Michael. Equally, the Grand Duke hesitated to be proclaimed Emperor without an expression of the people's will. This was the first step toward a republic, a step which many of those who had deposed the Emperor probably had not foreseen.

After his abdication, the Emperor returned from Pskov to Mohilev, where he handed over military command to General Alekseyev. Prince Dolgorukov has given an account of the terrible days there. The Emperor had a lingering hope of being able to serve his country as a soldier, but this was, of course, quite out of the question as his position was an impossible one. Many showed their personal loyalty to him, but many more avoided him and shunned the faithful ones as if they had the plague.

The Dowager-Empress arrived from Kiev and stayed with the Emperor. At Count Fredericks's suggestion, the members of the Court suite still dined with the Foreign Missions, the heads of which showed the greatest courtesy to the Emperor. Led by General Sir John Hanbury-Williams, the chiefs of the Allied Missions proposed to escort the Emperor to Tsarskoe Selo, and from there to the frontier, via Finland, but the Emperor would not agree to this as his children were too ill to be moved and he would not leave without his family. He hoped that when things had become quieter they would all be allowed to live in Russia.

The idea of leaving his country distressed the Emperor as much as it did the Empress. She would not entertain the idea for a moment and entirely refused to consider their departure for England when it was suggested to her as a possibility by General Kornilov on March 21. The Empress would not even listen to a suggestion, made a few days later by Mme. Narishkin, that if their Majesties were again given the opportunity of going, they should accept, leaving the children with her and Count Benckendorff, and that after their recovery Count Benckendorff and I should take the children to join their parents.

The offer to leave Russia was never officially made, as the unwillingness of the Emperor and Empress to agree to this suited the Provisional Government's purposes. To let them go, they would have had to fight against the Soviet of Workmen's Deputies, who had their own council in the building of the Duma and over which the Government very soon began to lose control. The various conversations between Sir George Buchanan and Miliukov, the Russian Minister for Foreign Affairs, on the subject of their departure were never heard about by the Imperial Family, nor did a telegram from King George to the Emperor ever reach him. Sir George Buchanan had given it to Miliukov, who declined to forward it, telling Sir George that it might be misconstrued. The Russian version of this story that was circulated at the time was that it was "wrongly addressed," as the King of England had designated the telegram to the Emperor of Russia. The only communication that the Emperor and Empress ever had from any of their relatives abroad was a message that Kerensky gave the Empress from Queen Mary, inquiring after her health.

During the first weeks after the Revolution, they were cut off completely from the world. Scraps of news were gathered from time-to-time by the doctors or tutors who were looked upon benevolently by the guards and who used sometimes to exchange a few words with the less hostile officers. Later, when the newspapers appeared again, it was difficult to grasp what was really going on owing to the wilful distortions of the Russian Press. The Emperor and Empress never knew if they still had any supporters in the country or abroad. The Empress still believed that the nation as a whole was faithful to the monarchy and could not believe that the upheaval was general, always trusting that there would be a sudden miraculous change and that the people would clamor for the return of the Emperor. It was only step-by-step, as their position became more difficult and as humiliations increased through their long months of imprisonment, that she realized their ever-growing danger and the hopelessness of their trying to avoid it.

The first days after the Emperor's return to Tsarskoe were the calm after the storm to the Empress. He was back at last and she felt that things must improve thereafter. Count Benckendorff, however, was afraid of visits to the Palace and of legal proceedings against the Emperor. He saw the increasing hostility and lawlessness of the soldiers and, as a soldier himself, understood that the officers were fast losing control over their men.

At his advice, the Empress destroyed those parts of her private correspondence that she felt were too sacred, for sentimental reasons, to be seen by prying eyes. These were her father's letters, Queen Victoria's letters, and the Emperor's letters written at the time of their engagement. She told me that she left the rest of her correspondence unburnt, for the Emperor's sake. Although she dreaded the idea of others seeing the intimate letters they had written as husband and wife, she felt it her duty not to destroy them, for, should the Emperor be tried – as Louis XVI had been – the letters would be a proof that his thoughts had always been for the welfare of his country.

The Emperor burnt nothing at all. He was the tidiest, most systematic of men, and all his papers were in perfect order, classified and with annotations. His daughters told me that, whenever he went to his writing table, he could find what he wanted at once.

Count Benckendorff spoke several times of the desirability of accepting the offer of going abroad, should it be made again. He foresaw clearly that the present moment was only a lull in the storm and knew that there was no example in history of a deposed sovereign being allowed to remain in his country.

The Empress once or twice, and very unwillingly, spoke to me of Count Benckendorff's views. She said the whole thing was such a nightmare to her that she prayed against it daily. Still, she questioned me tentatively about the possibility of their going to Norway, saying that if they should be "dragged away," she would prefer to go there as the climate would suit the Tsarevich and they would be able to live there quietly and unseen.

Prince Dolgorukov, who returned with the Emperor, had now been added to our permanent company. Colonel Narishkin, A.D.C. to the Emperor, who was expected to come on March 22, never appeared. Mme. Vyrubova's parents, who had been with her during her illness, were made to leave in March.

During those first weeks, the Emperor was allowed to go out with Prince Dolgorukov for a short daily walk in the Palace grounds, a detachment of soldiers with fixed bayonets accompanying them on thirty-minute outings. The Emperor generally got exercise by shoveling away the snow, as he did not care to walk round and round the limited space that was allotted to him. The Empress never went out at all. She had not walked for years, and to do so now, under escort of an armed guard, would have been very trying for her.

The Imperial Family spent the rest of each day in their rooms. The ladies and gentlemen of the Household squeezed into the rooms of the maids-of-honor, where they arranged a common sitting room and dining room. The Imperial Family had their meals with the invalids, who were now recovering, and Mme. Dehn, the Benckendorffs, Prince Dolgorukov, and we two ladies-in-waiting, had outings together, the doctors and M. Gilliard remaining by themselves.

In the evening, the Emperor and Empress used to go to see Mme. Vyrubova in her sickroom, and then came to spend an hour with us. Those evenings were unspeakably sad. The Empress was growing thinner and thinner, and was terribly aged in appearance, sitting almost in silence. No one dared to touch on the events of the day as it would have been impossible to discuss with the Emperor the anxiety that everyone felt for him, knowing the butchery of officers that was going on in Kronstadt and Vyborg, and hearing occasionally the talk of the soldiers in the guard room who were demanding that he be tried or sent to Kronstadt.

Armored truck-loads of soldiers still kept arriving from Petrograd. These were generally successfully turned away by the guard who considered the prisoners to be safe enough in their hands, but one particular batch included members of the soldiers' Soviet who refused to depart without having assured themselves with their own eyes that the Emperor was sufficiently guarded and need not be escorted by them to a safer place. Their attitude became threatening and they were ready to use their machine guns, so, in order to avoid violence, the Emperor was asked to pass through the corridor where they were amassed so that they should see him. They were pacified by this and finally went away.

On April 3, the Palace had its first visit from the rulers now in power, when Kerensky, the Minister of Justice, came to see the State prisoners. He wanted to satisfy himself that the orders of the Government were being carried out rigorously. The arrival of a representative of the new Government created great excitement among the guard and the servants, many of whom fawned obsequiously on him. Kerensky went through the whole of the Palace, accompanied by a mixed suite of people who followed his every step, perhaps to control his actions.

They were a curious and ill-favored crowd, some dressed like well-to-do workmen in black shirts with sheepskin caps pulled well back on their heads, and some soldiers and sailors – the latter with hand grenades, daggers and revolvers hanging all over them – strutting about the imperial apartments, investigating everything and talking loudly.

Kerensky himself was of medium size, thin and fair, with a pasty greenish complexion, shifty greenish eyes, and a loose-lipped mouth. He also wore the black blouse of a workman, but had removed his cap. He spoke in short, abrupt sentences, and stood in a Napoleonic pose with his hand thrust into the breast-pocket of his coat. His manner was commanding with everyone, but when he came into the Emperor's room, he was evidently ill-at-ease, although his speech became louder.

He had brought with him a new commander of the Palace in the person of Colonel Korovichenko, appointed to replace Kotzebue, of whom the soldiers had become suspicious as he had called on Mme. Vyrubova several times. Korovichenko immediately proceeded to the guardroom where he drew up a series of rules and regulations for the prisoners' regime. Meanwhile, Kerensky cross-questioned the Emperor about different matters in connection with orders given from Headquarters to the Ministers of the late Government. The Emperor replied to all the questions, evidently to Kerensky's satisfaction.

At the close of the conversation, Kreensky inquired after the children's health and did not insist on seeing the Grand Duchesses when he heard they were still in bed. The Emperor told me later that Kerensky was obviously nervous at the beginning of the interview, speaking fast and in jerky sentences, and shaking and flourishing a paper-cutter which he had picked up from the table, but that at the end he quieted down and was coldly civil.

Kerensky went through all the imperial rooms, except the bedrooms, and then to the part of the house where the Court suite lived. Here he was joined again by his staff who had spent the time while he was with the Emperor reviling the servants for waiting on the "Tyrants." After seeing the rooms of members of the Household, Kerensky, accompanied by Colonel Korovichenko and Count Benckendorff, went to see Mme. Vyrubova who had only just recovered from her bad attack of measles and was still very weak. Her presence in the Palace had been a source of continual anxiety to members the Household, on the Empress' account, for the soldiers not only openly attacked her but coupled the Empress' name with hers, and were continually threatening to murder first Mme. Vyrubova and then the Empress. They had occasionally become almost violent, excitedly accusing Mme. Vyrubova of high treason and of connivance with Rasputin, and saying that her presence in the Palace meant that plots were still going on and that Count Benckendorff had tried to persuade the Empress to have her friend quietly removed to a hospital outside the Palace where her parents could look after her.

The Empress would not hear of her being taken away. She believed that she would be safer in the Palace and that to abandon her would be to give her up to the wolves, and she scorned the idea that her friend's presence could be dangerous. Notwithstanding Mme. Vyrubova's state of health, Kerensky had her arrested and ordered her immediate transfer to the fortress of SS. Peter and Paul in Petrograd, and only with difficulty was permission obtained for her to say goodbye to the Empress.

They met for a few moments in Mlle. Schneider's room in the presence of Colonel Korovichenko and Colonel Kobylinsky. It was a tragic parting, and the loss of her friend seemed to the Empress one more of the crosses that she had to pray for strength to bear. Doctor Botkin had been asked, at the Empress' request, if he thought she could be moved, and had said he believed her health would stand it. Mme. Lili Dehn helped the trembling and crippled woman to pack her few belongings and went with her. She also was arrested on her arrival in the capital, and although she was soon set free, she found that she was not allowed to return to the Palace.

Mme. Vyrubova was treated with the utmost severity during the long months of her imprisonment but no proof could be found that she had played any part in politics and she was finally released.

It seemed to Count Benckendorff that Kerensky's visit and the cross-examination to which he had subjected the Emperor were preliminaries to a trial. He drew the Emperor's attention to this possibility and asked him to think about the person to whom he would, in such a case, wish to entrust his defense. The Emperor chose Senator Koni, a highly reputable lawyer, whose name had first come into prominence when, as a young man, he had defended Vera Zassulich, a revolutionary who was tried for political murder and in whose spirited defense he gained a great notoriety. The Emperor was never tried, but had he been, the beginning and end of Koni's career would have been in curious contrast.

On April 8, five days after his first visit, Kerensky came again. He sent for Mme. Narishkin, and after a few questions, told her that it would be necessary to part the Emperor and Empress, as the extreme elements were loud against the Empress' "counter-revolutionary" influence, and with the trials of the late Ministers in progress, he did not wish Their Majesties to be in communication with each other.

His first idea was to leave the Emperor with the children and remove the Empress, but Mme. Narishkin succeeded in dissuading him from this, pointing out that it would be cruel to part the sick children from their mother. He finally agreed to let the Empress stay with the children upstairs, while the Emperor was moved to another floor. Their Majesties were to meet twice a day, only at meals, and only in the presence of an officer of the guard (this was soon dropped), and they had to give their word of honor not to touch on any political subject during that time.

286

Their Majesties had to submit to this separation, which lasted until the inquiry into the Empress' conduct was dropped by the Government, nothing having been proved against her.

Kerensky's third visit took place on April 25, when he came to examine the Emperor's papers. The Emperor silently handed the key to his writing-table over to him, and Kerensky, seeing that the amount of material to go through would involve several hours' work, "entrusted" the task to Colonel Korovichenko, who was a lawyer, and to Colonel Kobylinsky. The Emperor did not ask that either he or his gentlemen should be present at these proceedings, so the two colonels did their work alone.

Meanwhile, Kerensky asked for an interview with the Empress and cross-examined her about the political role that she was accused of having played. He examined her minutely, and the precision and straightforwardness of her answers seemed to satisfy him.

The Emperor spent the time of this examination pacing up and down an adjoining room. Tatiana told me that he seemed ready to rush in to his wife's assistance, should any sounds of a heated discussion come from the room next door, and the time seemed endless to father and daughter, who both had at the back of their minds the fear that if some chance word should not please her accuser, the Empress might be arrested and taken away. However, when Kerensky came out, he greeted the Emperor with the words "Your wife does not lie." The Emperor quietly replied that he had always known it.

The painful situation created by their separation lasted for about a month. During that time, the Emperor and Empress scrupulously respected their promise and never exchanged a single word in private. This was the first time that orders were actually enforced and it was particularly trying on account of the children's illnesses, but it was pointed out to them that, were Kerensky unable to give the assurance that he had effectively separated the imperial couple, it might have been insisted that one or other of them should be taken to a fortress, which was a nightmare that oppressed them during the whole of their captivity.

During the time of her separation from the Emperor, the Empress lay nearly all day in her daughters' rooms. The inevitable physical collapse had come. The Emperor spent his time reading, except for his short daily outings and meals. Grand Duchess Tatiana sat with him in the evenings and he read aloud to her while she worked, or they sorted his books and photographs. "To learn blind submission" was a hard task for the Russian Autocrat and his family to acquire during nearly sixteen months of imprisonment. Even at Tsarskoe Selo, it was submission to orders given with scarcely a semblance of legality, as the soldiers' conduct was not in accordance with instructions from the Government, being rather their own interpretation of how State prisoners should be treated. Nonetheless, the lesson was learnt with wonderful courage and dignity, the children following the example of their parents.

The Provisional Government had laid down the rules to be followed in the Palace, but they had no time to see how their orders were carried out, and the abolition of the death penalty – one of the first of the new Government's decrees – certainly saved the Emperor's life. From the first moment, the extremists, drunk with power, would have gone to any lengths in their desire to enact judicial vengeance against the head of the Tsarist regime, and the ministers spent their days making endless speeches, which were listened to by admiring crowds, shouting themselves hoarse with cries of "Long live liberty!"

The guard of the Palace now consisted of the First, Second and Fourth Regiments of Rifles, to which a detachment of the Third Regiment of Rifles was added later. These had previously done service at the fortress and wanted to enforce full prison regulations on the Palace. It was they who first introduced a ten minute walk and who saw that all the things brought for the family's use were minutely examined. All their officers, most of them very young, had been elected by the men, and were, in consequence, treated completely without respect. The Second and Third Rifles were particularly hostile, and every time these two regiments were on duty, some incident occurred, some new rule was enforced, or some fresh thing was forbidden.

The soldiers who, barely a month before had been spick and span, perfectly disciplined troops, had degenerated into an untidy, undisciplined rabble. They were slovenly in their dress, their crushed caps were set awry on huge mops of unkempt hair, their coats were half-buttoned, and their nonchalant manner of performing their military duties was a continual irritation to the Emperor. They lolled out of the guardroom, and sat about smoking and reading papers.

One day Grand Duchess Tatiana and I saw from the window that one of the guards on duty in front of the Palace, struck evidently with the injustice of having to stand at his post, had brought a gilt armchair from the halls and had comfortably ensconced himself therein, leaning back, enjoying the view, with his rifle across his knee. I remarked that the man only lacked cushions to complete the picture. There was evidently telepathy in my eye, for when we looked out again, he had actually got some sofa cushions out of one of the rooms, and, with a footstool under his feet, was reading the newspapers, his discarded rifle lying on the ground.

Others, to while away the time, shot at everything they fancied, and the tame deer and swans of the park often thereby came to untimely ends. Every man considered himself his own master, free to roam about the Palace, and the officers' requests that they should remain in the guardroom were generally ignored. Protests from our side would have been still more pointless. The soldiers entered any room they fancied on the plea of "going their rounds." Once, a whole band of them, swearing and talking loudly, went into the Tsarevich's room in the early morning and were prevented, by Prince Dolgorukov, with some difficulty, from entering the Empress' room while she was dressing. As a vexatious measure, a sentry had been placed just outside the window of her dressing room, so that the Empress had to use the greatest ingenuity to find a corner where she was away from his watchful eye.

All this minor unpleasantness had to be borne in silence in order not to provoke a discussion that would inevitably give rise to stricter measures. As an example of our utter helplessness in the soldiers' hands, I can mention an incident that happened to me. One night, I was awakened by a raucous breathing in my bedroom. By ill luck the light near my bed was out of order. I asked who was there, heard stealthy steps, and the door of my dressing room closed. I jumped out of bed, ran to the dressing room, and switched on the light. The room was empty, but when I opened the door I saw the figure of a soldier disappearing around the corner of the corridor. Next morning I discovered that every small gold and silver thing in my sitting room had been stolen. The man had evidently meant to take also my watch and rings, which lay on my dressing-table, and must have made some noise that woke me. The gentlemen's boots, standing outside their doors, were also stolen, but we could not complain as we should undoubtedly have been taken to prison for casting aspersions on the honesty of the revolutionary army. I was an ex-Baroness and ex-lady-in-waiting to the ex-Empress (as a letter addressed to me said), and my word would never be taken against that of a free citizen.

Members of the Household, although they had voluntarily shared the arrest of the Imperial Family, were subject to the same rules and were allowed to see no one, although later one or two exceptions were made for special reasons. Prince Dolgorukov and Countess Hendrikov were allowed to see their brothers before they went to Siberia, and I was allowed to see my mother, and later my father, after my mother's death. These meetings took place in the guardroom. Both parties were brought in by soldiers with fixed bayonets, and they, with a member of the Soviet, were present at the short interview. Special permission could be given to the Court suite to telephone from the guardroom, a soldier standing by to listen in to the conversation. The servants, who were considered free, were not allowed to go out, although they might see their families on certain fixed days so long as they stood at some distance from them outside the Palace gates.

Petty humiliations and incidents were often harder to bear than more serious hardships. Every parcel that arrived was opened and closely examined by the soldiers, the officer on guard and the Commandant, and, after this, was delivered, or not, according to the mood of the moment. The guards were in deadly fear of conspiracy but these minute examinations were sometimes ridiculous. For instance, a tube of toothpaste would be ripped open although it came direct from the shop. Our yogurt generally had the trace of a finger that had stirred it up and chocolates were bitten open. The delivery of the laundry was a function at which all the guard assisted in a body.

The Imperial Family was allowed to keep its own cook, who daily received the necessary ingredients for the simple meals that were brought in to them by the soldiers. They were at first even forbidden fruit, which was a luxury that prisoners would not be allowed. All the plants in the rooms had been taken away for the same reason, and it was pathetic to see the joy of the poor Empress in summer, when one of the maids would come back from a walk in the grounds, bringing her some daisies or perhaps, as a great treat, a branch of lilac.

The ladies' maids had the privilege, as free citizens, of being taken for walks by the soldiers beyond the enclosure where the Imperial Family and the members of the Household were penned in. The rules varied. On one day one thing was forbidden, another day something else. One evening in the heat of summer, when Grand Duchess Tatiana and I sat on the window-sill of my room on the second floor, reading aloud and trying to get a little air – it was after five, and we were never allowed out a second time) – a sudden voice outside bellowed, "Take away your mugs or I shall fire." We looked out in surprise and saw the sentry pointing his rifle at us, shouting furiously. "Don't you know that you must shut the window?"

"But it is always allowed," I said. "It is so stifling."

"Obey orders," he shouted, "or I shall fire."

We closed the window, for we knew that he was quite capable of firing to frighten us and might well have killed us in his unskilled handling of his gun.

Church services had been allowed on Saturday evenings and Sunday, but were always made the occasion of long discussions, terminating in violent abuse, the echoes of which were heard as the guardroom was under the Empress' bedroom. After some time the guard insisted that their prisoners should be handed over daily by the existing detachment to the one replacing it. They were very insistent on this but Count Benckendorff managed to achieve a compromise. Every day, when the guard was changed, the old and the new officers came to Their Majesties' rooms to be presented to the Emperor and Empress and all the children.

A distressing incident occurred on one of these occasions, when one of the officers refused to take the hand that the Emperor stretched out in greeting, saying that he was of the people and would not lower himself to take the hand of a tyrant. These wilful humiliations and insults were intensely painful to those officers who were not extremists, and they did everything in their power not to be sent on guard at the Palace, doing their best to get transferred to the front as soon as they could. This meant, unfortunately, that gradually only the most hostile elements were represented in the guards and the treatment of the Imperial Family became steadily worse.

Chapter 29

Five weary months: March-August 1917

During the first months after the Revolution, the dread of the Emperor's being transferred to some prison, or of some violence being incurred against his person, was uppermost in the minds of all in the Palace, and although the Empress never spoke of it, she, too, realized the danger.

All disturbing rumors seemed mysteriously to reach her. Whenever there was any talk on subjects that would distress her, she always happened to come into the room. The members of the Household tried to hide the newspapers that contained the most violent attacks on the Emperor and Empress, but she always seemed to pick up the very worst.

The illustrated press, in particular, was full of dreadful, often obscene, caricatures, and although the commander had the decency not to send these upstairs, the soldiers took care that they should be seen.

The revolutionary press was giving vent to an orgy of abuse and calumny. What pained the Empress most in the accusations hurled against both of them were the utterly unfounded attacks made on the Emperor by the extremists in their search for something that might give them an excuse for starting legal proceedings against him. He, who had renounced everything for his country and whose loyalty to her allies was proved by his every action, was openly accused of disloyalty. Words were attributed to him that he could never have uttered.

These attacks were so monstrous that the Empress was forced to recognize that there were no lengths to which their enemies would not go. As for the Emperor, he gave onlookers the impression that, if there were danger, it concerned not him but someone else. When he did mention the incidents that so much alarmed his gentlemen, it was with a half-smile of pity for the worry given to those about him.

For months, every shot fired in the garden, every heated discussion in the guard room, might have been the first step towards disaster. On the whole, the local soldiers' Soviet gave its support to the Commander of the Palace, but no one knew how long this would last.

The Empress, like the Emperor, never showed any fears she may have felt. She was heroic, as she had been through all the early days of the Revolution when she and her children were in imminent danger. Her fortitude never deserted her and she would cheer up any of those in the Household whom she saw to be depressed and anxious. She had put those she loved into the hands of the Supreme Power, feeling the hopelessness of human help, and in her constant prayers found the wonderful serenity and courage that she kept to the end.

At first, neither the Emperor nor the Empress had any communication with people outside the Palace as no one dared write them. After a few days, however, some of the Empress' friends in the hospitals sent short notes to her and her daughters with the Commander's permission. He read all letters addressed to people in the Palace and all replies had to be sent to him, open. The soldiers generally read everything, too, and although, of course, only the barest commonplaces could be written, even these were often misunderstood and the most innocent words were twisted by the soldiers into quite different meanings, so that many of these notes were not mailed at all. The few letters the Empress received from her friends were rays of light to her, giving her a feeling of human sympathy that she longed for. She always believed that those who, after the Revolution, never sent a line or took any notice of her, did this because they were afraid that their loyalty would harm her or the Emperor.

Naturally, those who wrote had to be careful as to the wording of their letters and many really were prevented from writing for fear of causing additional trouble.

It was pitiful to see the gratitude that a few kind words could elicit from both the Emperor and Empress. Her Majesty was quite cheerful for a whole day after she had received a small icon sent by a lady to the Emperor, on the back of which was written a short prayer and her name. To balance these few words of sympathy, came hundreds of insulting letters, reviling the Emperor and Empress, and accusing them of the most fantastic crimes.

The Emperor never wrote to anyone, so fearful was he of compromising his correspondents, except once to the Dowager-Empress, who had been moved by the Government to the Crimea, when the Commander told him that she was anxious about him and that Kerensky had wished her to be pacified by the sight of a letter written in the Emperor's own hand.

The greatest anxiety the Empress Alexandra had was to know the fate of her friends and of all those in whom she had taken interest, and who might, for that reason, be in danger. She anxiously scanned the papers for details of Mme. Vyrubova's arrest, for she knew that she was hated and dared not think what might happen to her.

The fact that they had become a danger to their friends was brought home to the Imperial Family by the effect of any chance words spoken to officers of the guard. One of these officers was spoken to by one of the Grand Duchesses and was at once looked upon with suspicion. Another kissed the hand of one of the girls in greeting, as was the usual Russian custom, and the men wanted him imprisoned for his anti-revolutionary conduct. For hours shouts were heard from the guardroom, where the soldiers held a meeting to discuss the matter, and the officer in question, who had before this been quite unknown to the Imperial Family, was never seen again. In the end he was pardoned and escaped actual imprisonment, but he was removed from the Palace Guard and sent to the front.

Little by little the Empress began to realize the passionate animosity that was felt against her personally, but it did not make her angry.

"Poor creatures," she used to say, "they have been misled it is an illness like measles."

An insight into the Empress' mental attitude at the time can be gained by the following letter to Mme. Dehn:

Tsarskoe Selo,
June 5th, 1917

Oh, how pleased I am that they have appointed a new Commander-in-Chief of the Baltic fleet [Admiral Rostosov]. I hope to God it will be better now. He is a real sailor, and I hope he will succeed in restoring order now.

The heart of a soldier's daughter and wife is suffering terribly in seeing what is going on. Cannot get accustomed and do not wish to. They were such hero soldiers, and how they were spoilt just at a time when it was necessary to start to get rid of the enemy [Germans].

It will take many years to fight yet. You will understand how he [the Emperor] must suffer. He reads [newspapers] and tears stand in his eyes but I believe they will yet win [the war]. We have so many friends in the fighting line. I can imagine how terribly they must suffer.

Of course nobody can write. Yesterday we saw quite new people [new guard] – such a difference. It was at last quite a pleasure to see them. Am writing again what I ought not to, but this does not go by post or you would not have received it.

Of course I have nothing of interest to write. Today is a prayer at 12 o'clock. Anastasia is today 16 years old – how the time flies ... I am remembering the past. It is necessary to look more calmly on everything. What is to be done? Once He sent us such trials, evidently He thinks we are sufficiently prepared for it. It is a sort of examination – it is necessary to prove that we did not go through it in vain. One can find in everything something good and useful. Whatever sufferings we go through – let it be. He will give us force and patience and will not leave us. He is merciful. It is only necessary to bow to His wish without murmur and await there, on the other side. He is preparing to all who love Him indescribable joy. You are young and so are our children – how many I have besides my own. You will see better times yet here. I believe strongly the bad will pass and there will be clear and cloudless sky. But the thunderstorm has not passed yet and therefore it is stifling – but I know it will be better afterwards.

*One must only have a little patience-and is it really so difficult? For every day that passes quietly I thank God.
. . .*

Three months have passed now [since the Revolution]!! The people were promised that they would have more food and fuel, but all has become worse and more expensive. They have deceived everybody – I am so sorry for them. How many we have helped, but now it is all finished ... It is terrible to think about it! How many people depended on us. But now? But one does not speak about such things, but I am writing about it,

297

because I feel so sadly about those who will have it more difficult now to live. But it is God's will!

My dear own, I must finish now. Am kissing you and Titi most tenderly.

Christ be with you.

Most hearty greetings [from the Emperor].

Your loving

Aunt BABY.

During our long tête-à-têtes, she often spoke to me about the events that had preceded the Revolution. Neither she nor the Emperor ever said a bitter word to say about all those who had abandoned them so heartlessly, or about the ministers whose mismanagement of affairs had led to the Revolution, or even about the Generals who, like Russki, had played such a dark and fatal part in the drama. When their names were mentioned, they were passed over in silence.

When he left Mohilev, the Emperor had ordered everyone in his suite to give their faithful service to the Provisional Government. This seemed to him the only way to save Russia. He himself reverently made the sign of the cross when the Provisional Government was prayed for in church. He wanted to inculcate this spirit into all those around him, and noticing that I did not follow his example, he remarked upon it, saying that I should not forget that it was Russia for which I was praying.

Both the Emperor and Empress anxiously followed the trend of political events. They read the newspapers, no matter how painful they were to them personally, and the impression he gained of the helplessness and indecision of the Government filled the Emperor with anxiety. He dreaded the effect of the disorganization and demoralization of the army on the prosecution of the war. Taking the Palace Guard as specimens of what the army had become, its condition caused them both the greatest concern.

The Emperor realized that mistaken judgments on his own part had led in some measure to the cataclysm. For some time, however, the Empress continued to believe that all the harm had arisen from revolutionary propaganda and from the fact that the Duma had not supported the Government and had allowed sedition to work undisturbed. She was constantly thinking about these things, turning events over in her mind, but by degrees, I think, she began to see that she and the Emperor had made many political mistakes and given their confidence to people who had mismanaged affairs.

This thought was only an additional source of distress to her, and she was never completely disillusioned about the ministers who had given such fatal advice. For many years she had believed that bad luck pursued the Emperor and herself.

For Alexei, on the other hand, she had the greatest hopes. She was ready to suffer everything in order that he might come into his inheritance. His reign should be glorious; he should institute the reforms for which his parents would slowly prepare. She believed, with a fatalism that she shared with the Emperor, that they were the scapegoats for all the errors committed in previous reigns. Perhaps the lives of all princes were too easy; they had to suffer as an expiation for the good things taken without thought by preceding generations.

The Empress longed for church services and it was a comfort to her when in Holy Week they were allowed in the Palace chapel. The first service was held on Palm Sunday, April 8. Father Vassiliev was prevented by illness from coming, so the Cathedral priest, Father Beliaev, came with a deacon and four singers. The priest was an old man and there were tears in his eyes all the time he celebrated his first Mass under these conditions. It was a poignant moment when he brought out the Blessed Sacrament. This was the point in the service when he would have prayed for the Emperor. His emotion was so great that he could not utter the words of the new ritual and turned away in silence. He was a kindly man and the short morning sermon he preached every Sunday always contained a few words of consolation.

The clergy stayed in the Palace all through Holy Week, but were not allowed to see or speak to anyone between the services. The singers whiled away the time between Mass and Vespers by singing the saddest dirges which resounded all through the Palace. The Imperial Family was prayed for in church by their names and patronymics, but in order not to irritate the guard their titles were not used.

The Imperial Family and the whole Household went to church twice daily during Holy Week, preparatory to receiving the Sacrament. On Good Friday, all went to confession and I happened to go first. To my astonishment, a soldier followed me into the chapel and I waited for him to go before beginning my confession. The priest was waiting but the man showed no intention of departing. The idea then flashed through my mind that the soldier meant to listen to the confessions of the Emperor and Empress, and was beginning with me. This was too much. 1 turned politely to the man and told him that he had better leave as I was going to confess.

As I expected, he refused to do so.

A lively debate ensued, from which I emerged triumphant. I pointed out to the man that no order had been given by the Government for such an unheard-of thing as a public confession. Even condemned criminals had the right to see the priest without witnesses.

I asked him to call his superior, as I wished to ask him to telephone to Kerensky. Swearing loudly, the man brought his officer who decided the matter in my favor without calling Petrograd, and I secured at least the privilege of undisturbed confession for Their Majesties.

But the whole guard was pacified with difficulty and their suspicion of the clergy was so great that during Mass a soldier stood all the time behind the altar screen, watching the priest.

The inhabitants of the Palace were never able to forget the presence of hostile soldiers in the town, for detachments marched past the gates once or twice every day, stopping before the Palace to play the 'Marseillaise' or a particularly melancholy funeral march.

On Maundy Thursday, the usual Holy Communion was not celebrated as the funeral of the Tsarskoe Selo victims of the Revolution had been arranged for that day. The Communion service was postponed until the Saturday, and although Mass was said on the Thursday, it was at the same moment as the funeral, and the voice of the priest was often drowned out by the 'Marseillaise' and 'Internationale' played by the brass bands outside.

The victims were buried with great pomp in the Park in the center of a broad avenue leading to the Palace. The original idea had been to dig the graves under the Palace windows, but this had to be abandoned owing to a lack of space. The civic funeral ceremony lasted the best part of the morning and afternoon. Thousands of workmen and soldiers came to the function, carrying banners and placards on which were mottoes of every shade of socialistic and communistic thought. They made incendiary speeches in front of the red coffins, the bands playing appropriate music, varied from time to time by a funeral match.

This was the only concession to old-time prejudice, for every sign of anything reminiscent of a religious ceremony was carefully avoided. As the speeches became more and more heated, the commander and officers of the Palace Guard grew alarmed. They saw the increasing hostility of the crowd and feared an onslaught on the Palace. As the roars of the mourners grew louder and louder, the weather intervened and very probably saved the Imperial Family's lives. A wind arose which developed, in the course of half-an-hour, into a hurricane. The sky grew black and a tremendous snowstorm descended. The army of red banners fluttered desperately in the wind. Many were torn from their staves and the old trees swayed and creaked. The orators were blinded by the snow and obliged to cling to their caps and blankets in the ever-increasing blast, so the flow of eloquence stopped and one detachment after another tramped away, until the vast park was empty, leaving only a few torn red flags flapping in the wind on the site of the civic graves.

On Good Friday, the solemn procession of 'The Holy Winding-Sheet' took place in the Palace with nearly all the usual ceremonies. The servants in the black liveries of full court mourning headed the procession. The Emperor and his family, with members of the Household – the ladies in long black dresses – followed the priest, the lighted tapers they carried throwing fantastic shadows on the dimly-lit walls. A less militant detachment than usual was on guard, and some of the men stood about in the big empty halls and watched the procession pass without comment or interruption.

The customary night service was held on Easter Eve, and the authorities allowed Their Majesties to attend this and the usual Easter meal that followed it. This was a concession as it was at a time when the Emperor was not permitted to see the Empress, and was allowed only on condition that they should stand at some distance from each other in church, and that the Commander and officers on guard should be present at the supper.

This was a dismal repast, like a meal in a house of mourning. The Empress could scarcely bring herself to exchange a few words with Count Benckendorff, who sat beside her, her other neighbor being Father Beliaev to whom she dared not talk for fear it might compromise him. The Emperor and Grand Duchesses Tatiana and Anastasia, who alone of the children were present, were quite silent, and only the Commander, Colonel Korovitchenko, and Mme. Narishkin, kept up a strained conversation. The young officer of the guard seemed to choke at every morsel and was so ill-at-ease that he could scarcely manage to say even a couple of words.

Before sitting down to the Easter repast, the Emperor had kissed all the gentlemen of the Household, and the officers and men, three times according to Russian custom. The Empress did the same to the ladies, and, as she had always done, presented the gentlemen of the Household, the Commander and the officers, with china Easter eggs. The Commander accepted his, but even here he emphasized the changed circumstances by ostentatiously brushing past the Empress, who had stepped towards him to greet her ladies first, turning to her casually as an afterthought.

After Easter, the tedium of the long days was a little relieved by the whole Household's taking a share in the imperial children's lessons. Only M. Gilliard was left of their regular teachers and their parents did not want their education to lapse. The Emperor undertook to teach his son history, of which he himself had always been a student, the Empress taught him the Catechism, Mlle. Schneider mathematics, and Dr. Botkin Russian. Countess Hendrikov started art lessons with Grand Duchess Tatiana, and I was entrusted with piano lessons for all the three younger Grand Duchesses, and English lessons for them and Alexei. It helped to pass the time and in this way the whole day could be occupied.

In April, as the spring advanced, the Imperial Family was allowed to stay out longer in the garden. They had all suffered greatly from want of air and exercise. Every day, from three until four-thirty or five, the Imperial Family, with its Court suite and any servants who wished to do so, were allowed to go into the garden set apart for their use. Sentries were posted around it at short distances from one another, and in addition a detachment of soldiers, with one or two officers in command, kept close to them during the whole time they were out.

It would have been a pleasant change if it had not been for the conduct of many of the soldiers. Notwithstanding this, Their Majesties went out every day, the Empress in her bath-chair. She was not allowed to use her balcony, the door to which was sealed by order of the soldiers. The men seemed to be particularly irritated by her chair and her sad face, and swore loudly at her for not being made to walk. They always insulted the servant who pushed her chair, and once when he was replaced by the Tsarevich's sailor attendant, Nagorni, the men were so incensed at his serving "the Tyrant's wife" that he got letters from the men of his company condemning him to death.

All the inhabitants of the Palace assembled before these outings in the semi-circular hall. The guard and officers arrived, and, after unlocking the doors with much ceremony, made the imperial party and the servants file out before them, the soldiers bringing up the rear. There was often a deliberate delay in producing the key. Once it could not be found at all as the officer of the preceding guard had taken it with him, and the Emperor and Empress were ordered back to their rooms.

When they went out, there was generally a band of soldiers loitering about who made insulting remarks, gibing at the family as they passed. All the benches and the walls were scribbled over with the coarsest insults. The officers tried to herd the men back into the guardroom, but usually with little success, and when the party returned, they were again standing to watch them pass. The Emperor and Empress pretended that they neither saw nor heard them, but often, when the Empress' chair was drawn up under some shady tree, the lines on her face and her flushed cheeks would show that she had heard what had been said.

It hurt her beyond words to see the men's disrespect for the Emperor. Some would scarcely even answer his polite greeting with their usual "Good morning, Colonel." Once, at the beginning of his imprisonment, the Emperor got his bicycle and started to ride along the path. When he passed the sentry, the man put his bayonet through the wheel and it was only his extreme agility that saved the Emperor from a bad accident, while the men burst into loud guffaws. No one ever bicycled after that.

The garden was very small, and as walking or running around and around it for two hours was very dull, the idea was started of making a kitchen garden in which all could work. This was allowed, and the Emperor and his daughters worked vigorously there with the servants' help. The soldiers looked on and sometimes one or other of them would give the young Grand Duchesses advice about their work. On the whole they were better disposed toward the children than toward their parents, and the little Tsarevich was often looked upon kindly by the soldiers, although they always called him by his name, "Alexei," for fear that their comrades should consider them undemocratic.

Exercise in the garden did the Emperor a great deal of good. At the beginning, the soldiers had taken him for walks in the park, but while the trees were bare he could be seen, and the public began to assemble outside the railings to catch sight of him. Some came out of loyalty, the majority out of curiosity, and these walks were discontinued at the Emperor's request.

While the others gardened, the Empress sat nearby with her needlework. The soldiers always kept close to her, listening to her talk in Russian – we were only allowed to speak Russian – and they often smoked their vile tobacco straight into her face or exchanged rude jokes to see their effect on her. Once, when the Empress was sitting on a rug under a tree, I got up from my seat beside her to pick up something she had dropped. A soldier immediately took my place, remarking in reply to my protests that "now it was turn about."

The Empress edged a little bit away, making a sign to me to be silent, for she was afraid that the whole family would be taken home and the children robbed of an hour's fresh air. The man seemed to her not to have a bad face and she was soon engaged in conversation with him. At first he cross-questioned her, accusing her of despising the People, of showing, by not travelling about, that she did not want to know Russia.

The Empress quietly explained to him that, as in her young days she had had five children and nursed them all herself, she had not had time to travel around the country, and that afterward her health had prevented her from doing so.

He seemed to be struck by this reasoning and little-by-little he grew friendlier, asking the Empress about her life, her children, her attitudes toward Germany, and so on.

She answered simply that she had been a German in her youth, but that was long past. Her husband and her children were Russians, and she was a Russian too, now, with all her heart.

When I returned to the Empress with the officer, who seemed a decent man and to whom I had risked appealing for help, fearing that the soldier might annoy the Empress, I found them peacefully discussing religious questions. The soldier got to his feet on our approach and took the Empress' hand, saying, "Do you know, Alexandra Feodorovna, I had quite a different idea of you? I was mistaken about you." This was all the more striking because this man was the Deputy of the Soviet and when he came on guard the next time around he was quite polite.

It generally happened that when the soldiers talked to the Emperor or the children their hostility disappeared. They saw they were not the cruel monsters they had been taught to believe, but they were always more hostile to the Empress, and showed by their conduct the sort of propaganda that had been at work among them.

The Soviets feared that the guard might relax their vigilance, and nearly always deputed a *sovietsky* soldier to spy on the others and on the officers. This deputy was much more important than the rest of the guard. At one time a whole detachment was entirely composed of members of the Soviet. They began in a very aggressive way and at once laid down new rules, but the next day, for some unknown reason, they were more amenable and did not give any trouble.

As a rule the guard was always suspicious of its prisoners. Late one evening they created a great disturbance in the children's rooms as one of the men had raised a scare of 'signaling.' It turned out that one of the Grand Duchesses had inadvertently moved a lampshade that had seemed to give flashes of light from the window. The Tsarevich's little model rifle excited the greatest suspicion. It was taken away, and long discussions and shouts were heard from the guardroom, the soldiers maintaining that "they were armed." There were spies everywhere, and some of the underservants spied upon us, repeating what we said in the guardroom. We once found a footman kneeling at a door, listening to the conversation inside, so even in our rooms we had to be careful not to say anything that could be misinterpreted.

In the garden, the soldiers were continually on the watch. A word in French to M. Gilliard, whose Russian was very bad at that time, would be followed by great unpleasantness. Toward the end of our time at Tsarskoe Selo, the Assistant-Commander, Damadianz, was always hiding in the bushes when the Empress was in the garden, listening to everything she said. Neither parents nor children complained of all this. "Funny, isn't it?" was all the Grand Duchesses said, their one idea being not to make things harder for their parents.

The Emperor had always hoped through everything that his great sacrifice for his country would bear fruit and that the war would be won. Now nothing was heard of the great Russian advance that military headquarters had planned for the spring. In spite of high-sounding phrases, the war had become a secondary matter and the only thing anyone spoke about was the glorious Revolution.

Great was the Emperor's joy when, at last, after numerous appeals to the army, Kerensky, now Minister for War, succeeded in making a small advance in June. The Empress and the children were equally delighted, and the Emperor begged to be allowed to have a thanksgiving service at the Palace. His face seemed to light up during this service. It was the only time since the Revolution that he looked like his former self.

This was really Kerensky's victory. He had gone all through the country haranguing the soldiers, and he certainly had the talent of moving the masses by his oratory, to the extent that the Emperor and

Empress began to think he might be the man to save the country. During the interviews they had with him, Kerensky had impressed them with his patriotism. "That man loves Russia," the Emperor said, when Kerensky had spoken to him about the war. He had gained the Emperor's respect, and the Emperor used to say that, if they had met beforehand, he believed that, notwithstanding their very different political ideas, Kerensky could have been of great use to him in the Government.

The Empress also gradually veered around in favor of Kerensky, looking at him from an impersonal point of view, and she too hoped that he would be able to master the situation. In his dealings with the Emperor and herself, she had believed him to be honest and, as she said, "straight," and she believed that he meant to act with justice and equity toward the Emperor. He had always been a Socialist, with the courage of his opinions, and had not changed his views to meet the fashion of the moment.

Their Majesties never breathed a word of resentment when members of the Provisional Government took up their residence in the imperial apartments in the Winter Palace, using the Emperor's own car and their various private possessions, considering that if the Government in power could get the country out of its difficulties, it was welcome to anything. The Empress heard that Kerensky's health was bad and always spoke sympathetically about him, hoping that "the poor man would not break down before he had put things right."

Although the Bolshevik rising in July had been put down, the Government felt insecure and was uneasy at having the Emperor so near the capital, where extreme elements were always demanding stricter measures to be taken with the Imperial Family. On the other hand, they were in continual fear of attempts being made to free them. It therefore decided to remove the whole family to some out-of-the-way place from which escape would be impossible and where attacks by extremists could not be carried out.

Doctor Botkin had spoken to Kerensky, on the occasion of one of his visits, of the necessity of a change of air for both the Empress and the children, and had suggested their being taken to Livadia. The Emperor also had proposed this when Kerensky had spoken to him about the necessity for a move from Tsarskoe Selo. Kerensky seemed to have nothing against Livadia, although he mentioned the alternative of some landed gentleman's country seat in the interior of the country, far from factories and large towns. He said that the removal would be "for your good," asking the Emperor if he believed him. The Emperor replied that he did.

The whole family rejoiced at the idea of Livadia, the Empress in particular, for she hoped that they would be left there for good and that gradually they would be given more liberty. The mild climate would prevent them from suffering from the cold of winter as they had done at Tsarskoe Selo, for the new administration had cut off supplies of fuel and the rooms were insufficiently heated, and she began to plan how she would settle the house, for her ladies and Prince Dolgorukov were to accompany them, but they were to be bitterly disappointed.

Kerensky had sent Makarov, an engineer, accompanied by Count Benckendorff's assistant, to discuss details of the actual journey, but the destination to which they would be taken was not mentioned. It was only said that the ladies should take their furs, and it was clear from this that they were not going to Livadia. Although the five months spent at Tsarskoe Selo had been filled with disappointment and humiliation, the contrast between their past life and their present one being always before them, the move meant to the Empress the drawing of a line between old happy days and an unknown future. Still, removal to another place in Russia meant a further deferring of the exile abroad that was so much dreaded by them all.

At Makarov's orders, packing was begun very discreetly so as not to suggest to the soldiers that there was any suggestion of a departure. As August 12 was Grand Duke Alexei's thirteenth birthday, a *Te*

Deum was sung before the icon of Our Lady of Znamenie, which was specially brought to the Palace, and prayers for the success of the journey were added to the usual ones. The Emperor and Empress took leave of all the servants who were not going with them, and thanked them for their faithful service. The Empress sorted out her dresses, and sent parcels of them to humble friends and Polish refugees who were living at Tsarskoe Selo.

The departure was fixed for the night of August 13, but owing to some mistake on the part of the authorities, it was delayed for hours. There were not enough men to move the luggage that was to be taken at the last moment, and in the meantime the soldiers had got wind of the departure and were holding meetings in all the barracks to discuss whether or not it should be allowed.

The Emperor and Empress waited patiently for many hours until they were told they could leave. No one knew yet where they were being taken and they only heard the actual destination when they were on the train.

At 11:30pm Kerensky arrived with Grand Duke Michael to see the Emperor and was present at the meeting between the brothers, who had not met since the abdication of the Emperor. Kerensky sat at the far end of the room, and, as the Emperor told me, tried not to listen to the conversation, but the brothers were so upset that they could exchange only commonplace remarks.

The Grand Duke asked to see the Empress, but this was not permitted, neither was Alexei allowed to say goodbye to his uncle, whom he saw only through a chink in the doorway.

By this time the departure was fixed for midnight and the whole Imperial Family went down, already dressed, to the semi-circular hall. Here they sat for hours, false alarms being raised about every thirty minutes as the luggage was removed. There were quantities of it, mostly bedding or things belonging to the kitchen and pantry. All the doors were open, and officers and men were continually coming in and out.

The Empress and her children sat about, the poor little boy, green with fatigue, perched on a box and holding his favorite spaniel Joy by a leash, while the Emperor talked to his gentlemen through the long, weary wait. Once or twice they returned to their rooms to rest, but were immediately recalled by news that the cars were coming.

The delay was caused by Kerensky having to get the soldiers' Soviets to agree to their departure. He spent nearly the whole night haranguing the men and finally reappeared about six in the morning to say that they could now start on their journey.

All through that sad night the Empress had seen her life at Tsarskoe Selo passing before her and she left a letter for me with a few piteous words of farewell. In this, for the first time, she spoke of her feelings. "What shall the future bring to my poor children?" she wrote. "My heart breaks thinking of them."

Kerensky and Colonel Kuzmin, the commander of the Petrograd military district – a dark-faced, sinister-looking man – watched the departure from the background. Kerensky's naval A.D.C. looked on with mild interest, alert for the slightest sign from his chief. The "State prisoners" were hurried into the waiting cars and a mounted escort rode beside them at top speed to the station.

The Empress' face was ashy white as she went out of the door of her home for the last time. Count Benckendorff and I were left alone on the steps to see them drive away; all the others went with them. The Empress wrote to me later that she felt the whole force of their desolation when she saw our lonely figures and the expression on our faces. We were so much overcome by the tragedy we were watching that we both leaned against the wall, unable even to wave a hand or make a sign of farewell.

311

Chapter 30

Tobolsk: August 1917 to April 1918

The difficulties at Tsarskoe Selo before the departure showed how unwilling the extremists were to let the Imperial Family out of their clutches, and how little authority the Government really enjoyed.

The place of exile chosen by the Government was Tobolsk, a town set in the most deserted part of Siberia, where they arrived safely on August.

In Tobolsk, there was the shrine of St. John, to which the Empress had sent Mme. Vyrubova on a pilgrimage on her behalf in 1916, and she tried to see a good omen in this coincidence.

The Government had seen to the physical comfort of the Imperial Family during their long journey. They had a special train, made up of first-class sleeping cars, to which a restaurant car was attached. There were armed soldiers with them, but the men on duty were stationed at the end of each coach and not actually in the carriage. A member of the Duma, Vershinin, had been deputed to accompany them, as well as the engineer, Makarov, who had made all the arrangements for the journey, and two members of the Soviet.

In order not to excite suspicion and to avert the possibility of delay, the train was said to be taking a Japanese Red Cross mission across Siberia. There were, however, a few stoppages, and when the train passed through any large station all the blinds were drawn. The train was also stopped daily for about half-an-hour to allow the Emperor and the children to take exercise, the Emperor being asked by the deputies to keep away from the engine in case the driver might recognize him.

When they had got over their first grief at leaving Tsarskoe Selo, the Grand Duchesses, with the elastic spirit of youth, began to take an interest in their new surroundings, whereas the Empress lay all day in her carriage, utterly exhausted in both body and mind. She had been terribly disappointed at not going to Livadia; this was really exile and she felt that Siberia had been chosen to emphasize the point.

She gained some consolation from the fact that the deputies were civil to the Emperor and the few soldiers in the train were a vast improvement on the horde at Tsarskoe Selo, as Colonel Kobylinsky had carefully chosen the most reasonable men from the Rifle regiments to form their guard. Some of the men talked in a friendly way to the children, and even, at one stopping-place, picked some cornflowers and gave them to the Empress, who was leaning out of the window.

At Tyumen, the whole party was transferred to the steamer Russ, as there was no railway line to Tobolsk. It was said that the company had wanted to put their largest and finest boat at the Emperor's disposal, but the River Tobol was too shallow at that time of year, so the smaller Russ had to be used.

It was a fairly comfortable boat and the Imperial Family was delighted with this part of the journey. They had the illusion of freedom and the scenery reminded them of their trip on the Volga during the Romanov celebrations. The country along the banks was very thinly populated and they passed very few villages during their thirty-six hours' voyage.

One of these villages was Pokrovskoye, the birthplace of Rasputin, and the Empress could not help remembering that Rasputin had once said to her that, willingly or unwillingly, she and the Emperor would pass his house someday.

The population kept away from the river banks. They were not hostile to the Imperial Family, but even if they knew who the travelers on the Russ were, they feared getting into trouble by showing their sympathy with such political prisoners.

The first impression of Tobolsk, as seen from the steamer, was a favorable one. The town was picturesque, built for the most part on

313

the high banks of the river at the spot where the Tobol falls into the mighty Irtysh. The sunset gilded the domes of the churches, and the bells, ringing for vespers, reminded the Imperial Family of bell-ringing on official visits in happier times. It looked peaceful and pretty.

They discovered too soon, however, that this was an illusory impression as nothing had been prepared for them in the house destined for their use. The want of proper arrangements for their departure from Tsarskoe Selo had already demonstrated that the former Sovereign was no longer of importance even to those who were not aggressively hostile toward him. Prince Dolgorukov and General Tatistchev, who went to inspect the house with Colonel Kobylinsky, pronounced it uninhabitable in its present state. It had originally been the Governor's residence, but had since been used as a barracks and was indescribably filthy.

The Archbishop Hermogen, who had fallen into disfavor with the Court owing to his hostility to Rasputin, had been appointed by the Provisional Government to the See of Tobolsk and now offered his own residence to the Imperial Family. This house had the advantages of a private chapel and a garden, but the rooms, which were really only a series of large halls, were most uncomfortable and his offer had to be declined with many thanks. It was finally decided that the Governor's house should be painted and cleaned, and while this was being done the Imperial Family stayed on board the steamer.

This they really enjoyed. They were allowed to take short trips up the river and disembark for walks, the guard following them at a reasonable distance, and they were encouraged to hope that their conditions of captivity in Tobolsk might be milder, especially as the gentlemen-in-waiting were allowed to walk freely about the town while they were making the arrangements for the furnishing of the house.

All the necessary furniture was bought from private individuals in the town and the house was ready on August 26. The Imperial Family moved into it that day, the members of Household being lodged in a house opposite belonging to a merchant named Kornilov.

The Emperor and Empress went to see the quarters of their Court suite on the day of their arrival. This was to be the only time they were allowed to leave their house. There had been vague suggestions before leaving Tsarskoe Selo that the Grand Duchesses might be given more freedom. It had been pointed out several times by the Commandant that they were not under arrest, but had only joined their parents willingly, as had the members of the Household. Kobylinsky had even hoped that the Emperor might be allowed to have some shooting when he was settled at Tobolsk.

The actual conditions turned out to be very different. The imperial prisoners were not permitted to leave the house, except to go to church occasionally on Sundays, or on great holy days, and then they were accompanied by a strong armed escort. Indeed, the severity toward them actually increased as time went on.

The house itself was fairly comfortable and some private possessions, carpets, favorite pictures, etc. had been sent from Tsarskoe Selo by order of Makarov. Their Majesties had a bedroom, the Emperor a dressing room, the four Grand Duchesses shared a bedroom, and the Tsarevich had his own room, with his sailor servant in a room next door. There was a sitting room for the Empress and a study for the Emperor on the first floor, besides a large hall where later a portable church was erected. The dining room was on the ground floor.

M. Gilliard and some of the personal servants also lived in the Governor's house, the rest of the servants being accommodated with the members of the Household in the house opposite. Countess Hendrikov, Mlle. Schneider, and the gentlemen-in-waiting had all their meals with the Imperial Family and were allowed to cross the street unattended as the distance was quite short. For some time, indeed, the Court suite was allowed to take walks by themselves in the town, but this was gradually discontinued. At first they were allowed to go out on certain days only; then their walks had always to be taken under the escort of an armed soldier; and, after the New Year, even these restricted outings were very seldom allowed.

The Imperial Family got what air they could in the kitchen garden belonging to the Governor's house. This was a very small space with nothing in it but a few cabbages. A part of the adjacent street had been added, hastily enclosed by high wooden fences. This enclosure became a quagmire in autumn as it was unpaved. There was not a single tree or bush in it. Winter begins early in these northern regions, the first snow generally falling in September, but 1917 was an exceptionally mild year and there were no heavy snowfalls before the beginning of November. But the climate in Tobolsk is severe, and in January the temperature went down to 50 C. below freezing point. There was, however, no wind, which made it bearable, and the sun shone brightly every day for a couple of hours.

The great drawback of the house was its extreme chilliness. In the Governor's time, there had been a special system of heating, used probably regardless of cost, but now there was not much fuel and the whole family suffered terribly. The temperature in the rooms was often not more than +7 C. Even the Empress felt half-frozen and her fingers were so stiff with chilblains that she could not wear her rings and could scarcely move her knitting-needles. The Grand Duchesses, who always felt the cold, wore all the warm clothing they could find.

Tobolsk was a small town of about 30,000 inhabitants and was tucked quite away from the world. It was only during the four summer months that navigation of the river was possible, and during the rest of the year all communication with Tyumen, 287 versts away, had to be by horse. It would have been impossible for the prisoners to escape. If they had attempted it, the alarm could have been given by telegraph before they were twenty miles away, and there were very few villages on the long stretch of land from Tyumen to Tobolsk.

Any such idea, however, was far removed from the thoughts of the Emperor and Empress. They were glad to be away from the political

316

turmoil, and hoped that in this desolate place they might be forgotten and allowed to stay in Russia, their own wish to the last.

On New Year's Eve 1917, the Empress wrote to me, "Thank God we are still in Russia and all together."

The people of the town were not hostile. It was too far away for propaganda to have penetrated, and patriarchal customs still prevailed. The Emperor was still the Emperor in Tobolsk, and many people bared their heads when they passed the Governor's house. When the imperial party was taken to church, the crowd was kept at a distance, but there were many who crossed themselves as the Emperor went by. Many of the merchants, too, sent gifts of food, some openly, some anonymously. These were very welcome. In that severe climate, the only vegetables were cabbages and carrots. Potatoes had to be brought from Tyumen. Fish was plentiful, of course, and there was an abundance of game.

There was no garrison at Tobolsk, and the guard under Colonel Kobylinsky, consisting of 350 men from the Tsarskoe Selo Rifles, was the only authority. At first they seemed inclined to impose a gentler regime, and Colonel Kobylinsky and his officers kept control over their men, but under the influence of ceaseless propaganda, their authority weakened. The Provisional Government had appointed a civilian Kommissar in the person of Vassili Semenovich Pankratov, a former political prisoner, who had spent the best part of his life in Siberia. He was not a bad man, although his first term of detention in his youth had been on a charge of manslaughter. He had been imbued with the most extreme doctrines of Socialism and was really a fanatic with ideals. He and his assistant, a coarse, half-educated man called Nicholsky, insisted on reading Socialistic lectures to the soldiers. At first these did not affect them, but gradually, out of boredom, they began to discuss their rights, having little else to occupy them, with the result that the Commander's orders began to be disregarded and the little Soviet assumed greater importance. Pankratov himself was always afraid of the soldiers. He would have given more liberty to the imperial children, whom personally he rather liked, but he would not take upon himself the responsibility of authorizing it.

Much harm was unwittingly done at this time by the sudden arrival in Tobolsk of a girl friend of the Grand Duchesses, Marguerite (Rita) Serguevna Khitrovo, one of the honorary maids-of-honor. She had held no post at Court, but had nursed in the Empress' hospital and had conceived a great admiration for Grand Duchess Olga. During her journey she behaved most foolishly and wrote imprudently worded postcards to her family that excited the suspicion that she was traveling on a political mission. When she reached Tobolsk in September, she walked straight into the Kornilov house to see Countess Hendrikov. No one was allowed to enter the house without a special permit. She was, of course, seen by the soldiers, the alarm was given, and Mlle. Khitrovo was immediately arrested and taken to Moscow.

She had brought some perfectly innocent letters for the Imperial Family, which she intended to give to Kobylinsky to pass on to them, but she had broken the rules and her visit to Countess Hendrikov resulted in a cross-examination and a day's arrest in her room for the Countess, and many anxious moments for the Commander.

It was ultimately proved in Moscow that Mlle. Khitrovo was of no political importance at all, and that her journey was undertaken solely from a desire to see her beloved Grand Duchess, so she was released, but the prisoners at Tobolsk suffered from her escapade. Although the Imperial Family had not seen her, the soldiers were incensed by this breaking of the rules and increased their vigilance and severity. They feared that plotting was going on, and it was in consequence of Mlle. Khitrovo's visit that the Court suite was allowed out only under armed guard. When, in November, the Empress' dresser, Madeleine Zanotti, and two maids arrived from Tsarskoe Selo, they were not even admitted, although they had the necessary authority from Kerensky. A similar fate befell me also when I arrived. Although I was allowed to stay at the Kornilov house with the other members of the Household for some weeks, I had ultimately to lodge in the town, although I could see the members of the Court suite every day, and while I lived in the Kornilov house I was never once allowed to go out for a walk.

The morning after my arrival at the Kornilov house in Tobolsk the Empress wrote to me at 8am:

Xmas Eve, 1917
Dec. 11 /24

Good morning, dear Isa, I hope you slept well and don't feel too beaten and exhausted today.

I send you this image with my blessing, from the Saint of Tobolsk – John Maximovich – Metropolitan of Tobolsk. His relics lie in the cathedral on the hill (alas! we have not yet been there). Hang it up, and may he be your Guard and Guide. May you soon get strong, well, and fed up again here.

We have service at 12, wonder whether you may come to it, as the guard will just have changed and it would be nice to begin your entry by prayers.

A loving kiss, Darling, from

A.

No one from outside was allowed to see the Imperial Family, except occasionally dentists or an oculist for the Empress, all brought in by the Kommissar Pankratov and Kobylinsky. However, Doctor Derevenko's son Kolia was allowed to come and play with the Tsarevich. Even at Christmas the rule was not relaxed, and Doctor Botkin's son and daughter, who lived with their father in the Kornilov house, were not allowed into the Governor's house on the basis that they were not the imperial children's usual playfellows as they had never been invited to the Palace either at Tsarskoe Selo or at Livadia.

In November, the news of the Bolshevik revolution of November 7 reached Tobolsk. It was so far away that it produced no change. The officials of the Provisional Government, including the Governor, remained at their posts, the banks were open, and the law courts continued to work. Moscow was ignored, and while the money lasted Tobolsk ruled itself.

The guard had become used to their prisoners and was, on the whole, polite to them. There were, however, continual small conflicts and occasional rows. There was trouble, originated by Nicholsky, over some St. Raphael wine that was kept in reserve for the children and triumphantly poured out into the river, but on the whole things jogged along until Christmas, when the soldiers allowed the Imperial Family to spend as many hours as they liked in their enclosure, presented arms to the Emperor, and greeted him with the usual "Good morning, Colonel," in answer to his salute.

A more serious unpleasantness – and one that the Empress felt greatly – occurred at Christmas when the priest made an unfortunate slip of the tongue in praying for the Imperial Family whilst according them their former titles. It was never discovered if it was the priest or the deacon who had done this, but the soldiers raised a hue and cry, and the priest was threatened with imprisonment. With the greatest of difficulty the Archbishop managed to have his sentence commuted, but the priest was sent away and the Imperial Family was left bereft of the comfort of a "real" church. After that time, their church-going was a rare occurrence as the soldiers raised objections every time, and the Archbishop finally helped them out of their difficulties by allowing a temporary chapel to be erected in the house.

When the soldiers realized that the November revolution had installed the Bolsheviks permanently in Moscow, they began to understand that the authorities in Tobolsk were left with no

Government to back them up, and so the soldiers began to enforce their opinions more and more, and the officers had to conciliate them, knowing that they had now nothing to rely on but their personal prestige.

So long as the men's pay was in Colonel Kobylinsky's hands, and he could pay it regularly, things went on more or less as before. The soldiers had obliged the officers to take off their badges of rank and decorations, and the Emperor was asked to do the same so as not to tempt the men to force him to do so, but the men were clearly getting the upper hand. The Empress saw the change in the soldiers but she hoped it was only a passing phase.

She wrote to me at Christmas:

> *A blessed Xmas to you, Isa dearest! And a loving wish and kiss. Above all, I wish God to give you good health, peace of mind, "doushevny mir" [peace of the soul], which is the greatest gift. We can ask for patience, which we all need in this world of suffering (and utter madness), consolation, strength and happiness.*
>
> *A "Joyful Xmas" might sound like mockery, but it means joy over the New-born King, who died to save us all, and does not that renew one's trust and faith in God's infinite mercy? He is so far above all, is All in all: He will show mercy, when the right time comes, and we must patiently and resignedly await His good will. We are helpless to mend matters – can only trust, trust and pray and never lose faith or one's love to Him.*
>
> *Prayed for you, and shall again at mass – too hard you cannot go. I so hoped by a side door to another church.*

The Emperor and all the children send many a message and good wish. They share my regret.

God bless you. Won't you look out of your window and tell Nastinka [Countess Hendrikov] when? At one, let's say, and then we can peep at the corner window, and perhaps catch a glimpse of you.

Just off to church! God bless and protect you.

A loving kiss from your affectionate A. A

Happy Xmas to Miss Mather [my former governess, who had accompanied me on my journey to Siberia.]

The Empress' deep religious faith had come to her aid and helped her to bear her trials with fortitude and be hopeful to the end. In Tobolsk she gained that unearthly calm that sometimes comes to those who feel the Great Shadow before them, without perhaps entirely realizing how near it lurks. She had fought so hard against her human weaknesses that she had attained to real Christian humility and trained her proud spirit not to rebel. During those long months of introspection she learned to look in all sincerity at trials and hardships as a gift of God, a fit preparation for the future blessed life. She had always seen the Life Eternal as her ultimate goal, and now that her links with earthly things were slackening, she saw the Gates of Heaven very near.

Both the Emperor and Empress had realized the danger to their own lives from the beginning of the Revolution, but although the Empress expected no mercy from the extremists in Moscow, who were most of them not Russians at all, she still trusted that no real Russian would ever lay hands on his Tsar. She was also convinced that her children were in no actual danger. She foresaw a sad future for her daughters, spending their youths in such tragic circumstances, but she did not fear for their lives.

All through her own troubles, the Empress thought of others, not only those actually with her, but also those far away. Notwithstanding their ever-increasing financial difficulties, she managed to send parcels of food to humble friends at Tsarskoe Selo, where by this time people were nearly starving. Things were indescribably worse in Russia than they had ever been in imperial times. All the Empress' letters at this time are full of concern for her friends, and show more clearly than any words of mine the thoughts that filled her mind.

She wrote to Mme. Vyrubova from Tobolsk in March:

My heart is troubled, but my soul remains tranquil, as I feel God always near.

Yet, what are they deciding on at Moscow? God help us! ... Peace, and yet the Germans continue to advance further and further.

Again:

When will it all finish? How I love my country, with all its faults! It grows dearer and dearer to me, and I thank God daily, that He has allowed us to remain here and did not send us further away.

Believe in the people, darling. The nation is strong and young and as soft as wax. Just now, it is in bad hands, and darkness, anarchy reigns. But the King of Glory will come, and will save, strengthen and give wisdom to the people who are now deceived.

She liked to believe that the Lenten season and coming spring might work a change in men as well as in nature. She wrote to Mme. Vyrubova on March 15, 1918:

Soon spring is coming to rejoice our hearts. The way of the cross first, then joy and gladness.

It will soon be a year since we parted, but what is time? Life here is nothing – Eternity is everything, and what we are doing, is preparing our souls for the Kingdom of Heaven. Thus, nothing, after all, is terrible, and if they do take everything from us, they cannot take our souls.

Have patience, and these days of suffering will end. We shall forget all anguish and thank God. God help those who only see the bad and don't try and understand that all this will pass.

In another letter, she said:

All is in God's will. The deeper you look, the more you understand that this is so. All sorrows are sent us to free us from our sins or as a test of our faith, an example to others. It requires good food to make plants grow properly and the gardener, walking through His garden, wants to be pleased with His flowers. If they do not grow properly, He takes His pruning knife, and cuts, waiting for the sunshine to coax them into growth again. I should like to paint a picture of this beautiful garden and all that grows in it. I remember English gardens and at Livadia you saw an illustrated book I had, so you will understand.

*Just now eleven men passed on horseback – good faces,
mere boys. I have not seen the like for a long time. They
are the guard of the new Kommissar. Sometimes we see
men with the most awful faces. I would not include them
in my garden picture. The only place for them would be
outside, where the merciful sunshine could reach them
and make them clean from all dirt and evil, with which
they are covered.*

Count Benckendorff had said of the Empress after she had heard
the news of the Emperor's abdication: *"Elle est grande, grande ...
mais j'avais toujours dit que c'était un de ces caractères qui s'élevent
au sublime dans le malheur."* (She is great, great ... but I have always
said that she is one of those people who become sublime in the face of
hardships.) Those who were with her during her captivity at Tsarskoe
Selo and at Tobolsk can vouch for the truth of those words.

The Empress spent her long days in preparing the lessons she
continued to give her two children, German to Grand Duchess Tatiana
and the Catechism to the Tsarevich, since the priest could not be
counted on for lessons after the trouble caused by the imperial titles he
had used in church. She got up late at times and had her meals with
Alexei in her own room. She read a great deal, worked, copied out
music and practiced the singing of the responses for the church
services, at which she and her daughters joined in the chants. She very
seldom went out, but sometimes, when it was fine and warmer, sat in
the sun on her balcony, well wrapped up. When the others were out
she would often spend hours at the piano. She had no sheet music,
playing merely from memory, passing from one favorite piece to the
other as the spirit moved her. In the evenings, when all the members
of the Household were present, if the Emperor did not read aloud, the
Empress would play bezique with him. All her life she had a feeling
that cards were a little wicked, but she sacrificed her own conscience
in this case in order to amuse him and help him to pass the time.

325

The Emperor's days were terrible in their monotony. He read and gave history lessons to his son, but for a man so active in brain and body, such a life was unutterably wearisome. Happily, they could all go out into their courtyard whenever they wished, so that he could get exercise in the open, either in shoveling away the snow or in sawing wood. He also helped the children to build a small ice hill for the Tsarevich, which was a great pleasure to all the young people. It was a sign of the change of mood in the soldiers after the New Year that they destroyed this ice hill on the grounds that the children could see the people passing in the street from the top of it.

For a long time before Christmas the Empress and her daughters worked on Christmas presents for all the members Household and servants, making most of these gifts themselves. This gave the presents greater value and also saved money. There was a Christmas tree, and the Commander and the little Tsarevich's tutors took part in the family fête. The Botkin children and I were not allowed to join the party, so the Empress sent us little trees she had decorated herself. Even my old governess, whom she had never met, was not forgotten. The Empress drew her a little picture of holly to remind her of Christmas in England, which she sent with a note begging her to "allow a countrywoman's daughter to send her the small gift she had made for her, with her warm wishes."

The young people seemed cheerful enough, but the two elder ones realized how serious things were becoming. Grand Duchess Olga told me that they put on brave faces for their parents' sake. The younger children did not realize the danger they were in and Grand Duchess Marie once said to Mr. Gibbes in the early days of their stay that she would be quite content to remain forever in Tobolsk. During the course of the winter they even acted a few small plays in French and English, which made for a welcome diversion. The two tutors coached them and Grand Duchess Anastasia, in particular, displayed a decided talent for comedy. Even the Empress laughed during these performances and took great interest in them, for her children's sake, writing the programs and helping the actors to dress up. The sole audience was the Court suite and the servants living in the house, and of course the Commander was present.

After January, new difficulties arose for the Imperial Family and matters about which they had never even thought now forced themselves to their notice. Up until this time, the Government had paid for the upkeep of their establishment, but when the first Provisional Government was replaced by the Bolsheviks, funds ceased to come from Petrograd and Kobylinsky had difficulty in providing pay for his men. In order to supply the needs of the Household, Prince Dolgorukov and General Tatistchev signed bills in their own names, but the merchants were becoming anxious and the shops were reluctant to offer further credit. There was still some money left from that which Count Benckendorff had provided for the journey, but in order to make this last as long as possible it was necessary to practice the most rigid economy.

When Prince Dolgorukov explained this to the Empress, she talked the matter over with the gentlemen-in-waiting and it was settled that she, Prince Dolgorukov and M. Gilliard, a practical Swiss, would undertake the housekeeping together and work out the lines on which it could be managed with the minimum of expense. Some of the servants had to be discharged, the Empress giving them enough money to enable them to travel back to Petrograd, should they wish to go there. Those that remained offered to work without pay. This the Empress would not agree to, although she was much touched by their offer, and all salaries were cut down in proportion.

The members of the Household joined in paying the kitchen bills. The one o'clock dinner was the main meal, consisting of soup, a dish of meat or fish, and some stewed fruit. Supper was generally of macaroni or rice or pancakes, followed by vegetables. Often "gifts from Heaven," as the Empress called the anonymous presents of fish and game, came to supplement this somewhat meagre fare. When these were not forthcoming, there was only just enough to go round and no second helpings for anyone. There were no luxuries except when, as a very rare treat, a rich merchant sent some caviar or some especially fine fish. Sugar was very scarce, three lumps a day being doled out to each person. Coffee was unknown to everyone, except to the Empress, for whom it was considered a medicine. Butter was dispensed with, except when it came as a gift.

The Empress' fine under-linen gave way under the merciless washing of the local laundry. There was no money to buy new things, and in any case nearly all the shops, except those that sold necessaries, were closed, the few articles that were smuggled through from Japan being sold at fancy prices. As it happened, a few friends heard of this particular difficulty, and sent the Commander some under-linen and warm clothes for the Empress and her daughters. She was quite overcome with gratitude and afraid that their benefactors must have deprived themselves on her account.

Thus the long, dark, winter days dragged on monotonously, all striving to keep up intellectual interests in order not to be affected by the small, petty incidents of quasi-prison life.

What was particularly painful during those tedious months was the lack of reliable news as to what was happening in the world. Letters came irregularly. The Bolshevik regime had stopped the mail and there were so many *Tchekas* to be passed by letters before they reached Tobolsk that numerous pieces were lost on the way. When letters did get through, no one dared write openly, even to members of the Household. The newspapers that reached Tobolsk contained nothing but official telegrams, distorted and colored by the Bolshevik authorities. I remember, for instance, having seen an account giving full details of a revolution in Denmark in 1918, and was very much surprised when I arrived there the following year to hear that there had been nothing of the kind.

Still, these newspapers, such as they were, gave us all the news we had, and through them we were able to gain a slight impression of the effects of the Revolution. The Emperor and Empress were distressed beyond words at the state into which the country was drifting. This situation poisoned their lives as Russia's fate was still their main concern. All the Empress' notes to me were filled with this idea and her letters to Mme. Vyrubova show the same feeling, although more carefully worded, as these letters had to pass the censorship of the mail system. She wrote, "I cannot think calmly about it – such hideous pain in heart and soul. Yet I am sure God will not leave it like this. He will send wisdom and save Russia, I am sure." The Brest-Litovsk peace treaty with Germany came as a terrible blow, their real agony, because it showed that the Emperor's greatest sacrifice had been in vain.

In February, orders came from the regimental headquarters at Tsarskoe Selo that some of the older men of the guard were to be relieved as their time was up, while others would be sent to take their places. It seemed that the men had become rather uneasy at remaining under the orders of the old Provisional Government and had secretly sent two of their number to Moscow to see what was going on. These men had been well received and on their return had told their comrades that the new rulers seemed firmly established and had to be reckoned with in the future.

In the meantime Moscow had remembered Tobolsk. A Soviet was elected in the town by Moscow's orders, the Governor retired, and in the second half of February Pankratov and Nicholsky left hurriedly as the new soldiers from Tsarskoe Selo had threatened to imprison them. Soon afterward, a man called Doutzmann was appointed Commandant in succession to Pankratov and took up his quarters in the Kornilov house. These new soldiers were of the same type as those under whom we had suffered at Tsarskoe Selo. When the old guard left, some of the men came secretly to take leave of the Imperial Family. They had ended up having a real liking for the children and were altogether less hostile than they had been at first.

At the end of March more soldiers arrived in Tobolsk. Up until this time the town had been spared. In Tyumen, bands of sailors had struck terror into the inhabitants, looting and imprisoning them under the pretext of requisitions, but they had not undertaken the long horse journey to Tobolsk. Now Tobolsk had unwelcome visitors in its turn. No one knew if they were sent under orders from Moscow or not, but it was surmised that the new arrivals came of their own accord.

On Match 26, a band of soldiers arrived from Omsk, the chief town in Eastern Siberia and its administrative center. They took up their quarters in the girls' schools under the command of a certain Dementiev. Except that they saw that the orders of Bolshevik regime were carried out everywhere, their arrival did not cause many changes in the town, and they did not interfere with the Imperial Family's guard. They were followed by another detachment from the neighboring mining center, Ekaterinburg. The soldiers that formed these detachments were mostly Letts, some former sailors and some Ekaterinburg workmen. The people of Tobolsk were terrified of them. Well-to-do merchants were arrested and imprisoned every day in order that they might be bailed out by their families for large sums. Requisitions began and posters were hung up in the streets saying that all gold and silver and valuables must be given up to the authorities under penalty of death. The men started visiting people's homes, with – or often without – search warrants from the local Soviet which was now in command.

The Omsk and the Ekaterinburg bands did not seem to get on well together and in April the Ekaterinburg men departed to exact requisitions from Beresov, a town in the extreme north. They were replaced in a few days by another detachment from Ekaterinburg, with a Jew, Zaslavsky, at their head. Although every party of newcomers may have hoped secretly to get their hands on the possessions of the Emperor and his family, they did not try to do so forcibly, for the regular guard announced that if anyone tried to take its prisoners from it, it would kill the whole Imperial Family itself before it gave them up.

However, the soldiers of the guard were getting perceptibly nervous with all these new arrivals and they feared that they would be replaced if they did not show extreme severity in their treatment of the prisoners, so, in consequence, they forbade the Court suite to go out, were very severe with the servants, and even insisted on paying a visit to the Governor's house to ensure that there were no arms hidden away there.

Colonel Kobylinsky managed to pacify his men by providing them with new assignments, including charging them with guarding the wine stores in the town. This was a paid duty that had been carried out by Austrian prisoners, but as the latter were leaving in accordance with the treaty of Brest-Litovsk, they had to be replaced.

In April, orders came from Moscow for the arrest of the "citizens Dolgorukov, Tatistchev, and Hendrikov," and the two gentlemen and the two ladies (Mlle. Schneider being included by Kobylinsky) were taken over to the Governor's house on April 13. This house was now greatly overcrowded and the newcomers had to live two or three to a room as the ladies were accompanied by their maids.

The Empress was not blind to the meaning of these changes. She wrote to Mme. Vyrubova on April 3, 1918: "Though we know that the storm is coming nearer, our souls are at peace. Whatever happens will be through God's will. Thank God, at least, the little one is better." She was very anxious because the Tsarevich had added to her other burdens by falling dangerously ill. He had caught whooping cough from his playfellow, Kolia Derevenko, and had burst a blood vessel in coughing. The internal hemorrhage was nearly as bad as during his attack in Spala and Dr. Derevenko was in despair, for he lacked nearly every drug he needed in the badly stocked little town. Alexei had been very well up until this time, as had his sisters. They had succumbed to German measles in January, but on the whole had not suffered from the climate.

The Empress sat day and night with her boy, only allowing Grand Duchess Tatiana to relieve her for a few hours. The pain was intolerable, the fever was high, and the boy's life hung in the balance. Happily, Dr. Derevenko tried a new remedy that proved successful, and the bleeding stopped.

The fever remained high, however, and the patient very weak, when the blow fell. The leaders in Moscow had at last turned their attention to the prisoners in Tobolsk. No one in Tobolsk knew why they chose that particular time, nor what they meant to do. The arrival of the special envoy, Yakovlev, was a surprise to Kobylinsky, and apparently to everyone else, too.

Yakovlev appeared on April 22 with full powers. His arrival was shrouded in mystery. He was guarded by a band of mounted soldiers and had two assistants, a sailor called Khokhriakov and a former officer, Rodionov. The former had apparently been a stoker on The Alexander II. Yakovlev himself, although he too wore a blue jacket as a uniform, was of higher social standing. It appeared that he had been a political refugee and was a man of some culture.

Yakovlev's arrival completely threw Doutzmann into the shade. Yakovlev assembled the guard and loaded them with praises, telling them that the Government intended to pay them highly as a reward for their loyal service. He seemed to Colonel Kobylinsky to be a man accustomed to handling the masses. The soldiers and local Soviet were impressed by his credentials, signed by Sverdlov himself, according to which it was for him to give orders now and he had to be obeyed, as he could have anyone executed without trial if he wished.

Nothing was said at first about the purpose of his mission, but it was soon evident to Colonel Kobylinsky that he intended moving the Imperial Family away from Tobolsk, but he seemed to realize that it would be impossible to move Alexei in his current state, for, after having visited the Governor's house and seen the whole family, he returned a second time to see Alexei and then had long telegraphic communications with Moscow.

Yakovlev had told the guard that they and Colonel Kobylinsky would now be relieved of their duties. The Colonel remained nominally at his post until May 14, but all the orders were given by Yakovlev and Rodionov. Kobylinsky gained the impression that Yakovlev was not personally hostile to the Emperor, and that he was, in fact, rather optimistic after he had got over the first shock of the new regime. General Tatistchev was not so hopeful, and told me that he considered this the most dangerous crisis the Imperial Family had ever gone through.

On April 25, Yakovlev told the Emperor that he was going to move him elsewhere, although he did not say why or where. When the Emperor refused to leave, Yakovlev said that if he persisted in his refusal, he would have to use force as his instructions were to remove him. There was general consternation. Everyone thought that the Emperor was to be taken to Moscow, and who knew what might happen there?

This was the most terrible time of all for the Empress. She was torn between her feelings as a wife and as a mother. She felt that she could not allow the Emperor to go alone. On the other hand, her boy lay dangerously ill and the idea of leaving him in that state drove her nearly out of her senses. It was the only time that she completely lost her self-command, pacing up and down the room for hours in her consternation.

The Emperor's departure was imminent and some decision had to be taken. At last Grand Duchess Tatiana forced her mother to come to a decision. "You cannot go on tormenting yourself like this," she said.

The Empress summoned all her courage and went to the Emperor to tell him that she had made up her mind to go with him. The Tsarevich could be looked after by his sisters; she must be with the Emperor.

The girls settled among themselves that Grand Duchess Marie, who was the strongest physically of the sisters, should go with their parents. Olga was to take charge of the house and Tatiana was to look after her brother. Anastasia was too young to be taken into account.

Prince Dolgorukov had asked the Emperor which of the gentlemen should go with him and the Emperor had chosen him. Dr. Botkin also appeared, carrying his famous small black bag, and when he was asked why he had brought it, he said that as he was naturally going with his patient – meaning the Empress – he might need it.

The Imperial Family spent the rest of the day alone. The sick boy had to be prepared for his parents' leaving and the Empress spent most of her time with him, trying to treat her departure in a casual way so as not to frighten him, and telling him that he and his sisters would soon follow her.

In the evening the members of the Household joined the Imperial Family at tea. The Grand Duchesses all sat as close to their mother as they could, looking the picture of despair. About three a.m. Their Majesties took leave of the members of their Household and the servants. About four a.m. some springless carts were drawn up before the main entrance. The one destined for the Empress had a hood and she was lifted into it. Dr. Botkin said that it was impossible that she should travel in such discomfort – the carts had no seats – so some straw was brought from a pigsty to layer in the bottom of the cart, over which some rugs and pillows were arranged. The Empress motioned to the Emperor to follow her, but Yakovlev said that the Emperor had to travel with him, and Grand Duchess Marie got in beside her mother.

Yakovlev stood at attention when the Emperor came out and the sentry presented arms. Yakovlev was, on the whole, respectful in his manner to His Majesty, and was even considerate, insisting that the Emperor should take an extra coat. Prince Dolgorukov and Dr. Botkin took their seats in the third *tarantas*, as the springless Siberian carts are called. In the fourth one there were Matveyev, an officer of the Tobolsk guard, and one of the Empress' maids, Anna Stepanovna

Demidova. The Emperor's valet, Chemodurov, and a servant, Sednev, completed the party.

A mounted escort, consisting of some of Yakovlev's men and a few of the Rifles, who had insisted on accompanying the Emperor, surrounded the carts and the whole convoy drove off at four a.m. at full speed, clattering over the streets in the dim, morning light. The remaining three Grand Duchesses stood watching them as they left, and it was a long time before their lonely figures disappeared behind the open door.

The journey was terrible and it can be imagined what the Empress suffered when she was rattled at full speed over the awful Siberian roads. These roads are shocking at the best of times, and just then were at their worst, for the snow and ice melted during the daytime and froze again into hard lumps at night. The Empress sent me a line from Tyumen saying that all her "soul had been shaken out." Several times wheels came off and broke, and the harness gave way.

They travelled all day, spending some hours at night in a peasant's house where they slept on the camp beds they had brought with them, the Emperor and Empress sharing one room with their daughter, the gentlemen in another. The ladies were nearly frozen. Someone who saw them at one of their stops said that when the Grand Duchess got out to arrange her mother's cushions, her hands were so cold that she had to rub her numbed fingers for a long time before she could use them at all as she and the Empress wore only thin coats of Persian lamb barely suitable for motor car driving in Petrograd.

They had to get over several rivers, where the ice was so unsafe that they were obliged to cross them on planks on foot. At one place the Emperor had to wade knee-deep in ice-cold water, carrying the Empress in his arms.

The state in which they reached Tyumen can be imagined, yet the Empress begged Yakovlev to send an encouraging telegram to her children, saying that they had "arrived all well." A train was awaiting them at Tyumen.

It seems likely that it was Yakovlev's original intention to take them to Moscow. There are two ways of reaching Moscow from Tyumen, the one westward through Ekaterinburg, the other by going first eastward to Omsk and branching off from there via Cheliabinsk. Yakovlev chose the latter to avoid Ekaterinburg, where there was an ultra-Red Soviet. They reached the station before Omsk safely, but the authorities at Omsk were evidently afraid that the prisoners might escape further east and would not allow them to be taken beyond their town. Yakovlev had many discussions with the Omsk Soviet and spoke directly to Moscow. As a result of the instructions he received, the train was turned back towards Ekaterinburg, which had evidently been warned of their arrival.

When the train stopped outside the town, a large band of soldiers surrounded it. Yakovlev went to the local Soviet, and there, apparently, resigned his powers, and the Emperor and Empress were handed over to the Ural (Ekaterinburg) authorities. The Emperor, Empress and their daughter, plus Dr. Botkin, the maid and the two men-servants were taken in motor cars to the house of a local engineer named Ipatiev where they were imprisoned. Prince Dolgorukov was taken to the prison in the town on April 30.

The Empress was utterly weary in body and spirit and was hardly able to stand when she left the car. She had no news of Alexei. The letters she had written daily to her children were not being answered and she was desperately anxious. Happily, a telegram soon came from Grand Duchess Olga describing an improvement in the boy's health, but she never got most of the letters the children wrote her. Still, she seems at first to have had the hope that the stay in Ekaterinburg would not be a long one, and her chief trouble seems to have been her children's absence and apprehension as to their own journey.

Chapter 31

Ekaterinburg: April to July 1918

The house in Ekaterinburg was much smaller than the one in Tobolsk. It had belonged to a well-to-do engineer named Ipatiev and had been requisitioned by the Soviet.

Two days before the Imperial Family arrived, I was told it had been hastily put, more or less, into order and a high wooden fence was erected all around it so that only the upper panes of the windows could be seen from the street.

The party had the use of three rooms: a bedroom, that was occupied by the Emperor, the Empress and their daughter; a sitting room, where Dr. Botkin and the men-servants slept at night; and a room, meant for the Emperor's dressing room, in which the maid Anna Demidova slept on a camp-bed. The remainder of the house was occupied by the Kommissars and the guard.

The furniture had belonged to the former owners. The Imperial Family did not realize at all where they were staying as nothing could be seen from the windows except the gilt cross on top of the belfry of a church in the square opposite. There was a small garden belonging to the house, which later they were allowed to use at stated hours: they could not go freely in and out as they had done at Tobolsk. All the things they had brought with them were thoroughly searched. The men even wrenched the Empress' gray suede handbag rudely out of her hands, although she kept only her heart-drops, pocket handkerchief and smelling salts inside it.

This was the only time that the Emperor showed acute irritation. The rudeness to his wife thoroughly roused him, and he said sharply to the Kommissar that up until now they had at least been treated with common civility.

The man retorted rudely that they were the masters now and could do as they pleased, and was so aggressive that the Empress had to pacify the Emperor for fear of causing trouble.

From that time the valet Chemodourov told me the Kommissars were always rude to them.

Their Majesties' dinner was brought in to them from a Soviet restaurant. It was coarse food and the Empress could scarcely touch it. It arrived at most irregular hours, seemingly according to the whim of the guard, and was sometimes delayed until three or four p.m. They often had to go without tea for breakfast as the soldiers used up all the hot water. Supper consisted of the remains of the midday meal, warmed up by the maid.

The servants had to sit at table with the Imperial Family, by order of the Kommissar. At first they refused to do this, out of respect for their masters, and agreed only when the Emperor expressly commanded that they should. There were neither tablecloths nor napkins, and only five forks for seven people.

Dr. Botkin pleaded for better food and for some comforts for the Empress, but his appeals went unheeded. Not only did the Kommissar and the guard help themselves to the dishes before they even reached the imperial table, but often one of them would come in during the meal and, pushing the Emperor aside, pick some piece he fancied out of the dish with his fork, declaring that by now they had had enough.

The Imperial Family had to be up and dressed by 8:15 am, when the new Kommissar would make an inspection. He was a drunken workman called Avdeev from one of the factories near the town, and was rude and totally lacking in any consideration. The eight riflemen who had come with Yakovlev's men from Tobolsk were imprisoned for several days in the basement of the Ipatiev House, and were then sent back with their officer Matveev to Tobolsk. The men now on guard were men from the Syssert and Zlokazov factories. The men outer guard was often changed. The inner guard had been specially chosen from among the most militant Bolsheviks, and they spared the Emperor and Empress no vexation or unpleasantness.

The doors between the rooms had been taken off their hinges so that they might see all the rooms at one glance when they came in. They would appear at any moment and without warning. A sentry was posted at the door of the lavatory and followed the Empress and her daughter at every step. Their remarks were rude and disgusting, and Dr. Botkin's complaints to the Kommissar were ignored.

The little money the Imperial Family had brought with them was taken away, so that they could not buy anything they needed. The only red letter days for the Empress were the rare ones on which she received a small note from her children at Tobolsk. Holy Week came, but no church was allowed. They asked to be given fasting food, but could only get a little gruel for the Empress. On Maundy Thursday they arranged all their icons on a table in the sitting room and at vesper's time the Emperor and Dr. Botkin read the Gospel for the day. Even now the Empress does not seem quite to have abandoned hope that, when the children joined them, they would be moved somewhere else and that things would improve.

The children, meanwhile, were leading a desperately anxious life in Tobolsk. Stories of the Emperor's treatment were repeated to them by the returning soldiers and their future looked very black. Alexei's improvement was slow. His temperature was still high, and he was extremely weak from loss of blood and unable even to sit up in bed.

Colonel Kobylinsky and his men were replaced on May 14 by a mixed guard of Letts and sailors. The new-comers were a great deal more severe than their predecessors, who had been openly sympathetic toward the children since their parents left. The stoker Khokhriakov was nominally the chief, but it was evident that Rodionov, who had replaced Kobylinsky, was the head man. He knew no pity, but on the contrary seemed to take pleasure in tormenting and humiliating those under his rule.

He started the system of a daily roll call in which the Grand Duchesses had to assemble in the sitting room and to reply to his question, "Are you Olga Nicholaevna? Tatiana Nicholaevna, etc.?" while he added contemptuously that there were so many of them he could not remember either their names or their faces.

Sentries were posted inside the house and all the doors had to be open. The servants were not allowed out. Nagorny once took a bunch of radishes with three lines written by the Tsarevich to the doctor's son. The man was searched and it was with the greatest difficulty that General Tatistchev managed to persuade Rodionov not to court-martial poor Nagorny.

A priest and four nuns were allowed to come for the Easter services, and Grand Duchess Olga gave the members of the Household the presents that the Empress had prepared. All the inhabitants of the town sent the young people gifts of food and their Easter table was laden with Easter cakes (*Paschas*), etc.

Olga was in a state of great anxiety. She longed to join her parents, for whose fate she trembled, and on the other hand she feared the move for her brother, both on account of his health and also recognizing what the move might lead to. However, the decision was not to rest with her. The river was by this time nearly free of ice and the Kommissars seemed very anxious to get the children away as soon as possible, although Dr. Derevenko said it was still out of the question to move the Tsarevich.

On May 16, Alexei had no fever and felt stronger, and implored Grand Duchess Tatiana to allow him to sit up a little in an armchair. She gave in. He had not been allowed to do this before as the Kommissars had said that, when he had been up for a few hours, he could be moved the next day, and the doctor thought he was still too weak to stand a long journey.

As ill luck would have it, the Kommissar, who as a rule never came at that time of day, appeared just as Alexei had got into his chair, and at once announced that they should all start out the next day. Dr. Derevenko managed to have the journey postponed until May 20, but even then the boy was extremely weak and palpably unfit to travel, having been in bed since April 12.

The boat The Russ had just arrived with some German prisoners of war and was used for the journey to Tyumen. General Tatistchev, Countess Hendrikov, Mlle. Schneider, Dr. Derevenko, M. Gilliard, Mr. Gibbes, and myself, along with thirteen servants and the Tsarevich's nursery governess, A. A. Tegleva, made up the party. I had received Yakovlev's permission to join the rest of the members of the Household, but Rodionov would not allow me to live in the house for lack of space, and I only joined the others on the Russ.

Rodionov, Khokhriakov, and their men formed our escort, and the Governor's and Kornilov's houses were looted by them on their departure. Everything, whether belonging to the Imperial Family or not, was taken away, even including the horse and carriage that the Archbishop lent to take the children to the landing-stage. All these things, as well as most of the Imperial Family's own belongings, were divided by the men in Ekaterinburg as "spoil," some of it, as I saw myself, being transferred to the Soviet.

The Grand Duchesses were not allowed to shut the doors of their cabins and guards were posted everywhere, even inside the dressing rooms, from which we expelled them with difficulty. When we were on deck, a man sat at the end of our benches and we were obliged to speak very loudly in Russian so that the guard could follow the conversation. It was fine weather, so the Tsarevich was able to sit out during the day in a wheel chair. At night Rodionov locked him up in his cabin, much to the distress of Nagorny, who continually had violent altercations with Rodionov.

When the ship left the landing-stage, the men fired volleys with their machine guns for some unknown reason, but Khokhriakov, who was more considerate than Rodionov, approached the sick boy   to tell him not to be frightened.

There was a delay at Tyumen, where the party arrived the next day, as the local Soviet wished to arrest everybody. After much parleying, a train was arranged somehow and we were all taken on board on May 27. Meanwhile, the news that the Emperor's children were in the town had spread and a crowd had gathered. Some ladies threw flowers at the children but were rudely pushed aside by the soldiers. A mixed compartment contained the Tsarevich and his sisters, General Tatistchev, Countess Hendrikov, Mlle. Schneider and myself, as well as Dr. Derevenko, a maid, and Nagorny, each of us entering separately under armed guard. The tutors were put with the servants in a fourth-class carriage that had no communication with ours.

Happily, at the last moment, the Empress' page, Volkov, ran up and gave us a bottle of milk and some cold veal, otherwise the travelers would have had no food for two days. The milk was a godsend to the little Tsarevich and the others refused to have any so that he could drink it all.

The carriage was inexpressibly filthy, no words can describe it, and the soldiers deliberately did all they could to make it more impossible, jeering at our disgust. Here again all the doors had to be open and sentries stood inside the carriages, and we could exchange only brief, insignificant remarks. The Tsarevich missed M. Gilliard very much. He felt ill and it was difficult to draw his attention away from his depressing surroundings. He felt the humiliations that surrounded him intensely and Grand Duchess Tatiana and I could only keep him contented by playing games of cards with him all day.

At last, on the night of May 23, we reached Ekaterinburg. We were not allowed to leave the train at once, however, as members of the local Soviet had to come to discuss matters with the Kommissars, and it was only the next morning, between eight and nine, that the imperial children were allowed to disembark.

Some ill-favored Kommissars and soldiers arrived, a line of *izvostechiks* (cabs) was drawn up, and the Grand Duchesses were led out of the carriage by armed soldiers. They were rudely ordered to carry their own luggage and had to struggle alone with heavy bags and the three dogs they were leading, Nagorny being pushed aside roughly when he wanted to help. The Tsarevich was carried out by Nagorny and then the Court suite followed, one by one.

The Grand Duchesses and the Tsarevich were taken by the soldiers to the Ipatiev House to join their parents, while General Tatistchev, Countess Hendrikov, and Mlle. Schneider were taken off to prison. I myself was imprisoned for a few hours in the train and was then set free, joining the tutors and the servants in their fourth-class carriage in which we were allowed to stay for eleven days. After this we received orders to leave the province of Perm (of which Ekaterinburg is the capital) within twelve hours. We had to comply and never saw the Imperial Family again.

Nearly a month had passed, from April 26 May 23, since parents and children had been parted. The Empress knew the children were leaving Tobolsk, but it was a joyful surprise to her that May morning when they walked in and the delight of being together again made them forget their hardships for the moment. Four of the servants who had come with the second party were brought to the house later in the day. These were the cook, Kharitonov, and his assistant, Leonide Sednev, Nagorny and a servant named Trupp, to replace the Emperor's valet, Chemodurov, who had fallen ill and been taken to the prison hospital. The Emperor asked for his suite to be allowed to join him, and particularly for M. Gilliard, who was indispensable to the Tsarevich, but this request was refused. Three rooms had been added to their accommodation. One was for the Grand Duchesses, another was used as a dining room, and the third room was where the men-servants slept. They also had the use of the kitchen bathroom, but firewood had to be collected for this, and it was very seldom that the men condescended to heat the water. Indeed, it was such a rare treat that the Empress noted the "bath days" in her diary.

The house was very damp and no beds were provided initially for the new-comers, so the Grand Duchesses slept on rugs on the floor, the Grand Duchess Marie giving up her bed in her parents' room to her brother. Camp beds were eventually brought from the train, their other luggage, however, was taken to the Soviet and most of it never reappeared. Some things were taken to the Ipatiev House, but were put in the loft, where the prisoners could not get them, and were eventually looted by the soldiers.

On the night after his arrival, Alexei slipped getting out of bed and hurt his knee badly. Dr. Derevenko was summoned, but the Kommissar Avdeev only allowed him to enter the house on the express condition that he should not exchange a word with the Imperial Family, except on medical matters, threatening that he should not be allowed to visit his patient again if he infringed this rule. Medical men always had a privileged position, even under the Soviet rule, and Dr. Derevenko lived at liberty in the town. Naturally he kept his promise and on this account caused a great shock to the Empress. She did not know the conditions under which he had come and anxiously asked him about the fate of the ladies. The children had been expecting us to join them all day as we had at all stops on the journey. Dr. Derevenko made a deprecating movement with his hands. The Empress took this to mean that we were condemned to death and burst into a flood of tears. This was an added trial to her, and I do not know if she ever knew that we were still alive. Countess Hendrikov and Mlle. Schneider did indeed later pay for their loyalty with their lives.

Alexei recovered slowly. His fall caused a hemorrhage in his knee that weakened him to such a degree that he was in bed for weeks. A priest, who was allowed to come and say Mass at the end of May, says that he was then so thin as to seem nearly transparent. The same priest said at the beginning of July that he looked stronger, but was still in his wheelchair. Naturally, the bad food gave him little chance of recovery. Later on, the nuns of a convent near Ekaterinburg brought some milk and eggs for him every day, but what actually reached the prisoners is unknown, for in the Empress' diaries she mentions the difficulty of getting food for him.

Avdeev, the Commandant, was amenable to reason only when he was sober. Sokolov, the judge who conducted the subsequent inquiry, says that all the witnesses declared that he took pleasure in refusing the Imperial Family's modest requests. After the children arrived, a second fence was added to the first one around the house. Later, the windows were painted so that even the sky could only be seen through the topmost panes. No newspapers were allowed to reach the prisoners and they received no letters. Dr. Derevenko was at first allowed to see his patient regularly, but these visits became fewer as time went on. Whenever he came, a Kommissar watched him closely to prevent his exchanging any remarks with anyone else in the house. The faithful Nagorny, who had always looked after the Tsarevich, was soon arrested, as was the second servant, Sednev. They were taken to prison, where both were shot.

When Alexei got better, he had to be carried as his knee had grown quite stiff and Dr. Derevenko was not allowed to treat it with electricity. This was one of the requests that was unreasonably refused. Grand Duchess Anastasia asked for a second pair of shoes to be fetched out of one of the boxes in the loft, but was told that those she was wearing would last the rest of her life.

These events all took place under Avdeev's rule, however, on the grounds that he had allowed some mismanagement on the part of the soldiers (the Empress in her diaries seems to think that it was because he had allowed their belongings to be stolen), he was replaced at the beginning of July by a Jew named Yurovski, the very spirit of evil.

If Avdeev's rule had been harsh, Yurovski's was harsher. His first act was to order the prisoners to give up all their jewelry, when all the gold they had possessed, even the chain on which some small icons were hung over the Tsarevich's bed, had already been seized in Avdeev's time.

Very soon after their arrival, Dr. Botkin had obtained permission for them to have an hour's outing in the small garden. In the height of summer, at the end of June, this time was increased to an hour-and-a-half, but he could never get leave for the sick boy, or for the Empress, to be allowed to sit on the balcony that ran outside their rooms, notwithstanding the fact that it was shut off from the street by a double line of fences, and that not only were sentries placed outside, but that two soldiers were posted on the balcony itself, armed with machine guns. The heat in Ekaterinburg is almost tropical in June and July, and it was with the greatest difficulty that permission was obtained even for a window to be opened at night. It was evident that the Soviet was terrified at the idea of their prisoners escaping. Alas, this was impossible, for who was there who could help them?

The soldiers became more and more neglectful. In the Empress' diary, on July 10, she noted that for a couple of days they did not bring them their meals at all and that the family had to live on the meagre supplies (mostly macaroni) that the cook had brought from Tobolsk in May. Next day she rejoiced that some eggs were brought by the nuns "for baby," but "only enough to put in his soup for six days."

The Grand Duchesses helped Demidova with the housework. They washed and ironed the linen, mended the clothes, washed the plates, and took turns in reading to, and amusing, their brother. They seem to have taken part in the cooking too, and on one occasion to have helped in baking bread, probably with some flour brought by the nuns. Sometimes the guards seem to have ordered the Grand Duchesses to play the piano for their amusement. The guardroom was so near to the sitting room that the men could hear the music clearly from their quarters through the open doors,

The Empress seems to have been physically very ailing all this time, and she lay, fully dressed, on her bed for most of the day. The Emperor was also ill in June and was laid up for several days with fever and kidney trouble. These illnesses caused great complications when everyone was living at such close quarters, and when there was so much difficulty in getting medicine and suitable food. Still, not a word of complaint was ever heard.

The Empress only noted the daily happenings without any comment in her diaries and she spoke of the blessing of having had Church services for the first time on May 24. They had asked for this at Easter but had been refused. A priest from a neighboring church was sent for by the Commandant and officiated with a deacon, but they were not allowed to approach the Imperial Family. The Grand Duchesses sang the responses. Church service was again allowed on July 14. All looked sad and dejected, and this time the young girls did not sing. This priest was the last reliable person to see the Imperial Family alive.

During the last week they seem to have heard movements of soldiers marching outside. The guards were very nervous and redoubled their watchfulness. The Czechoslovak troops were approaching Ekaterinburg, but the Imperial Family probably did not know this. (The town was soon after taken by the Czechs.) The guards were said to have heard the Grand Duchesses singing sad Church music when they went their rounds.

I can explain, on the basis of the last entries in the Empress' diaries, the impression of sadness the priest picked up. Her short notes, in their bald statements of fact, gave a poignant picture of these last days.

June 28. We heard, at night, the sentries under our rooms being ordered to keep a particularly vigilant and constant watch under our windows-they have again become very suspicious -since our window is open-and do not allow us even to sit on the window sill.

July 4. A new Commandant [Yurovski]. All the inner sentries are gone. (Probably one has discovered that they have taken all our things out of the loft) – the Commandant and his young assistant made us show all our jewels we had on and the younger one noted all down and then they were taken from us. Why? For how long? Where? – I do not know-they left me only two bracelets from Uncle Leopold [the late Duke of Albany] which I cannot take off, and left each of the children the bracelets we gave them, and which cannot be slipped off, also N's engagement ring, which he could not take off. They took away our keys from our boxes in the loft, which they had still left us – but promised to return them. Very hot, went early to bed, as I was frightfully tired and had pains in the heart.

July 5. The Commandant came with our jewels, sealed them up in our presence and left them on our table. He will come every day to see that we have not opened the parcel. At 10-30 A.M. – Workmen have appeared outside and put iron bars in front of our open windows. They certainly always fear we shall climb out or get into touch with the guard!

Being so completely cut off from the outer world, the Empress was still spared the full realization of how the clouds had thickened, and mercifully seems to have had no premonition of the approaching tragedy. She was sincere in her belief that all was for the best, and must have hoped to the last that the children would be spared:

July 16. Every day the Commandant comes into our rooms 8 P.M. Suddenly Lewka Sednev [the 15-year-old kitchen boy] was told he could see his uncle and flew away – would like to know if this is true and if we shall ever see the boy again? Played bezique with N. 10 1/2 to bed – 15 degrees of heat.

These are the last lines ever written by the Empress. Thus the curtain falls on the life of a great and noble character, a woman whose love for her husband and his country, and whose trust in the mercy of God, were stronger than her fear of death.

The dark tragedy of Ekaterinburg is believed to have occurred three hours later

Lightning Source UK Ltd.
Milton Keynes UK
UKHW02f1915070618
323908UK00029B/459/P